His first Wife

Jacob's Family

A Novel

By

Renate M. Schulz

ISBN: 0-7596-8363-8 (e-book)
ISBN: 0-7596-8364-6 (Paperback)

This book is printed on acid free paper.

Second Edition

For ordering information, contact 1stBooks Library
by phone at 1-888-280-7715
or visit www.1stbooks.com

1stBooks - rev. 06/09/03

Disclaimer

This story is a biblical biographical novel only, created by the author below, without input from other writers of similar topics.

Any similarities, real or perceived, to portions of the Holy Scriptures or any other stories by the same or similar title of other authors are purely coincidental, written for entertainment purposes, and are not necessarily intended to portray accurate biblical events.

February 6, 2001
Renate M. Schulz

Dedication

This story is dedicated to my very dear niece
and God-child Dr. Matthea Cara Rauchholz,
a physician in obstetrics and gynecology.

Table of Contents

<u>13</u> Children of Jacob Israel

<u>From Leah seven children</u>

1. Reuben
2. Simeon
3. Levi
4. Judah

<u>From Maid Bilhah two children</u>

5. Dan
6. Naphtali

<u>From Maid Zilpah two children</u>

7. Gad
8. Asher

9. Issachar
10. Zebulon
11. Dinah

<u>From Rachel two children</u>

12. Joseph
13. Benjamin <u>Rachel died</u>
    <u>+ in childbed</u>

<u>Leah died + at ripe age</u>

<u>Jacob died at age 147, Genesis 47:28</u>

Note: This page is true history.

Ancestral Roots, Around 1996 B.C.

A grove of palm trees was swaying in the wind, bending the trees back and forth. Now and then the wind managed to loosen a coconut, and it crashed down into the soft sand underneath. A young boy with dark curly hair and wearing a short grey, roughly woven tunic ran barefoot under palmtrees toward the city. Just then another coconut came loose, hit some leaves, and almost landed on the boy's head. But he, quick as lightning, bent sideways, and the palmnut crashed on the ground, hit a rock and split apart.

Terah, an older man with thick grey hair, tall and broad- shouldered, sat in the open doorway of his hut. He had to laugh at the speed of the young lad escaping the hard coconut. "That's the kind of boy I need for my cattle drives, fast and sharp," he thought.

"Hey, young fellow," he called, "do you have a master to work for as yet?"

"No, sir."

"What's your name?" Terah asked.

"Abqa Eliezer," he replied.

"Where are you running to?"

"I am going to the festival. They have a big dance to the moongod tonight. It is a full moon tonight..."

"Go and see what they are doing at the market place. Then come and tell me. I will reward you," said Terah. The boy ran off.

Later on, Abqa came back and told Terah about it. "The town mayor was there, all his scribes, the guards with their swords and spears. Then came the moon priests. Everyone bowed down to the priests and threw money into their open bags. My sharp eyes scanned the ground and I found two gold pieces." Abqa put his hand into his pocket and showed Terah the gold. "This is my lucky day."

"You said all the scribes and townspeople were there, Abqa? Even Mosha, my relative, the mayor's secretary?"

The lad thought about it, then replied, "Yes, Mosha was there, too." Terah shook his head, gave the boy a silver coin, and asked him if he would like to work for him some time. "And Abqa, there is no god in the moon, only the God Jahweh who created the earth is God."

"But aren't all those powerful men smart? Would they give money to the moon priests if there was no god in the moon?" Abqa asked.

"They are wrong, Abqa. And, think it over if you want to work for me."
"Maybe, someday, sir. I have to go home and hide my money first."
And he ran off.

Just then loud metallic "bangs" disturbed the peaceful, sunny afternoon. People looked out of their tan colored, burned- clay brick hovels to see what the sudden noise was. A town crier came down the street, banging a piece of iron against another piece which he held on a rope, announcing the start of the moon god festival and everyone's attendance is expected. Terah arose and disappeared into the dark interior of his hut, so he could not be seen, but could observe others if they would follow the order. Terah saw many folks leaving their huts and walking toward the marketplace. He shook his head. "I am not going," he mumbled to his wife. She looked at him curiously. "This 'old lion' has taken ill," and he layed down on his mat.

Just then clouds sailed across the sky, and more coming from the south, covering up the blue afternoon sky and the emerging moon. Terah knew if there is no full moon visible, the priests will say the moon god is angry and people have to sacrifice more and donate more money to the priests. "What a waste of intelligence," thought Terah. He was thinking as to what his future would bring for himself and his young sons.

Terah was rich in comparison to others, but that also made others notice him more. He lived within the city, although he had his cattle herds outside of town but still within the perimeter of the city's protective soldiers. They would help guard his cattle and servants from wild marauders and thieves. He would, in turn, supply the town with meat and food. The city's ruling men would expect allegiance from him. The name of the city was Ur, in the country known today as Iraq.

Terah was a man of vision. He could see that certain men, hungry for power, were using religion to gain power, money and prestige. They used their man-made religion to control the people into submission. Their scheme seemed to be working because these otherwise sane human beings, were obeying their pagan religious leaders to worship the moon and the stars instead of the God of creation. Then they tried to force others to follow those practices. The money this brought in made the religious leaders rich. Terah saw all that and did not like it. He was not going to go along with that scheme. Terah could remember well the history of mankind told to him by his fathers and ancestors. What these contemporaries taught was not the truth. He saw that his future and that of his children would not be a good one in this environment. Terah discussed all this with his sons Abraham, Nahor and Haran. They had made the same observations, he knew that. Then Terah told his sons, "I am not going to put up with this new religion and I cannot fight it, and I don't think we would prevail if we tried. I say, we are leaving. The land is wide open toward the northwest. Let us go!"

So the whole family group packed up and left with all their possessions. It was a long journey north, then they turned westward and stopped in a new area that seemed to be uninhabited where they settled. They named their new city Haran.

Then some time later, the Lord of creation told Abraham, the oldest son of Terah who was now older and of age, to move out even from Haran, while leaving his father and relatives. He had heard God's voice with his ears, it was not an imagination, so he obeyed. Abraham left, with his wife and servants as well as with his goods, possessions, and cattle. However, he took his young nephew Lot along. Lot's father had died young, and Abraham now as the oldest uncle felt responsible for him.

Abraham became a traveling nomad, moving south, and staying wherever his large number of cattle would find grazing grounds. He was wealthy, but childless.

God had promised Abraham and his wife Sarah a child, but the child did not come. Abraham and wife Sarah were getting older and older. Sarah was realizing it did not go with her the women's way anymore. God's promise of a child had not come either. The idea of a miracle did not occur to her, and the promise of God seemed too far fetched for them. So finally, in their impatience, they thought they would do what others did in those days: use another woman. Sarah wanted so much to have a child to cradlele and to hold, so she told Abraham to go sleep with her maid Hagar. Abraham was willing to engage in this little excursion, which turned out not to be so "little" after all. The maid Hagar promptly got pregnant. Then she began to be resentful and disrespectful towards Sarah. Sarah then mistreated her slave Hagar in return. Hagar was an Egyptian slave servant, and Sarah could order her to do everything she wished since she had the power. After nine months, Ishmael was born. The attending midwife cleaned up the baby and handed it to Hagar for his first nursing. After the baby seemed satisfied, Sarah stepped over to Hagar and took the child from her. Now she had finally a child to coddle and to hold, and to proudly show around. In-between he was being nursed by Hagar.

Hagar was tall, with light brown skin, with black straight hair, narrow nose and a rectangular face, rather good-looking. The baby boy was named Ishmael. He had dark curly hair, inherited from his father. Sarah liked this feature. She combed her fingers through his dark curls and held little Ishmael tightly to her bosom. Hagar said to her "You are hurting the baby." Then Sarah realized all her metallic armbands and necklaces had to go, they do hurt the child. "Mind your own business, you slave," ordered Sarah. But

3

then she walked to her bedroom chamber, took off her arm and neck jewelry and placed them in her ivory and ebony jewelry boxes. Hagar, still on her mat and exhausted from the birth, watched with contempt as her mistress coddled the child of her womb.

There was little joy in the relationship between the two women.

Hagar watched Ishmael closely and whenever she saw an angle to criticize Sarah, she did. For instance, in the way Sarah wrapped the baby, or in the way she supported his little head, or as to when he ought to sleep or nurse. Sarah could not beat up Hagar because that might interfere with good nursing and the flow of milk. So, Sarah had to swallow down a lot of rebukes from Hagar.

Abraham looked in on little Ishmael, held him, kissed him and handed him back to Hagar for nursing. Hagar saw her advantage and used every opportunity to have a fight with Sarah.

Finally, the gray-haired but still good looking Sarah could not take it any longer and confronted her husband about Hagar; what a fresh thing she has become, as if she is the boss and not Sarah. Abraham told her, since she is her slave, she could do with her whatever she wanted. Sarah squeezed her pretty lips together, made a determined face, put the baby in his crib, grabbed her leather strap, marched over to where Hagar was, and beat her up good while yelling at her all the swear words she could think of. Hagar was not going to take it and ran away, into the desert that was not far from there. Now she was free, however childless and homeless. What was she to do now? An angel of the Lord appeared to her and told her to go back and submit to her mistress. Hagar cried, the humiliation was too much for her, but she had no choice. What would she do in the desert? Dance with the hyenas? So, after she had cried her fill, she walked back to Abraham's homestead and apologized to Sarah, at least with her lips, even if her heart was not in it. She did her work as ordered and loved Ishmael at a distance. The little guy enjoyed the attention he received from the three people and seemed to love his "mother's" maid also.

Abraham was careful not to show any extra attention to Hagar as not to offend his wife.

After a long time God gave Abraham and Sarah the promised child, a real miracle baby. Both were quite old already and still God made Sarah pregnant from her husband. It was a miracle. Both old people Abraham and Sarah were ecstatic. Even though Sarah was very old, the birth was normal and, except for childbed woes, uneventful. Then neighbors came filing in, all wanted to see this miracle child. Sarah proudly showed baby Isaac around. There was great joy, even laughter when they looked at old Sarah and perfect new little baby boy Isaac. After about three years, Abraham made a big party for everyone, when Isaac was weaned from the breast.

Now there was new trouble! Hagar saw that Isaac was healthy and strong, he would not die as some young babies often did. Therefore, he would replace Ishmael. She did not like this new real heir to the family fortune. Ishmael made fun of little Isaac, probably instigated on by his mother Hagar. Sarah was extremely angry and told her husband to chase that woman and child out into the desert. Abraham gave Hagar and his son some food and some water, and off they went, into the lonely wilderness of the desert. Hagar wondered, why a rich man like Abraham did not at least give her a donkey to carry a tent and a goat or two for some milk? This rather stingy banishment bothered Hagar a lot. However, the Lord stepped in and showed her a well of pure water. That saved her life and the life of her son. With a good well they could make a life in the desert. They were satisfied and now had their peace. Hagar taught Ishamael how to trap and shoot. He was intelligent and learned fast. They built themselves a sturdy hut from rocks and furs near the well. They both enjoyed their freedom and became proud of their ability to fend for themselves. Hagar and Ishmael felt they were better off poor and free than well-fed and under bondage.

At Abraham's headquarters there was now peace also. Little Isaac was the lovely child of Abraham and Sarah, the heir in his large household. He did not seem to be spoiled, nor was he dictatorial or domineering.

When Isaac was an adult, his father did not want him to marry a woman from the local area because they believed in non-existing gods which led them to lead a lifestyle Abraham did not approve of. He wanted Isaac to marry a woman from his former neighborhood in Haran, where he believed might be some God-fearing people left.

Abraham's head servant, Eliezer of Damascus was sent away to find a bride for his son Isaac. Parents chose their childrens' spouses. Love and romance was not considered very important to Abraham either. He presumed romance or love could develop. Isaac was not seeking a woman on his own. So Eliezer traveled with camels and other servants to Haran. He stopped at the city well to rest and to get fresh drinking water. Eliezer was worried how he would find a fitting woman of so many fair maidens in that town. He asked God for the following sign:

"Please give me a little water from your jar and for my camels also." And if the maiden would answer:

"Drink, my Lord," that would be the right maiden, the wife for his master Isaac. The Lord agreed to these events to show His will.

Just then, a young woman came to fetch water from the well. Eliezer approached her and said his sentence.

"Please give me a little water from the jar." Even though the man was a total stranger to her, the young lady reached her pitcher over to this man and said:

"Drink, my Lord." Eliezer drank. After he had quenched his thirst, the young lady said:

"I will draw water for your camels also, until they have finished drinking."

Eliezer's thirsty camels drank a lot. The girl poured pitcher after pitcher of water for the camels without tiring or complaining. Eliezer was amazed and glad as he watched her. Eliezer knew this must be the woman that God had ordained. He asked her for her name and whose daughter she was.

She explained that she was the daughter of Bethuel, the son that Milcah bore to Nahor, Nahor being the younger brother of Abraham, and he had a son named Bethuel, her father. She explained that Bethuel had two children, a boy named Laban and a girl named Rebekah, which was her. This all made sense to Eliezer.

Wonderful, he thought, *she is a relative. God has blessed my mission. I am sure she will learn to love Isaac eventually. This must be the one! If she is faithful watering the camels, she will be faithful in marriage.* Eliezer was sure he was on the right path now.

The father of Rebekah then invited Eliezer and his entourage to his house and yard. Then Eliezer stated his mission and started negotiating with Bethuel about his daughter Rebekah to be the wife of his master Isaac. Eliezer was granted his wish and wanted to avoid any change of mind, so he suggested he would take Rebekah the next day. Rebekah was unafraid and she was willing to go for this new adventure. When Rebekah left her family to travel with this stranger to meet her future husband, her family wished her the following:

"Our sister, may you increase to thousand upon thousands; may your offspring possess the gates of their enemies."

Rebekah packed her personal belongings, as well as her maids packed theirs. The next morning, after a hearty breakfast, Eliezer and his camel drivers loaded all baggage on the camels so the trip back south to home could proceed. After a number of hard travelling days on bumpy camels' backs, the troop came near the Abraham compound. In the distance stood a man as if waiting for someone. Eliezer pointed out that it is her future husband, Isaac. Rebekah, quickly pulled out her veil from her baggage and slung it around her head, because in the custom of those days, the groom should not see his bride on the wedding day. Eliezer presented the veiled woman to Isaac as his bride. Isaac smiled and was all excited, but held on to himself as not to appear love-stricken in front of the servants. He made a deep bow to Rebekah, and she was walked over to his old father Abraham. Eliezer told Abraham all that he had experienced, and how the Lord had led him to this woman. Abraham was convinced his servant had made the right choice and she was the woman the Lord had chosen for his beloved son. Abraham put the groom's and the bride's hands together, put his hands on both of their shoulders and prayed the Lord's blessing on them. He then called his cook to prepare a delicious wedding meal for all, while Isaac and Rebekah were led into his wife's tent. The tent was empty for awhile because Abraham's wife Sarah had passed away. It had been hard on Isaac and he had missed his mother. But now he was comforted, no empty home for him anymore and his heart would be at rest.

Renate M. Schulz

Rebekah's Twins Born

The wish of her family in regards to fruitfulness and children did not come to be for a long time. Isaac and Rebekah were married about nineteen years and still had no child. Isaac remembered that when his father Abraham had the same problem, he went to God, and God helped. Isaac was not going to make the hasty mistake of sleeping with a maid like his father had. Isaac rather prayed to God to make his wife pregnant. And God listened and rewarded Isaac's bedtime efforts with success this time. After twenty years of married life Rebekah finally got pregnant. They felt excited and full of joy, and grateful to God who had heard their plea so fast. Rebekah hoped the pregnancy and birth would be normal; after all, her late mother-in-law's birth of Isaac was, so why should not hers? Isaac also assured her of God's provision and they would have nothing to fear. The couple spent the nine long months of waiting in blissful happiness. Isaac took her walking sometimes, picked her flowers and wove her a wreath to put on her brown hair. "You are my queen," he said, and she rewarded him with a kiss. Isaac did not care if some men thought he was catering to a woman. Most husbands tried not to do that in order to look tough. This was his woman, his lovely Rebekah, and he did not care what others thought. Then Isaac had to leave again and turn back to his business of digging wells in a dry land and overseeing the servants and the cattle.

When the nine months were finally over, Rebekah waited anxiously to deliver. The last months were difficult and what was inside her womb moved around too much. Sometimes she felt like a hurtful push against her back or belly. Rebekah wished all this would be over. The midwife was there and comforted her. Rebekah wished for her mother, but she was far away. Then the midwife made Rebekah lie down on her back and she placed her hand on her abdomen. She noticed that Rebekah was unusually large and what she felt was irregular. The midwife felt her again and, yes, there was life in Rebekah's womb. She kept feeling it again and again, then said to Rebekah that she has twins. Rebekah had thought that much, now it was confirmed. She also called in Isaac and told him so. He was happy. Rebekah was a little scared, but the midwife assured her that all would probably go well. However, the babies would not show. They were positioned improperly in the womb, and the midwife could not do much about that. The head of a baby should show first. Rebekah felt very tired, very pained, very due. However, the babies were not showing, but finally a foot showed, but retreated again. Rebekah knew if hard labor continued she

8

would eventually die, and the babies also, maybe even that day. However, Rebekah surmised that if God gave them these children because of her husband's prayer, He would also provide a mother to raise them. Rebekah trusted God for help. She got up from her bed and walked behind her house to the private place that stood under a large tree, put the hook into the loop so no one could enter. She wanted to talk to God in private. The midwife ran after her and implored her not to drop the babies in the sand or endanger herself. But Rebekah told her to leave her alone and go back to the house. Then Rebekah prayed to God about the stalled birthing process. Right then the Lord said to her:

"Two nations are in your womb, two peoples will be separated from your body. One people shall be stronger than the other, and the older shall serve the younger."

It had gotten dark outside and Rebekah stumbled into the house, still pregnant, to the relief of the midwife. Isaac had questioned her already how she could allow his wife to stumble around in the dark in her conditon.

Rebekah told Isaac that the Lord had spoken to her, and the one born later would be the heir and ruler of the family, as per the Lord's prophesy. Isaac thought to himself, *My wife is in childbed woes, getting visions. This scares me. I hope, I hope…"* Then, turning to the midwife, he whispered with a troubled face "My wife sees visions, a bad omen. Is she all right? Did you give her fresh broth to drink? Could she be thirsty? Could she be hungry?"

However, a midwife is not easily influenced by scared husbands, visions or bad omes.

"A bad omen, Master Isaac? A bad omen?" she said with a determined voice, while she pointed to the door, and gently shoved Isaac out. Men did not belong in a birthing room, especially not when there were complications. So, Isaac obediently left with a troubled heart.

It had gotten pitch black outside by now with a clouded sky. As Isaac stepped across the threshold, someone tripped him and hit him in the head with a hard object. Isaac stumbled, exhaled a swearword, pulled his knife and turned on his attacker. But it was only a large rake someone had left standing, leaning with the tines up, against the wall and the rake handle hit him in the head. Relieved that it was only a rake, he rubbed his bruise, the prophesy of Rachel forgotten.

He walked back and forth outside. He loved his wife so much, he wanted to hold her hand, kiss her, stroke her and encourage her, although he knew he could not really help her.

Finally, the first baby was born. Rebekah named him Esau, because he was red and hairy. The second baby held on to the heel of the first one as if he wanted to hold him back. The midwife was relieved because it meant the second child would come head-first also. She marveled what a strong little guy this one must be, and told it to Rachel to encourage her to keep on pushing. "Not even out of the womb and already grabbing things." They named him Jacob. Rebekah recovered. Both boys grew up strong and healthy. The older one was a rugged outdoors man and his father's favorite. The second boy Jacob looked less coarse in appearance and was his mother's favorite. Since Esau was Isaac's favorite, he took him hunting and to all possible outdoor activities. Jacob was Rebekah's favorite and she taught him how to cook and care for lifestock. Both boys had a happy childhood. Things went their normal way until their teenage years.

Esau's Wives

Eventually, Esau got married to two local girls of the Hittite tribe; he was not too choosey in regards to character. Beauty counted more to him. Their names were Adah and Oholibamah. However, these two women caused Rebekah a lot of grief. They were not helpful daughters-in-law. Nor were they friendly or loving. They also were not obeying the customs of the family in which they married into as was expected of a daughter-in-law. When Rebekah gave them any advice on cooking, washing or child rearing, they resisted her and would make it a point of doing the opposite. Or if Rebekah wanted some help, the wives of Esau always had some excuse why they could not help.

There was also the matter of village festivities where Esau's two wives wanted to continue to attend after the wedding. The problem was the locals were centering their party around idols, some statues of make-believe gods. Esau as well as his parents and Jacob did not like this, dancing around some idol until deep into the night. They would not have minded the dancing, but not to dance in honor of an idol. To honor that piece of wood and iron instead of the true God? No! Abraham and Esau would not allow this, but the daughters-in-law wanted to. Esau suggested they have a dancing party right in their own backyard with flutes and drums. There were several servants talented in music. However, the two wives Ada and Oholibamah wanted no part of it, they felt it was too boring with just the servants and husband.

Then Esau told them that in one of those recent parties around the idol, the villagers gave a baby to the priest and he sacrificed it to the idol in the fire. It was Sebura's little, youngest son. The women countered that Sebura has so many children, he has a hard time feeding them as is. And it would bring good luck to the village to sacrifice a child to the god named Moloch.

Now Esau exploded, "You must be out of your mind! Adah and Oholibamah, don't you see that it is God who created people, and killing a baby, like throwing it into the fire, to serve a non-existing god is pure murder? Never, never will I allow you two to participate in that, nor will I allow any of my sons or daughters to be murdered that way. You two watch your babies, I want all of them, and I want them alive and well. That is an order, or else…" threatened Esau's booming voice.

Adah and Oholibamah tried to understandand, nodding their heads. They also realized that their common husband Esau is serious about this. But still they muttered complaints under their breath about missing out on the festival.

11

"Their wine at the party is really good," said Oholibamah.

"Don't you dare drink it. I want no drunk women in my household or else..." threatened Esau again. Then, with a consolatory voice he added, "You don't have to go overboard, but a little orderliness is appreciated." Jacob could not help it, but he had overheard that loud conversation and decided to stay single for the time being. He did not want to marry local women who did not believe in the real God, the one who spoke to his grandfather and father. Heathen women would not respect his parents nor their household duties toward them, as he saw his two sisters-in-law doing. No, Jacob did not try to get a local woman for a wife.

Rebekah also was getting older. She wanted some help picking berries and drying them for winter. So she walked over and asked Oholibamah and Adah to come and help.

"Oh, mother-in-law, don't you see that we have babies to take care of? We are so tired..." and similar excuses. Rebekah was upset that she always got a negative answer and had to talk and talk and cajole, until the women would do something for her. *A lazy bunch, these two women! Must have been sneaking out last night and going to the village dances. If my son Esau did not go to the dances, and I know he does not like liquor, with whom did my daughters'in-law communicate? Nothing but worries, that's what they give me. And all the dirty swear words they allow their children to say. Esau is too soft on them.*

The Blessing

A number of years passed with nothing extraordinary happening. Esau and Jacob, the brothers, got along well with each other. Jacob stayed single and was not looking for a wife. He also compared every young virgin with his mother and could not find such a noble woman anywhere. He watched his two sisters-in-law and how they raised their children, and he could only shake his head at times. The women would allow their children to use real dirty words without rebuke and sometimes they allowed them to lie without punishment. *I would know how to do a better job if I was a parent. I will train my children right, you folks just wait and see how noble and orderly my children will be, once I am married.*

Isaac noticed that lately the morning sun was not quite as bright, and the night was darker then he was used to. Even the bright stars in the firmament were not as light and sparkling as they used to be. He asked his wife Rebekah about that. She felt the sun was as bright as ever. It made Isaac think. He thought that, maybe, he is getting old and may someday, turn blind altogether. He would need someone to take charge of him, lead him, be the executor for him when he cannot see anymore, which of course, will be his oldest son Esau. That is the way things are done: The oldest son will be "in charge." He ought to make a will. Isaac's eyesight deteriorated more and more. Finally, he was totally blind. Isaac realized the time has come to give his first-born son The Blessing, which makes him the executor and the one responsible for the whole clan.

Isaac called his son Esau:

"Esau! Come here! I want to make my last will. I want to bless you. So, go out into the fields and hunt me a deer. Cook it for me the way I love it, and I want to give you The Blessing."

"Yes, Father," Esau said, joy filling his heart. "I will do it, my Father."

Esau left from his home. His wives saw him taking up his bow and arrows and asked him where he is going.

"I am going hunting for Father. He will give me The Blessing. Do you know what that means?"

"Yes, we know, you will inherit. It's about time. Your father cannot even see where he is going; he is with one foot in the grave already."

"Do not talk about my father in that tone, Adah."

The other wife Oholibamah also said, "Good, then I don't have to listen to my mother-in-law Rebekah anymore and can do what I want."

"Stop talking nonsense, Oholibamah, or I make you," threatened Esau, and left to hunt that game.

Eliphaz (son of Adah) heard all this while hiding behind a curtain and immediately ran off to his favorite stepbrother Jalam and broke the news. Word went around in a hurry. Now Rebekah also heard it through the grapevine. She was shocked and alarmed. *The Lord told me that the younger son was to get the birthright, inherit the estate and be our caregiver in old age. Why now this? I cannot stand those two women Adah and Oholibamah, I must go talk to Isaac about this. I rather die than lay my later years into their care. I must go and talk to Isaac.*

Rebekah found Isaac. He just had his mid-morning rest in the shade of his hut.

"Please Isaac, I have to talk to you. I just heard that you are making your will, and are giving Esau The Blessing because he is the firstborn. Is that so?"

"Yes, Rebekah, that is what I want. Esau, my firstborn, just left to hunt a deer and cook it the way I like it best. Then he will get The Blessing that God put on my grandfather Abraham, then on me, and now on Esau, so that the name of the Lord be proclaimed in future generations."

Rebekah was crushed but did not say anything to her husband and left. Back in her kitchen Rebekah was all upset, she just stood there, shocked. Had she really heard right? She looked through a window. Esau's children were playing 'chieftain,' one exclaiming, "I have the blessing, and you obey." Then the other boy did not want to bow down and a fight ensued. "This is for real," said Rebekah. Something had to be done and fast, she determined in her mind. She quickly called her son Jacob over to her kitchen, and told him in a whisper what Isaac, his father, had said. Jacob was as alarmed as she was, because the birthright was to be his. His mother had told him that many times.

"Yes, I remember, Mother. I was to inherit the estate," said Jacob.

"I also remember the day when I had cooked that delicious meal and Esau wanted some of it. I gave him some and in turn Esau gave me the birthright. Esau had no qualms about giving that birthright to me, because he was very hungry and an immediate meal was apparently more important to him than a future birthright."

Mother and son looked at each other perplexedly.

An angry frown came over Jacob's face. "Yes, something has to be done."

Rebekah wanted to hear the details of the sale of the birthright once again. And Jacob repeated, "Esau had gone hunting and caught nothing. He was famished. He begged me for the delicious meal of lentil stew that I had cooked. I remember as clearly as ever what Esau had said:

"Quick, let me have some of that red stew! I'm famished!"

I replied, "First sell me your birthright."

"Look, I am about to die," said Esau, "what good is the birthright to me?"

So, I said to Esau, "Swear to me first."

"So Esau swore an oath to me, selling his birthright to me. Then I gave Esau some bread and some lentil stew. He ate and drank, and then got up and left."

"Everyone knows, and it was understood, that the birthright also includes taking care of one's old parents. In this case your blind Father, also me when I turn old and weak. God's spiritual blessing will go with it. Esau apparently did not value that too much either," said Rebekah.

"This is a proper trade as I can see it," she continued. "Then there was the vision at the time of Esau's and your birth. I did not make that up. The Lord told me so. I told it to your father. He heard me."

"Listen, my son Jacob," said Rebekah, "I will cook a meal of young goat meat and spice it up so it tastes just like wild deer. Your father won't know the difference. Trust me. Go and kill me two young kids, quickly."

"But, Mother, what if we tell Father that I was to inherit and that Esau sold me his birthright?"

"It will never work. Eliphaz heard it and already went running to his mother and everybody knows about it. Those two wives of Esau's will give us problems, and they are so very mean. I would rather die than live with them and entrust my old age into their careless hands."

Rebekah continued, "You will take those young kid furs, which are soft and pliable, like human hair, and we will wrap them around your arms. Your father is blind, and when he touches you to see if you are Esau, he will feel the hair. Then he will think these are the hairy arms of your brother. Just be calm and collected. Remember, God told me during childbirth that the younger one should inherit, so it is not totally wrong."

"Just a little bit wrong?" asked Jacob.

"Basically, we are doing what the Lord wants. It's your father and relatives who are against the prophesy, and we will help the Lord along," explained Rachel.

"If you put it that way...but what if Father finds out? I would get a curse instead of a blessing."

"Let the curse fall on me," said Rebekah. Mother and son parted, she into her kitchen, Jacob behind the yard by the fences to catch and kill two young goats. He then brought them to his mother.

Rebekah had made a good fire, took the meat, added some vinegar and spices, soaked it a few minutes, then added grease to the pan, then the meat. She put her whole soul into that meal and did not leave the stove for anything, so it would neither burn nor get tough. She tasted, and tasted again, to make the meat taste just like wild game. Finally, it was done. *I hope Esau does not come in before Jacob comes. I hope he has a hard time catching a deer."*

Jacob was scared and nervous. He practiced his words as to what he would say. He wanted the birthright, no matter what the cost. He rehearsed the sound of Esau's voice. Finally, the dinner was ready. Rebekah took the best clothes of Esau which she had found in the house. She was relieved to find them. *Good, his party tunics are still in my house or else this would never work. His wives would have surely let the children soil them.*

She put the clothes on Jacob. She was hasty, nervous and very scared, hoping that nobody would see this and that Esau would not come home soon. She wrapped the goat kid fur around Jacob's arms and around his neck. Then she handed her son the tasty food and the bread she had made. Jacob went into his father's room and said:

"My Father."

"Yes, my son," Isaac answered.

"Who is it?" Isaac asked.

"I am Esau, your firstborn. I have done as you told me. Please sit up and eat some of my game so that you may give me The Blessing." Isaac asked his son. "How did you find it so quickly, my son?"

"The Lord, your God, gave me success," he replied.

Then Isaac said to Jacob, "Come near so I can touch you, my son, to know whether you really are my son Esau or not." Jacob put the tray with the food down on a small table in front of Isaac. Then Jacob had to step close to his father, who touched him and said:

"The voice is the voice of Jacob, but the hands are the hands of Esau. You must be Esau, he is hairy. Are you really my son Esau?" he asked.

"I am," Jacob lied.

Then he said, "My son, bring me some of your game to eat, so that I may give you my blessing."

Meanwhile Rebekah stood nervous and idle in her kitchen, looking out the window, scanning the horizon for Esau. Every movement in the distance, from the wind tossing the leaves on bushes, became suspicious to her. But so far, she did not see Esau coming, it was just a wayward goat knibbling on branches.

In Isaac's tent, Jacob handed the food to his father and Isaac ate. He ate slowly and did not complain. Jacob was silent and watched his father eat,

16

wishing he would hurry up. Now and then Jacob bent his head toward the door of the tent to see if Esau is coming. Finally, his father asked for some wine to rinse down all the food.

Rebekah had put their best wine on the tray also. Jacob handed him the wine and Isaac drank. Then his father said to Jacob:

"Come here, my son, and kiss me."

So Jacob went close to his father and kissed him. When Isaac caught the smell of his clothes that smelled like Esau's, he became convinced it was Esau. Esau, as an outdoorsman, often sat by open fires after a hunt, roasting the fresh game he had shot. His clothes had a smokey odor on them, mixed with sweat. While Jacob's clothes smelled more like cattle.

"Ah, the smell of my son is like the smell of a field that the LORD has blessed. May God give you of heaven's dew and of earth's richness—an abundance of grain and new wine. May nations serve you and people bow down to you. Be lord over your brothers, and may the sons of your mother bow down to you. May those who curse you be cursed and those who bless you be blessed."

Jacob listened intently to his father's blessing. When his father stopped speaking, Jacob exhaled a sigh of relief, because now not much could go wrong anymore. The father had spoken. Then Jacob bent his knees before his father, touched his hands and thanked him for The Blessing and added, "May I be a worthy bearer of the high responsibility your blessing requires of me." Then Jacob quickly disappeared to his mother. He pulled off the kid fur from his arms and stripped off his brother's clothes. His mother quickly placed them back where they were before and efficiently removed all the leftovers of the hasty meal. Then she sat down, took her spindle and tried spinning wool, as if nothing happened. However, Rebekah's ears were wide open. Jacob also made himself scarce, grabbed an ax and walked to the back of their compound to chop wood, waiting for what would happen. It was not quite over yet. He had hardly chopped two pieces in half when Esau came back from the hunt, carrying a freshly-killed deer on his shoulders.

Esau, without haste, pulled the skin off the deer, cut up the meat, and prepared venison the way his father liked it. It was an arduous task and took quite awhile. A beautiful new aroma penetrated the compound. When done, he went into his father's partition of the tent to his bedside and said to him:

"My Father, sit up and eat some of my game, so that you may give me your blessing."

"Who are you?" asked Isaac fearfully, knowing that something must be terribly wrong.

17

"I am Esau, your firstborn son. You wanted to give me The Blessing."

At that moment a violent trembling shook old Isaac and he said, "Who was it, then, that hunted game and brought it to me? I ate it just before you came and I blessed him—and indeed he will stay blessed!"

When Esau heard his father's words, he burst out with a loud and bitter cry that reverberated across the yard and said to his father:

"Bless me - me too, my Father!"

Rebekah and Jacob heard it and it felt as if someone cut a knife into their hearts. They had been so hasty in their plan and had not considered the consequences of Esau's reaction. They were shocked that Esau took it so hard, but they made themselves hard, and figured, what is done is done. "We got our wish and nothing can change it."

Then Rebekah heard Isaac say:

"Your brother came deceitfully and took your blessing."

Esau said, "Isn't he rightly named Jacob"? You called him Jacob when he was born because he tried to be born before me but it did not work. Even then you thought the name fit: Jacob, the deceiver.

He took my birthright and now he's taken my blessing!" Then he asked:

"Haven't you reserved any blessing for me?"

Isaac answered Esau.

"I have made him lord over you and have made all your relatives his servants, and I have sustained him with grain and new wine. So what can I possibly do for you, my son?"

Esau said to his father, "Do you have only one blessing, my father? Bless me too, my Father!" Then Esau, while kneeling in front of his father, wept aloud. He was crushed and felt as if the world had come to an end for him.

His father answered him, "Your dwelling will be away from the earth's richness, away from the dew of heaven above. You will live by the sword and you will serve your brother. But when you grow restless, you will throw his yoke from off your neck."

Esau, red with anger, walked back to his house. His two wives, expectantly happy about their good fortune, awaited their common husband with anticipation. Then they saw Esau coming home, mad and angry. They were alarmed and asked with one voice, "What happened?"

Esau explained. Now Adah and Oholibamah were angry, cursing Jacob and belittling their husband Esau.

"Wimp, little mouse," one yelled, "and you let that happen to you?" "You act like a dog with his tail pulled in. Go kill Jacob. Must we tell you everything? You scaredy-cat!"

Esau's anger really exploded. He kicked Oholibamah powerfully in the rear and punched Adah in the nose. She started bleeding and her face swelled up. Oholibamah had fallen against a clay water jug, which broke into a hundred pieces spilling the water all over the place. All this damage calmed Esau down suddenly, and he left the campground. In the back he had a fenced-in area with an Arabic mare, a lovely brown animal with four white feet. When the mare saw Esau she cantered over, expecting a treat. This time he had none, but he stroked her shiny fur and talked to her and spilled his disappointed heart out to her. The mare acted as if she understood. Esau became calmer. He sat down and tried to remember how things had been when he sold the birthright. Now it came back to him.

Jacob had cooked. He remembered asking for some food, for he had been very hungry. He remembered now how Jacob wanted his birthright from him for the food. *What a deceitful guy Jacob is, taking advantage of a hungry man!* Esau was angry. He was thinking how to punish Jacob for this. He figured *Father is old and blind, he won't live too long. After the funeral I will kill Jacob.* Eventually Esau went home, ate his supper and went to sleep.

The next day when he was in a better mood, his wives wanted to do some nasty trick to Jacob in revenge. They were discussing as to what they could do to him. Esau heard it but would not allow his women to mix into this, his personal affair. "I can handle it myself, and don't need you women for this."

So, the women and Esau decided that superficial order and peace has to prevail: they must show a good face, even if underneath their emotions were broiling.

Later that day, Rebekah went into her husband's sleeping quarters and sat down. With her friendliest, most tender voice she told Isaac about her birth experience when the Lord had told her that her second-born son should be the heir. She reminded him that she had told the prophesy to him. Now he remembered what she had told him on that worrisome and joyful day, and that he had not paid attention. He assumed that since his wife was in labor pains she did not know what she was saying. It all became clear to him now. So, the Lord did have his hand in all of this after all. It stirred a wonder in his soul; he was speechless, even in this thing, and became somewhat comforted.

Jacob's Flight and New Home

Mother Rebekah was a good organizer. She now told her son Jacob that he should go away and find himself a wife. It ought to be a good wife, not like those locals that his brother Esau married with whom she and his father just could not get along. She told him to travel to her hometown of Haran and find a woman from her relatives. She believed that somewhere there ought to be a suitable helpmate for him. His father Isaac blessed him again and sent him on his way.

Rebekah rightly feared also for Jacob's life; she had seen the bitter but silent face of her son Esau. When he wore that face, trouble was brewing. Jacob had to go and he had to go quickly! Jacob took a small bundle of clothes, some food, a skin of water, the golden heirloom bracelet and some money from his mother, and started to walk away. Esau's children, their mothers and Esau saw Jacob leaving. They asked Rebekah where Jacob was going and why? Rebekah told them, "Jacob is going to find himself a wife. He is old enough to get married now, it is really time."

Esau understood that answer. He realized that marrying those two women was not in his parent's best interest. His mother Rebekah obviously suffered more with his two wives around than he had realized. Now however, he wanted to be more in his parent's favor. So, he got himself another wife, this time from the relatives of Ishmael, his father's half-brother's children. He built his first two wives a hut further away from his parents so they would be out of sight. Then he brought the new, hopefully nicer, wife home to his parents.

After all this, the relationship between Esau and his mother had cooled down somewhat and he often sent his new wife over to his mother if there were things to discuss.

~~~

Jacob now traveled alone, in a northerly direction on foot. At night he slept outside, since there were few inns. There were many crimes committed in cities where a traveling man would be easy prey. Jacob preferred to sleep in hiding by some bushes near an outcropping of rocks, out of sight of people. It was dark by now. Jacob ate some of his mother's bread and drank some water from his leather pouch. It tasted old, but for now it was better than nothing. Tomorrow morning he had to find fresh water. Jacob felt his hidden pouch under his outer garment with the silver coins and the golden heirloom bracelet from his mother. It was the one she received many years ago from Eliezer when he brought Isaac's proposal of marriage to her. His mother had given it to him to give to his future bride as a bride price. This bracelet was precious. He cherished it. Then he cuddled up under his coat and fell asleep. The next morning Jacob awoke, a little stiff from the hard ground, but hopeful and eager to move on. He tasted the stale water and ate some bread. He touched his coat pocket with the pouch inside. It was flat!

"Flat...what is that? All was in there last night!"

He opened his leather jacket to look, the pocket was empty, the pouch gone, with the bracelet and the coins.

"What happened?" Bewildered Jacob looked around. The place was empty of men and animals except some chirping and singing birds, bumble bees and butterflies.

"There must be an explanation?" Jacob looked around on the ground. He saw no footprints of any kind. Jacob circled his nighttime area further out. There was some soft sand from an empty streambed.

"There, what is that? A human footprint in the sand!"

He balanced his foot over it.

"No, it is not mine. So, someone was here at night while I slept, and robbed me. Who could that have been? Someone secretly followed me and I didn't hear a thing, nor did I suspect anything. How could I be so naive? I could punch myself!"

Jacob checked the human tracks again. He had an idea who it might have been; in fact, he was sure by now.

"So, they are still after me. I better put space between me and them and move away from here fast. What am I going to give the woman of my dreams now? The heirloom bracelet is gone, my traveling money is gone. I am a pauper. No man of means will give me his daughter now. Who will believe me that my father is rich and I will inherit? Jacob, you are in a mess," he said to himself.

Jacob left quickly. He took some fresh water from a brook, filled up his pouch and moved on. That evening Jacob slept a second night outside, resting his head on a stone. He was afraid and felt dejected. "I now have no bride price. Where is my God?"

However, he had a beautiful dream that night: A long white ladder dropped down from heaven above and landed right in front of him. Heavenly beings in extremely white gowns went up and down upon the ladder and were looking at him. It was beautiful! Up on top of the ladder stood someone that looked more brilliant than the heavenly beings, and he spoke with authority as he introduced himself to Jacob as the God of Abraham, Isaac and Jacob. He told him he will get all the land where his feet stand on to the west, the east, the north and the south; that his seeds will be like the sand on the beach of an ocean. Immediately Jacob awoke and knew now that God was for him, that God would protect him, no matter where he went. Jacob smiled, raised his fist and made a triumphant face toward home and the nephew, whom he presumed had snuck up to him while he slept and stole his bridal treasures from him.

"You wished me bad luck, "kazzer", but you got only my money and the bracelet, haw, haw, haw. I wanted God's blessing, by hook or by crook, and now I will get it. You cannot steal that from me."

In the morning Jacob made a promise to God, and said:

"If God will be with me and will watch over me on this journey I am taking, and will give me food to eat and clothes to wear, so that I return safely to my father's house, then the LORD will be my God and this stone that I have set up as a pillar will be God's house, and of all that you give me, I will give you a tenth."

The next day Jacob traveled on. He took water from brooks and rivers, he even begged at a hamlet for food. It worked out fine for him because a young bull had escaped. Men were trying to catch him. Jacob came just at the right time and helped rope him. He was allowed to stay overnight at that place as well as receive a warm meal. At another hamlet, men were trying to put up beams for a home. They seemed to need another helper. Jacob offered himself. They let him help, stay overnight and receive another warm meal.

Gradually Jacob traveled a little east and came to the area called Paddan Aram, his destination.

There he saw a well in the field, with three flocks of sheep lying near it. The sheep were just lying down and waiting to be watered. Over the opening there lay a huge stone. When all the flocks were gathered there, the shepherds would roll the stone away from the well's opening and water the sheep. Then they would return the stone to its place over the well.

After Jacob watched the shepherds for awhile he asked them:

"My brothers, where are you from?"

"We are from Haran," they replied.

"Do you know a man by the name of Laban, the grandson of Nahor?

"Yes, we know him," they answered.

"Is he well?" asked Jacob.

"Yes, he is," they said, "and here comes his daughter Rachel with the sheep." Jacob looked and in the distance he saw a flock of sheep advancing in his direction, leaving behind a cloud of dust.

"Look," said Jacob, "the sun is still high; it is not time for the flocks to be watered. Why don't you water the sheep and take them back to pasture?" This unusual behaviour did not make sense to Jacob.

"We cannot," they replied, "until all the flocks are gathered and the stone has been rolled away from the mouth of the well. Then we will water all of the sheep at the same time." Now Jacob knew the reason for the shepherd's unusual behavior. He figured being timid gets you nowhere, being inquisitive helps.

While he was still talking with the shepherds, Rachel arrived with her father's sheep. When Jacob saw Rachel (daughter of Laban, his mother's brother) and Laban's sheep, he quickly stepped to the well and rolled the heavy stone away himself and proceeded to water all of his uncle's sheep.

Afterwards he introduced himself to the young shepherdess and told this young lady that he is her cousin, son of Rebekah. Then he kissed Rachel and began to weep aloud unashamedly. He was also extremely grateful to God for letting him find his relatives so soon and effortlessly. Rachel was also surprised to suddenly see a cousin, rather old but handsome, whom she had never seen before. She quickly ran away to her father and told him about Jacob. She was all excited and forgot to dust off her feet before entering the carpeted front room. Her father, when he saw his daughter rushing into the house like that, at first frowned, but his face soon changed to a quizzical smile.

As soon as Laban heard this news he hurried out to greet him. Laban embraced Jacob, kissed him and brought him into his home. Dinner was almost ready. His aunt and her other daughter were setting the table and getting ready. Then the whole family sat down to dinner. Jacob noticed that his uncle was bald already with medium brown hair and a nicely trimmed short beard. He was tall, slim, and broad shouldered. In manner he was agile, talkative and animated. His wife, Mother Laban, was medium size, dark hair and olive-skinned. She seemed to be a quiet person with few but well chosen words. Jacob noticed the older sister was serving at the table. Then he saw a young girl, a grandfather and his servant also sitting down at the table. The older daughter had pale blondish hair, light grey-green eyes, lighter skin than Rachel, actually pale in his opinion, and the same figure and size as Rachel. He noticed that whenever the older daughter (they called her Leah) looked at something in the distance she squinted her eyes and held things rather close to her eyes as if she could not see well. *No wonder she is looking so pale in her face, she is in the house too much. That must be why she is not helping with the sheep. She could not tell a wolf or a sheep apart at the distance. Her nose is slightly bent, like her mother's, but her skin color is from her father. The little girl looks like a mixture between the parents, but her eyes are definitely her father's. I better not stare.*

Jacob quickly bent his head and concentrated on his food. The dinner tasted good, very good indeed. His aunt and that pale-looking cousin certainly knew how to cook.

After the hearty meal Laban leaned back on his chair and asked Jacob, "Now tell us, Jacob, how did you get here and what brings you here? This is really a great news, meeting our nephew whom we did not know existed. Though we guessed that my sister Rebekah must have had children. The Lord would give them to her."

Jacob explained that no children had been born to his mother for twenty years. Only after Isaac prayed to God did children come, twins. Jacob told them that he is a twin, the second-born. He explained that God had told his mother just before their birth that the second-born was to get "The Blessing." Jacob then mentioned the unhappy marriages of his brother Esau with the two non-believing wives, which is the reason he chose to stay single for the time being. However, his mother told him it is time he should go and look for a bride in an area where there might be women more suitable to his and his parent's liking. At that moment Rachel and Leah, who sat next to each other at the table, kicked each other's knees but their faces remained still. Then Jacob told them about the incident of how he connived the birthright away from his brother Esau and the trouble that he is in right now because of it. However, Jacob told them of his significant angelic dream that God would still be with him in spite of it all. He concluded that he left home for two reasons: to get away from his angry brother and his wives who feel they got cheated out of their inheritance, and because his parents want him to get a suitable wife who will care for their olden days with tender hands.

Laban rubbed his short beard and thought about all this silently.

*So, he is a refugee, I hear no money jingling in his pocket. What might he have for a brideprice? Does he want us to help him find a woman around here? Where will he stay? Where will he work? He obviously cannot go home or his brother will most likely kill him...*Finally, Laban said to Jacob, "You are my own flesh and blood, you stay here, you are welcome." A great "lump" disappeared from Jacob's heart. Jacob smiled, bowed his head slightly toward Laban and thanked his uncle and said. "I am looking forward to working for you, Master Laban."

Jacob immediately made himself useful by looking around as to what needs to be done, what jobs he could do. His uncle suggested Rachel take him along to the fields shepherding and showing him around. Jacob did not shy away from any job. He was tall, muscular, with light skin, but slightly sunburned on his cheek bones from his trip over here. He wore a short beard with shoulder-long wavy hair. His clothes was partly leather, partly linen, well-made, like rich men used to wear. Jacob wanted to show his uncle Laban that he is worth his keep and more so, by working hard.

Whenever he was near Rachel his heart was rejoicing. He fell head over heals in love with her. Sometimes he had to remind himself that he is here to work, not to romance. Rachel also noticed and cherished the affection of her cousin, even though he was much older than she. Laban saw Jacob's diligent labor and realized that he should pay him something for his work. He could not let him work for nothing, it would not be right. "What shall be your pay?" asked Laban.

"I will let you know about the price of my humble labor, Master Laban" replied Jacob.

~~~

Laban had three daughters. The name of the older one was Leah, and the middle child was Rachel. The youngest was Denah. Jacob saw that Leah did indeed have weak eyes, as he had guessed right away. However, Leah did not seem to suffer from it; she could do all jobs women are supposed to do. Rachel was the beautiful one with a dark sun-tanned face and lovely black hair. Jacob had fallen in love with Rachel at first sight, right on the first day. He worked with her in the fields, with the sheep and the herds. Her personality impressed him so much. He knew he ought to bring a good woman home to his parents, and this should be her!

Jacob compared the two sisters and saw they were of the same size and figure only their faces and skin color were different. Leah's nose was slightly bent, her eyebrows too light for his taste. Leah's voice was lower, while Rachel's had that melodic sound, that sound that drove him to a dreamland. He could look at Rachel from the front, the sides or the back. She was a perfect dark beauty. At night on his mat Jacob seriously thought about uncle Laban's question for his wages. *Laban had asked me for a price for my labors the other day. I better give him an answer. I must not show my love for Rachel, or the price will be too high. After all, Rachel is just a woman to Laban. Father's forget all about love when it comes to money and a bride price. His sister was given the heirloom bracelet and other precious things when she left to marry Father. This man won't give his daughter away for the shepherd's staff I have in my hand. Whatever a reasonable price he will ask, Rachel should be worth every dinar.*

The next day Jacob turned to Laban with a business-like face and bowed to his uncle. "I have made up my mind about my labors for you, sir. I do not need money. The price for my labors is the hand of your younger daughter Rachel in marriage."

Laban answered, "It is better that I give her to you than to some other man. Stay here with me. Seven years of work for my daughter." Now Jacob worked for his future father-in-law, for the woman he loved. He enjoyed working there and seeing his beloved.

Laban's wife then asked her husband the details of the working price for his nephew. He told her, "the hand of their younger daughter Rachel for seven years of work."

"Of course," Mother Laban said, "she is pretty. I have noticed many young men looking in her direction. Leah is older but still young, we will marry her off in time too."

Leah worked around the house with her mother, cooking, weaving, washing, sewing, planting a garden. Everyone could see that Jacob and Rachel were in love. Everyone knew that Jacob had to work for a wife for seven years.

The cattle had to be driven from one place to another, wherever there was enough grazing pasture and water.

Once again, Jacob and Rachel and servants drove the sheep to another pasture further away for several days. They took two donkeys along and a cart to carry their tents and food.

Leah's Beauty Parlor

After they had left, Laban's other workers brought in more firewood on a cart pulled by two oxen. This time it was birch. Laban cut and pulled off some of the white sections of the bark. He would sell it to traveling merchants, as a material for writing on, in the absence of expensive papyrus.

When Leah saw the birchwood she was happy. She immediately cleaned out the fireplace and oven very carefully because birchwood ashes have a bleaching agent in them, and she wanted it. Her mother's recent comment about her having pale skin bothered her.

Mother Laban was also looking forward to the birch ashes for laundry purposes. Leah watched out and fetched some birch ashes as soon as the fire had cooled down before her mother could get the "lion's share" of it. Leah wanted her pale ashblond hair color bleached to a nice summer-blond. She heard of blond beauties living way up in northern countries that were sometimes captured or their blond hair chopped off and sold.

Two days later in the evening, Leah washed her hair and laid down on her back over a shallow bowl, and Denah had to soak her hair in the solution of birch ashes.

After what seemed a long time for her, Denah thought Leah's hair was now blonder and probably light enough. In the morning Leah would decide if it was blond enough or they would have to try again the next evening. Denah quickly folded a towel around her sister's hair and carefully pressed it to dry. It should not get tousled up for the night. Leah was happy and smiled, but it was too dark to see her image in the metal mirror or her reflection in the water bucket.

What will Jacob now think when he comes back and sees me? I look stunning, except of course, (and Leah made a sigh) for my homely face. Why did the Creator give me such a face and such pale, nearsighted eyes? Why? Leah looked up to the sky, but there was no answer. Women say I am born under an unlucky star. But I overheard Jacob tell my father that there is no other god or unlucky star, but Jahwe, and he should not listen to what some neighbors may say about different gods. It is the one God that spoke to his grandfather and father. That makes more sense to me.

The next day after it got dark and her mother had left the kitchen, Leah boiled some onion peals and added a slice of red beet. It gave the water a light red color. Leah added some of her father's gale to it to keep it fresh in a jar. Then, when Jacob returned from the trip, she would rub that concoction on her cheeks. She could also use it on merchant's day when the traveling merchants came around. Denah watched her older sister, how she cooked the concoction and saw her pour it into an earthen jar and hide it under some blankets.

That ought to take care of my pale skin. It's a shame I am not more beautiful, but I will work on myself. Rachel looks better with dark red cheeks. I look more stylish with light red cheeks.

Leah saw Denah watching her every move with quiet anticipation. "And, Denah dear, don't you take any of my beauty aides. I know exactly how much I have. It's for me only. Besides you are too young to use color. You look just fine for your age." She gave Denah a hug, and the girl was satisfied. Leah felt jealous of Rachel. *No wonder our cousin Jacob is mesmerized by her and I am a nobody in his eyes. Sure, he says 'please' and 'thank you' to me and behaves properly, but his eyes are always on Rachel. And on market day some men try to talk to me, just so they can be near my sister Rachel, who scorns them all, since she met Jacob.*

Finding a Husband for Leah

In those days girls did not go around finding and dating young men. Women were married off to whomever their father liked best as a son-in-law. Often there were business deals that made men decide whom to give their son or daughter in marriage to. Now it was time for Laban to find a husband for Leah also. His wife reminded Laban from time to time to get busy and find Leah a man. Laban knew it was his duty. Next time he went to the marketplace, he met another landowner like himself.

"Peace be with you, Amram."

"Peace be with you, too, Laban."

Laban knew Amram had a single son in the right age for his daughter, Leah. So Laban struck up a friendly conversation about the weather at first, how his fields are doing, how his flocks are multiplying and how his son Amrak is enjoying the work. Amram, when he heard the name of his son Amrak mentioned by Laban, he immediately sensed Laban's intentions. He knew his not-so-pretty daughter Leah, and knew what Laban was after.

"Oh, my son Amrak, he is such a 'windbag' and such an unreliable boy as yet. I have to go and see that he does things properly; all he thinks of is enjoying himself with friends. I better be going to look after my herds. Good bye, Laban, it was good talking with you, see you soon." And Amram was gone. Laban felt the politely unspoken rejection.

Another farmer was selling some of his sheep to the Ishmaeli salesmen.

"What lovely sheep you raised, Kenan. I also have some sheep for sale, thanks to my efficient nephew Jacob," said Laban.

"And a lovely daughter you have also, Laban. What is her name again? Isn't it Rachel?"

"No, her name is Leah." Kenan's face clouded up. He started talking about his good sheep, his lovely pastures, the rain that happened to come this year, just at the right time. Then Kenan looked at the sky and said:

"The sun is sinking, I better be going, see you later, Laban." He also turned, busily dealt with the merchant and then went straight home. Laban was disappointed, twice turned down. He could sense that no one wanted his daughter Leah. When it was time for supper, Laban came home and his wife asked him if he found a suitor for Leah? He said, "No, my wife, I did not, and don't bother me with that, or I'll get angry."

His wife sensed that her husband had not been successful and she better say nothing more, today. He could get fresh to her if pushed too much.

On other days, his wife made suggestions as to whom Laban could also talk to about Leah's marriage situation. But still nothing worked out on

Laban's pursuit. Nor did they want Leah to be married to a poor man, much below their own standard of living.

~~~

Leah, in the meantime, worked at home, diligently and orderly. She helped mother with the cooking and the serving. She, too, enjoyed looking at handsome Jacob and trying to snatch a smile or a glimpse from him once in awhile. Jacob was polite to her, of course, and acted like a future brother-in-law should. He did not notice Leah's longing glances in his direction. Jacob's eyes were on Rachel. Leah wondered if there was another man somewhere else even if no young man in this area liked her. It made her sad. Sometimes she cried when no one was around. She made sure she was always dressed well. She looked critically at herself and compared herself with Rachel. Yes, Rachel had a prettier face even though she was so dark. Rachel also had an easy way of talking and it made cousin Jacob laugh. *Why can't I make jokes like that? Why did God give me such pale skin and a homely face?*

Jacob's eyes were on her sister, Rachel. She was enough woman to see that. She knew Rachel would get married before her even though she is younger. It is not right, she thought, but there is nothing she could do. Sure, she was the daughter of a well-to-do man, but money does not always attract if beauty is missing. Sometimes Leah fought the feeling of getting bitter, and condemning all men who looked past her. But she knew that would not be reasonable. She did not want to become a sour-looking spinster and carry her heart's sorrows for everyone to see. Leah wanted to work hard and efficiently. She knew she was needed. Every working hand was needed, even children. Leah knew she had a steady job, weaving, cooking, grinding grain into flour and other important jobs. The ground had to be dug up and hoed. Seeds for vegetables had to be planted and raised. They had to be weeded and watered. Leah was busy.

Sometimes Leah looked up from her labor to straighten her back while gardening. There in the distance she saw sheep grazing and two figures against the far horizon: her sister Rachel, the other the new cousin Jacob. Sometimes she saw the two sitting together, having lunch or directing the servants. Sometimes she saw Rachel and Jacob looking at each other at the dinner table for just a short moment, and then shyly avoiding their eyes from each other as not to appear "in love."

A good girl was not supposed to flirt with a man. Leah saw the special looks. Her heart ached for something similar. Leah thought that her father would also find her a man that loves her. She hoped it would be soon.

Jacob, in his efficiency, had become the head herdsman for Laban. Under Jacob's care the flocks increased. His hard work paid off. Every year sheep could be sheared which gave them plenty of wool for clothing and selling.

The Bewitched Meadow

One time Jacob hiked up towards a nearby mountain to better get to know the area around his new home. He also wanted to see if there is any good grazing ground around that he had not spotted as yet. He followed a beaten path up a steep hill, then climbed up higher. He then stood and looked around in all directions. Not too far below he saw a beautiful green large meadow with a small brook in the middle. "What an awsome sight!" he exclaimed. "No one showed this to me as yet. I will drive the cattle over this steep mountain pass and let them graze there below. It looks lovely down there."

Jacob quickly walked home and told Laban about that luscious pasture where they never were and no one had told him about. Rachel was nearby and heard it also.

"Oh," Laban said, "that is the Job pasture. No one grazes his cattle there. The meadow is bewitched."

Rachel added, "Whoever grazes his sheep there suffers heavy losses."

"Bewitched?" replied Jacob. "I cannot believe it! We could stay there for at least three days. The lovely brook in the valley…the cattle could get fat down there. Besides, the Lord is with me; He promised it to me on my way over here. I would like to try the Job meadow."

When Rachel saw Jacob's confidence, she got all excited and said to her father, "Please, let him go and let me go with him, this time. The sheep know my voice, they will follow me. My presence will be valuable there. Please, Father."

Laban said, "All right, Jacob, but if you loose any cattle you will have to repay me. Also, if Rachel helps in the drive protect her from harm. That is an order."

Rachel immediately ran to her mother and Leah and exclaimed, "I am allowed to go to a three or four day cattle drive. I am tired of sitting in the house, spinning a thread, on and on. I want to go outside and be free." Then she stretched out her arms and turned in a circle. "Free like the birds in the sky."

"But, daughter, you have to spin and weave for your dowery, don't forget."

"Oh, that dowery," and she waved with her hand. "That dowery can wait."

"I also want to go on a cattle drive some day, and be free, Mother," said Leah. "Rachel always gets to go out, I am the one that always has to stay home and dig in the muddy garden. I want to be kissed by the sunshine also."

"No, Leah, we need you here at home. Besides, there is sunshine in the garden. Your vegetables are growing well. We need them. Rachel has to learn the patience of growing things as yet. You are irreplaceable, my dear daughter."

Rachel, fortunately, had not heard the last sentence. She was already up and about collecting provisions for the long cattle drive. She knew how to pack. Her mother and Leah had a stash of cheeses and bread saved in a cave. Inside the small cave another den-like opening was dug into the earthen wall with a heavy wooden door in front, held up with a rock. It was cold in there, Rachel shivered. She needed a lot of provisions for Jacob, the men and herself. Then she filled up water jugs and added some vinegar so the water would stay fresh on hot summer days. She needed a cooking pot and implements, and also a small tent for herself. Everything was stored on a cart, being pulled by donkeys. Jacob wanted four of Laban's soldiers along, but got only three. Laban said he needed the extra man to help guard his western borders.

When all provisions were packed, the cattle drive could start. They left very early the next morning. Leah noticed that Jacob had a happy face and so did her sister. It was a hidden smile only, but she could tell. Then the sheep and some cows were rounded up and slowly driven toward the mountains. The foothills were steep and the cattle drive went slowly because the sun shone brightly on a cloudless sky. All men surrounded the cattle so none would be lost. Jacob led the way. Rachel stayed with the wagon near the end. It was hard going. People got sweaty and used their water pouches often. The men had to use their sticks and voices to keep the sheep together. Finally, they reached the top of the rocky pass. When the cattle saw the green pasture down below and smelled the water from the brook, they started running and needed no more prodding. The men encountered no wild animals on their drive because marauders usually go hunting in the early morning and at night. It was midday by now.

Jacob had taken along two long thin trees with the branches chopped off and tied together. The men were wondering what he was needing that for. The meadow was surrounded by mountains with a lot of large rocks on the slopes. Then Jacob scratched a large circle in the ground, indicating where he wanted a corral built for the nights. He and the three soldiers climbed the mountain and with full force rammed the tied-together beams against the rocks, which then rolled down the mountain. The men rolled the rocks unto the circle on the ground and placed them on top of each other with the opening toward the meadow. They built the rock corral higher and higher, large rocks on the bottom, smaller ones on top. They would then drive the sheep and cows with their calves into the corral to protect them against carnivores at night. They did this all day long. It was hard work.

Finally, the corral was ready and the sun began to sink. It was time for supper. Rachel had it all ready for the hungry and tired men. Jacob and his three soldiers were sweaty, dirty and hot. They looked at the sparkling, cool water from the brook.

"Yes, that's for us," Jacob exclaimed. They ran toward the shallow brook and laid down flat in it on their backs. The water was cold and refreshing.

"Now we are ready for the food, men. Let's go," said Jacob.

When they arrived at the wagon, Jacob saw Rachel had been guarding sheep all day and had the dinner ready. She looked tired and sweaty and had seen the guys laying down in the brook. Jacob saw a longing in her eyes. He was thinking. Then, with a mischievous look, grabbed a large water jug and poured the vinegar water suddenly over Rachel. She got soaking wet from head to toe and squeeled in shock.

"Aieee! Look what you did. Now I am totally wet and I smell like vinegar and cucumber pickles. Now I have to also run to the brook and get a bath, you, you..." she said with a smirk. Then Rachel ran to the brook and also laid down in it until she felt cooled, clean and refreshed again. Dripping wet she came back to the men and the food wagon. Now the happy eating could begin.

Rachel would otherwise never have laid down in the brook as a lady. Jacob knew that, so he had helped her along. His love had found a way.

After supper the cattle were driven into the corral. Jacob ordered the men to place themselves around the corral from all sides, taking turns watching. Some were afraid because of the, supposedly, bewitched meadow. Jacob did not permit anyone to talk about their fears. He was the chief here and what he said had to be done. Rachel slept on the wagon under her little tent. All seemed in order and peaceful. A night wind came up and cooled the meadow to a comfortable temperature. Laban's prize bull stood in front of the opening of the corral, guarding his cows. Every man had made a little fire at his guard post with a torch by his side. Jacob sat near the front of the corral, near the bull, watching and listening.

Then he saw a dark, long, low shadow approaching the bull. He held on to his torch tightly, stood up very, very slowly. By now he saw the thing was a leopard, crawling nearer toward the bull, getting ready to jump him. The bull did not move. Jacob felt the wind was blowing from the corral toward the leopard, that's why the bull did not smell the cat. Jacob could not wait any longer, he ran, with torch in hand, toward the now jumping cat and pushed his burning torch into the belly of the animal. There was the smell of melting hair and burning flesh. The leopard howled, raised himself up toward Jacob, but Jacob kept pushing his torch into the cat. Finally, the cat ran away. Jacob exhaled a sigh of relief. The bull got wild and tried to run after the leopard, but the other men raced over and drove him back toward the corral. The sheep and cows had heard the commotion and tried to get wild. The men then called out, in their special voice, "shalom, shalom, shalom." They always used those words to calm down the cattle. It worked also this time.

"This is truly the bewitched meadow," the shepherds said, looking accusingly at Jacob.

"Nothing bewitched," exclaimed Jacob, "just a leopard. My Lord was at my side. Now you all go back to your lookout places. I'll take the first night watch. You, Shamo, the second. Here is the whistle. Use it if need be."

"You could have gotten hurt, Jacob, by saving that prize bull," whispered Rachel to Jacob.

"I have to, my dear. I must save that 'prize woman' and you know who that is!?" The rest of the night was uneventful.

On the next night a bear had smelled Rachel's food, and walked closer to the corral. The men chased the bear away with their torches. Another night wolves tried to come near. The men had rocks sitting by the fires and hurled them at the wolves. One man managed to shoot one wolf with an arrow. It howled out loud, tried to run away, collapsed and died. That scared the other wolves. They decided to find other prey for the night.

After several days, most of the grass was grazed off and Jacob gave orders to round up the cattle and drive it up the hills for home. So far he had not lost a single piece. He was happy. When they were almost home, he could not help it, he embraced Rachel and kissed her when no one was looking. She let herself be hugged in happiness. However, suddenly, she realized what he had done and she tore herself off from Jacob, and said, "What are you doing? This is not our wedding night." Her eyes, though, could not hide her pleasure.

When they arrived home Laban counted the cattle. All was in order. He was pleased but would not say so. He figured if he praised Jacob too much, Jacob might want a higher reward for his labors.

Several months later Jacob again climbed the hills to look down on the bewitched meadow. What he saw amazed him. His carefully built corral was wrecked. He walked home and told it to the folks.

Laban then insisted that the meadow is bewitched, after all.

"No witch or spirit will move those rocks. No, Master Laban. That is done by people. But who and why?"

Then, finally, someone explained, that many years ago there was a rich man by the name of Job. He had many children. His oldest son had his homestead on that meadow. There was a great festival. Suddenly, a strong wind blew the house down and all Job's children died. There were also other great losses. Since that time the meadow is bewitched and no one ever lives there, nor grazes his cattle there.

The Wedding

Soon the seven-year engagement was over and Jacob, having earned Laban's respect, was now ready and able to marry Rachel. Jacob and Rachel were still in love. It did not even seem seven long years for Jacob to have been there; time flew by fast. He and Rachel often had long conversations together when their working place made it possible for them to be together. Often they sat together while watching and discussing the sheep, and looking at the sky. Will it bring rain or wind or a touch of frost? Since sheep graze close to the ground, they have to be moved often as not to dry out the land and create a desert. So, Rachel, Jacob and their farmhands were always on the move.

At lunchtime they sat together watching the larks fly up straight into the air, singing their shrill songs, while flying large circles in the sky, yet never colliding. After many circles in the sky, the the larks flew down again tending their little nests on the ground, somewhere, but hard to find for a human eye. Rachel also longed to make a little "nest" for herself, as she was soon to be married to Jacob.

Rachel was brown from being outside a lot, a real shepherdess. She did not always have to tend sheep, only on special occasions, now that Jacob was there. If they were ever alone somewhere, they never slept together nor did they inappropriately touch each other. Jacob was getting excited now, because soon he would marry Rachel, soon he would hold her in his arms, she would be his.

"How good is life! God is really blessing me," he said to himself. He was not young anymore, some gray hair colored his temples. Rachel was his first love and Jacob created a small song about Rachel. He was not a poet, but love helped him along.

"Let me kiss you with the kisses of my mouth
For your love is more delightful than wine.
You most beautiful of all women.
Dark like the tents of Kedor, darkened by the sun.
Pleasing is the fragrance of your perfumes.
Your name is like a rose of Sharon, grown for me.
I follow the tracks of your sheep that graze by the tents of the shepherds.
Like a lily among thorns is my darling among the maidens."

Soon preparations were made for a large wedding. Laban hired a butcher to take care of the meat. He bought more slave maids for his wife to help with baking and cooking. Now Rachel had no more time for shepherding. She had to sit and sew the shirts for her groom. A good wife had to know how to do that. Mother Laban and Leah helped her along. There was excitement and anticipation. Jacob looked forward to this event for which he had labored for seven years. Jacob thought of his mother and father and how good it would be if they knew about him and his love. However, they were too far away. Rachel also looked forward to it, because soon she would be in the arms of her lover. A lot of wine was bought. Wine was purer than some wellwater and therefore, more valued. When Rachel passed by the deep water barrel she looked into it to see her reflection. She tried to comb her hair one way, then another way when no one was looking, because she did not want to appear vain. A good bride acted humble. However, she wanted to be a beautiful bride, the prettiest woman around.

Leah watched the happiness of her younger sister. She wished so much that she, too, would some day be able to happily prepare a wedding feast for herself. But so far, nothing developed. She rationalized she was in the house too much and therefore, not noticed.

"Rachel is a shepherdess, outside most of the time. She gets to see young men, and when the tradespeople come she has to help line up the sheep, so she is visible and I am not." Leah felt she was not visible enough to single men. However, she knew, it is her father's duty to get her a husband. It is really up to him. On her own she did not manage to make herself available too much, or it did not work. Men seem to look right through her as if she was thin air. In the meantime, Leah tried to learn everything that had to do with housekeeping, so that some blessed day, she would be able to be a good wife, whenever her time came. *A man ought to love such an efficient wife.* The guests for the wedding were invited. The foods were being prepared and stored. Everyone in Laban's family was excited and very busy.

Finally, Mother Laban produced the bridal veil that she had carefully laid away in a tight wooden box she had bought from an Egyptian merchant. Rachel and Leah admired it. It was a tight box and well-made. No moths or insects could get into it. Now Mother Laban carefully spread out the veil and hung it over a frame so it would not show any wrinkles. Rachel, when done with her work, would sneak into the room and put it on herself and looked into the mirror, a metal plate, polished to a shine. Yes, she looked beautiful. And then her dress! She would look glorious! Leah also snuck into the room when her mother was not around and looked at the beautiful veil. She, too, put it on her head and saw herself wearing it. She realized that no matter how pretty the veil is, her face stayed the same, not quite as pretty as Rachel's. Leah heard a sound. She quickly put the veil back on the frame, grabbed a broom and tried sweeping. *Mother must not see me trying on the veil.*

When all was ready for the wedding the guests arrived: their relatives, cousins, aunts and uncles, with a good number of children. Young Denah was put in charge of the children, which she did with eagerness. When the children saw the piles of grape clusters, pomegranates and figs, they wanted to dive right into them. But Denah took them aside, gave each child some fruit and explained, "dinner first, then the desert." Mother Laban and Rachel took the lady guests into her special chamber and showed them the official wedding gown that the bride would wear. The wedding gown was white (for purity). It had live green leaves on long vines with flowers attached to the waist by black ribbons and hanging down over a full skirt, symbolizing fruitfulness. The black ribbons symbolizing seriousness, the woman now being attached to her husband. All women admired the dress, tested the material with their fingers and were satisfied. The ladies then went into one tent, the men seated themselves in another. The men were served first with roast lamb spiced with mint, and beef, raisin breads and wines. They had a good, happy time talking, laughing, eating and drinking. Everyone urged Jacob to drink another cup, and another, because he is the groom, this is his happy day. The young girls helped serve the men. They were also all dressed up in their holiday dress and wore a flower in their hair. The mood was good. And the time went fast. Soon it got dark outside. Torches were lit and stuck into the ground. Their flames burned brightly, casting dark shadows in all the corners between the groups of guests. A slight wind was blowing and drove the smoke out of the tents. The party continued.

Rachel was all excited. She combed her hair again and used more Egyptian perfume on herself as did the other maidens. She wore a fine dress in pink, her pre-nuptial outfit. The color suited her well. It was not the dress she thought she ought to wear. Her mother kept that official bridal gown in white under strict supervision. Mother Laban wanted her daughters to help in the background with serving and food arrangements. It was necessary because of the many guests and to keep children away from hot pots and pans, they tried to dart in and out and between them, making the cook upset. That way Mother Laban could also show the guests what well-trained daughters she had, always humble and serving. Leah also wore a new dress in pale green. Leah, as well as the maids, were serving the men in the wedding tent. Mother Laban kept Rachel with her in the background helping there. She, as the hostess, was rather nervous and tight-lipped. It was up to her to keep everything running smoothly and under control. She had to make sure every guest had all the food and drinks, especially the men.

Then someone started beating the drum and another man played harp. This was the cue for the girls to start dancing. All the young girls of the guests came forward, held hands and danced in circles and different rhythms to the beat of the music, while the men clapped their hands and enjoyed watching them.

They danced in different ways. Sometimes they separated, all to the beat of the music, and then came back together again in rows or circles. One could see they had practiced well.

"Mother," Rachel whispered to her mother, "isn't it time for me to put on that official wedding gown and the veil?"

"You impatient young daughter, you will soil it, not yet…Go rather into the ladies' tent and pour them more wine, and see if there is enough meat and cakes around. We don't want anyone to go hungry. Go, check it out. Marlah, the maid, will help you."

Impatiently and with a deep sigh, Rachel and Marlah took the wine pitchers and more food platters into the tents to serve the ladies, then to serve the men. Rachel saw Jacob eating and drinking merrily, from a distance. She could hardly contain herself, but as a good and well-trained daughter and wife, she had to control her emotions and pay attention to the serving. By all means she must not spill any gravy on her dress, or spill wine or grease on some guest! Then she and Marlah walked to the back room, as Mother Laban had told them to check out the food supply.

While Leah carried a large bowl of grapes into the men's tent, she saw a tall, broad-shouldered young man with brown hair. As she pondered who he might be, she remembered it was Kadesh whose wife had died during childbirth with her first child. Leah knew he was still unmarried. He looked impressive to her. She carried the fruit bowl to his side and gave him a friendly smile. He thanked her. However, the man did not seem to "see" her. *Am I invisible?*

Mother Laban kept Leah by her side to help with food preparation. Leah also longed to be seen by fellows in the wedding tent, so some young men might notice her. Leah was glad that Rachel would be getting married today, then other young men would not be attracted to her beautiful sister anymore and maybe they would notice her.

In the wedding tent the men got louder and started calling for the bride.

"The bride, Laban, bring the bride!" Laban, the pleasant host, urged the men to have more drinks, especially his good son-in-law.

"Here, Jacob, have another cup of wine. This is your big day, you don't have to herd cattle today, enjoy yourself." Jacob did.

When the chorus of "the bride, bring the bride" continued. Laban thought it was time. He arose from his seat and walked to the back room where his wife was directing servants with Leah's help. He looked at her and gave her a wink to bring the bride. Mother Laban then took Leah by the arm and asked her to follow her for another task. Rachel and Marlah were again in the pantry room, cutting more bread. Leah followed her mother to her mother's bedroom where the bridal gown was hung over a frame. Mother Laban quickly and silently put the real bridal gown on Leah and the veil and draped it tightly around her, as was the custom.

"Mother," exclaimed Leah, "what are you doing? This is Rachel's wedding."

"Be silent, my daughter, and obey your father. Behave yourself, and be silent like a good married bride should be, and obey your husband from now on."

Then Mother Laban took her veiled daughter to her husband Laban.

Leah was all wrapped up in the veil, like all brides, her facial features and figure not showing. When she appeared, nobody saw her tenseness, her agitation, her fear. But she behaved like a good bride should and was silent. When she appeared, all the men started shouting and clapping hands.

"Long live the bride, long live Jacob, may the Lord of Abraham and Isaac bless you and give you many children that your quiver may be full." Then Father Laban took his veiled daughter, led her to Jacob to hand her over to him.

Jacob arose, leaned against a large water vase, for he was unsteady from all the wine, and tired from sitting so long. He put his arm around his new bride and while the men all kept clapping their hands and yelling good wishes, Jacob walked with her into the dark wedding tent. Who needs light for this anyhow? Leah was silent and obediently allowed Jacob to do with her as he pleased, as she and Rachel were previously instructed by their mother and a thousand other brides by their mothers. Jacob gently folded her garments aside, as needed, and officially consummated his marriage act. It felt good to Jacob as he always had hoped it would. It was slightly painful for Leah because she was a virgin. Leah understood it would be that way for the first time and was silent, as Mother had told her to be. Jacob felt all was perfect, Leah was a virgin as expected. Jacob was tired, oh so tired, from all that celebrating and eating and drinking. He also was somewhat drunk, not used to so much alcohol. After his marriage act he fell promptly asleep. He soon started snoring. Leah was glad.

In the meantime Rachel saw that her groom Jacob was missing. She figured he must have just stepped out. But he did not return. Rachel ran to Mother Laban and with a curious face asked her why Jacob is not there or is staying out so long. Mother Laban took Rachel alone into a shed further away, out of earshot, and explained to her that Father had determined that Leah should be married to Jacob, since she is older: "You know the rule, the older daughter has to be married first?"

"No," Rachel screamed, "he is my husband to be, not Leah's." Big tears rolled down her cheeks. "This is a trick," she screamed. "You ruined my day, the most beautiful day of my life."

"Sh, sh, my dear daughter Rachel, your father determined it that way. You know that the father is the chieftain in the house. You know the rules. Just be patient, you will get married when it is your time."

Rachel bent over and cried and raged while Mother Laban tried to hold her hand over her mouth and ordered her to behave herself. Finally, she took her by the arm and led her back to her private bedroom and told her not to come out until she has cooled her temper.

~~~

Leah was overwhelmed from the sudden turn of events. Now she had time to think. She was grateful on the one hand, that her father finally did what a father is supposed to do.

If Father had only said something to me before, or at least mother! What will Rachel think? How will it be when Jacob wakes up? Rachel acted as if she would be the bride. Will Jacob love me? He took me. I am his legal wife now. He must have known.

Leah lay there, awake. She could not sleep.

Undoubtedly, her father had told Jacob that he gets her as his wife. Therefore, it had been wrong of Jacob to romanticize her sister all the time, while knowing that it is me he would marry. Jacob must have known. Why did my mother not say anything? What is going on?

Leah stayed awake. She was contemplating life. *How often did I give Jacob the largest piece of mutton, how I served him the cider, while my sister just rested at the table and ate her plate empty...maybe it all paid off now.*

Rachel, she stayed outside a lot, cared for sheep, came inside mostly for eating and sleeping. So, it had paid off for me to have served Jacob well at the tables. Now I became his wife.

I hear the wedding guests leaving, most men seem drunk except my father Laban, of course. He never looses control. I hear him wishing our guests a pleasant night.

Leah heard the maids, her mother and women relatives putting the leftovers away and chatting merrily. They were chasing stray dogs away who wanted the leftovers from the wedding meal, until even her mother went to sleep. Tomorrow the celebrating would continue, and so on for six more days. Leah folded the cloth of the wedding tent aside a little bit and saw over them the sky with millions of stars shining down on them as if heaven, where Abraham's God lived, had windows.

No, there are too many stars for even Jacob's grandfather Abraham to count as God had told him to. And so, Leah's thoughts turned round and round in circles about this sudden turn of events. It took a long time for her to finally fall asleep.

The sun rose from the east, turning the land into deep gray first, then lighter and lighter until the golden sun stood over the homes of the people. The morning was cool and refreshed. Herds of sheep and cows were awakening, waiting to be milked and the shepherds getting busy about their morning chores. Leah also awoke, planning her first day of marriage.

There was a stir in Jacob's body. He rolled over on his other side, stretched, rubbed his eyes and noticed the sun already out. "I have overslept!" he exclaimed. His hand went to his head, it hurt. But now he remembered, his wedding day! *Yes, and all the food I had. This is because of all the wine I drank yesterday, serves me right. Never will I drink so much again!*

He remembered, yesterday was his wedding day. *Now I will see my beloved Rachel as a brand-new wife in daylight.* He put his arm around her. *But, oh horror! What is that? That is not Rachel. That is Leah!* He pulled his arm away from her.

"What are you doing in my tent, in my bed? You are not Rachel, you are Leah," he roared. "What did you do? You deceived me. I know I should not have had the last two cups of wine, I did not know what I was doing."

"I was married to you yesterday," said Leah. "Don't you remember?"

"Do you mean to say I had sex with you?" screamed Jacob.

"Yes, you did, Jacob. Here, look at that spotted sheet - it is all legal, you consummated our marriage," replied Leah.

Suddenly the real truth dawned on Leah: Her father never told Jacob that he would exchange the bride.

"I did not deceive you, Jacob," implored Leah. "My father did it. I had no idea he was doing that; it is his fault.

Go to him. I could not disobey him; Mother is in on it. I thought you knew. Father grabbed me by the arm and took me over to you. I am so sorry, Jacob, but wait and see what a good wife I will be to you."

"I do not want you, Leah, I want Rachel," insisted Jacob coldly. These words cut Leah's heart and tears poured out of her eyes. Jacob stormed out of the tent to find his father-in-law. Leah sat on a little stool, held the wedding gown to her eyes and cried and cried. The maid who worked nearby did her tasks as quietly as possible to hear all that was said between the new couple. She just had to hear it. This was beginning to be exciting.

Father Laban was sitting at his breakfast table, being served food by Mother Laban. Laban had gotten up extra early as not to be disturbed during his breakfast. He knew young Jacob would soon appear to have words with him. But Laban was prepared. Laban just finished eating his breakfast, pushed back his plate and leaned back in his chair. Mother Laban saw Jacob emerging from the wedding tent. Then she quickly disappeared from the kitchen and closed the door.

Just then Jacob came storming in, red in his face, shouting: "Laban, what have you done? You cheated me! You knew I told you I would work for Rachel seven years. I worked for Rachel for seven years, now she is mine. You gave me the wrong bride. I don't want Leah."

"Take it easy, young Jacob, don't get so upset, so early on this beautiful morning. You mean you could not tell it was Leah? What is the matter with you? You did consummate the marriage, didn't you? Besides, you got a good woman. Don't you know that the custom in this country is to marry off the older sister first? Should I neglect custom and good manners?" Jacob stood there, his hands in fists, getting red in his face and angry.

"Calm down, Jacob," said Laban. "I have a proposal for you that is so good you cannot turn it down. Live and stay married to Leah for seven days, be orderly and control yourself like a good husband should. After seven days I give you Rachel. No extra wedding feast, of course. You can just take her. For Rachel you will serve me another seven years. You cannot deny that I gave you a good deal. You are employed, you don't have to go around and look for another master, you have a job here, for another seven years, and two good women as wives. You are really a lucky man. Do you see that?"

Jacob's anger slowly subsided somewhat with that buttersmooth talk of his father-in-law, even though he still felt cheated by that "old fox." Laban also made another proposal to Jacob. He would not have Leah only; he also would give him a maid for Leah, so that Leah would not be overtired and unavailable with cooking and housework, so Jacob could sleep with Leah any time he wanted.

"Zilpah," Laban called to the young slave girl, "come here. From now on you will be the maid of my married daughter Leah. Serve her well."

"Yes, Master Laban," she said, and bent down deeply and then went to the wedding tent to Leah to get her orders.

Jacob left. He had to get away for a time, away from the tents, the new wife, his cheating father-in-law, from the still sleeping wedding guests, to just clear his head. He saw the sheepherders guiding the flocks, since he was on wedding-leave. Jacob walked farther out into the fields where he could be alone. He had to be alone to let off steam and anger. He felt so taken advantage of. Jacob grabbed some small rocks and slammed them against a large boulder, hitting it right in the middle. *That is what I would like to do to Laban. However, what can I do? Where will I go if I don't agree? Back to my brother Esau? It is only about seven years ago since I cheated him; that man has not forgotten. I know he hasn't. I have no weapons. I have nothing, just one wife and another wife in seven days. I cannot return. If I make a big scene all the wedding guests will know that I am stupid and can be taken advantage of. I will be the biggest laugh in town. What am I going to do? If that man thinks I will in time get to love his daughter because he wants me to, he is wrong, wrong, wrong! I will not like or love her! He must see that he cannot dictate my lovelife, my privacy. Imagine, not asking me about it! I can have two wives, but only one love. So, the best would be that I act as though all is well, as if it was planned that way, to put up a good front.*

Slowly Jacob calmed down somewhat after he had surveyed his situation. He unclenched his fists, practiced looking normal and walked back to the wedding tents. By the time he arrived, Jacob even had a forced smile on his face. Leah looked at her new husband and saw his eyes were not smiling, just his mouth. She was glad he got control of himself though, in front of all those people.

However, in a country where walls are thin and domestic problems of others are the only entertaining news, words and whisperings went around anyhow. Jacob acted like the normal married man is supposed to, even if his eyes shot invisible "darts" in the direction of Laban.

Rachel, in the meantime, decided she could not go back to the wedding tent. Her embarrassment was too great. She did not want to look Jacob in the eyes while serving food. It would make her sick to see him acting 'in love' with her sister in front of all the guests. *I am sick, too sick to go over there, that's it. I am not feeling well; I got my special time of the month with pain, they will believe me.* She stayed in her bed, covered herself up and waited. Eventually other relatives noticed Rachel missing. They asked Mother Laban. They walked over to Rachel's room. There she lay, with a miserable face.

"What ails you, Rachel? We missed you so. Are you ill?"

"Yes, oh yes, I am ill and hurting. It's that time of the month for me. What a shame to get sick on such a beautiful day! Can someone bring me a tea to drink, please?"

They brought her a caraway tea with a bit of mint and some honey in it. It was used for such occasions. Rachel took a sip, then leaned back and moaned a "thank you." When the women guests left, Mother Laban brought her breakfast. She ate. But it was hard for Rachel to stay in bed more than three days; her healthy body desired to be up and running, and she did.

On the seventh and last day of the long wedding celebration, Laban talked to his wife to get Rachel ready for Jacob. Rachel had been pouting and been angry all six days, with no friendly smile passing to her sister. Six days ago the two sisters had become enemies. Nor did Rachel talk to her father at all and looked the other way when he appeared near her.

Then Laban called another slave girl by the name of Bilhah and told her that she would be the servant of his daughter Rachel. She also bowed down to Laban and acknowledged, "Yes, Master Laban." Now Rachel had a personal maid also.

Leah's Married Life

Leah now had a new heartache. She saw that Jacob gladly left her and went to his long-love Rachel. Such a rejection, knowing that she is only the number two person in the man's life, was hard for Leah. She cried when she was alone, too ashamed to show the maid her sorrow. But in her heart she cried a lot. She saw that Rachel and Jacob were the happy lovers they were before the wedding.

Why, oh why, did God not make me as pretty as Rachel? Why did He not give me better eyes, a prettier face? I am a good woman. I can cook, weave, wash, plant, all those things that a married man wants his wife to know. Rachel just knows mostly how to herd sheep and cattle. She is just practicing cooking right now. I smell another waft of burnt meat that the wind sent over. Will Jacob come back to me to sleep tonight?—No, it does not appear that way; he only sees my sister.

And true to her guess, he did not come. Jacob slept at Rachel's dwelling, and the next night, and the next, and the next. *Maybe he will come the day after.*

Leah made a delicious lamb roast, the aroma spread throughout the whole settlement. Did it attract Jacob? No. So, just she and Zilpah ate the delicious roast by themselves, rather quietly. They gave the leftovers to the shepherds who always seemed to be hungry. Everyone knew now that Jacob's love went for Rachel and not for Leah. You cannot hide such things. And when Mistress Rachel, the love-wife, asked for something, everybody jumped and brought it to her and obeyed quickly. They knew Rachel is the one wife that the head-man of this new family appreciated. Leah, well, yes, if she had wishes, they were obeyed but not as quickly. She may have been Jacob's first wife but in reality she was only number two. Servants did not jump for her. So Leah lived on in loneliness and dejection.

One day she could not take it anymore. She walked to a large figtree that grew by a rockface. She bent the large leaves apart and hid under them and talked to God.

"When my father and my mother forsake me, then you Lord take me up…please. For in this time of trouble, hide me in your pavilion and set my feet upon a rock. Deliver me not unto the will of those that despise me." Then Leah fell silent, and it was as if someone said to her:

"Wait on the Lord, be of good courage and he shall strengthen thine heart: wait, I say, on the Lord."

Leah left the figtree bush and walked back to her home, to work and to wait.

Leah was really not completely alone, she knew it now. There was someone up there on high who saw her situation. He saw that Leah needed a boost. This one was God. In those days people believed that a good wife gets pregnant and makes babies. God has the strange ability to bend toward a person, even if that person's belief is false. God knows how to communicate to everyone, no matter how strange he appears to others. So it was here with Leah. The Lord gave into Jacob's heart the wish for children.

So far Jacob had lived with Rachel every day for several months. He noticed that she did not get pregnant. Jacob wanted children. This was no problem for Jacob, he would just go and sleep with Leah. *If one wife does not make babies for me another one surely will. I don't have to love Leah— and I certainly will not try. I will show my father-in-law he cannot wrap me around his finger.*

So Jacob went to Leah that night to sleep with her. Leah was so excited and happy. She tried to fix the dinner just right and made the bed soft and inviting. Jacob also tried to be nice, after all, he wanted something definite from her and received it. Leah was happy. The next day, however, Jacob left again. Rachel was after him with longing eyes, with smiles, with humor, with female enticement. Jacob succumbed to her and stayed in her home again. Rachel was eagerly watching that her lover-man would not shift his basic interest to her sister. The next night Jacob went back to Rachel.

Leah was sad again, *Yes, if he wants something from me, he comes, but otherwise I am like thin air to him.* The next morning she felt a tightening in her breasts. She prepared her lonely breakfast with her and Zilpah again. They ate. And the next day and the next. The food would not taste so good to Leah. *Oh well, maybe I am getting a cold from the shifting wind.* However, the funny feeling in the morning continued. It was time for her monthly event. Nothing. She waited several days - nothing. Her eyes widened, her hope exploded in her mind like a bright light. *Could it be? No, it could not. I don't want to be disappointed. Let me wait.* Leah ate a little less breakfast than before, but she tried to keep it from Zilpah.

Leah waited a few more days, full of hidden excitement. Then she hiked over to her mother's house.

"Good day, my dear Mother, I wanted to visit you. How are things going since we are gone?" Her mother offered her a bench and told her about other children, about Father, about everything. Then she turned to Leah.

"And you Leah, my dear daughter, how is it with you? I know that your husband loves you less, but don't take it to heart. Lots of women experience similar circumstances. You are not alone. That is the way things are in this life. Don't you think it is better to be married to an unloving husband than not to be married at all?"

"Yes, mother, but it is still so hard, but..." Then Leah stopped talking, a smile entered her eyes and she looked at her mother.

"You don't, Leah, do you?" said Mother Laban with a quick look toward Leah's waist. A hidden smile entered Mother Laban's eyes, another quick look glanced across Leah's waist again. Both women started laughing and falling into each other's arms, words were not necessary. Mother Laban gently pushed down Leah to sit and offered her milk to drink. "Here, my child, eat this, drink that...you have to eat for two."

"Thank you, Mother, I am not hungry enough right now."

"Does he know?"

"No, not yet. I had no opportunity to get him away from Rachel as yet to tell him."

"You will, you will, my child, just give yourself time and to be sure about it. Now Jacob will see what a good wife you are, getting pregnant for him."

"I sure hope that is true, Mother."

"And let us keep this beautiful secret between the two of us a little while longer. Agreed?"

"Agreed," said Leah, and walked home comforted, happy from the visit with Mother, happy for her condition, and grateful to their God of Abraham, Isaac and her husband Jacob, nevertheless. Jacob had told Leah about the dream he had on his way over here, when a ladder to heaven was by his side and God's angels went up and down by him. So Leah knew, as Jacob's wife, that blessing would be on her also. Her first joyful pregnancy!

Some days later Rachel visited her mother. They talked a bit. Rachel told her about the big disappointment of being cheated out of a beautiful wedding. "The wedding, the most beautiful day of my life, you two made me miss it!"

"Oh, my daughter, the wedding is not the most beautiful day of your life. Every day on which you are successful and healthy and have the love of your husband is the most beautiful day of your life. And I know you will have many such days."

Then Mother Laban reminded her again, that it is the father who determines as to who marries whom, and that is it.

"And, Rachel my girl," and Mother Laban put her arm over Rachel's shoulder, "God is there, in all the non-beautiful days of our life. I believe in him. Somehow, I sense there is hope in God. So, don't be sad."

"Besides, Rachel, don't 'hog' your husband all the time. You two own him together and Leah is his first wife and gets to have the first priority. You know that is how it's supposed to be in our society. One woman for one man would be better, but what can we do?" Rachel made a pouting face, and Mother Laban told her that life is tough, and that is that.

"Mother, I came over to ask you how to pickle cucumbers. Can you show me? And when I weave a cloth it wants to get narrower toward the middle. How do I avoid that?"

So Mother Laban told her about the pickling. And then she promised to go over to her place and help her with the weaving. "You will learn to keep house, my little shepherdess. In fact, I have to teach Bilhah also. Is she any good?"

"Well, she complains that her father played cards and lost lots of money and he gave her as payment and now she has to be a maid. She thinks she is something special. The sun is in the west, I have to prepare supper and must go home. Good day, Mother." Then Rachel left.

When Jacob came home at night, he ate his supper at Rachel's home. Later however, Rachel suggested that he go check out her sister's place, see if she needs anything, meat, or whatever. So Jacob, like a man with more wives is obligated to, left for Leah's home. Leah's eyes got bright and happy when she saw her husband coming over. She served him some more food that was leftover from her and her maid's supper. Jacob looked around, asked questions about meat, grain, flour, wine. Finally, it got rather dark, the fire was burning low and it was time for bed.

When Leah and Jacob were all alone in their bedroom niche, Leah asked him:

"Do you know something, Jacob? Can you guess a little news?"

"No, Leah, I cannot guess anything. What do you want to tell me?"

She took his hand and placed it on her stomach.

"Can you guess now?"

"Leah, you are not pregnant? You are. Great! My first son."

He smiled and impulsively embraced her and lay close to her and kissed her on both cheeks. Leah was so happy.

"What if it is a girl?"

"It won't be, my God promised that he will make a mighty nation out of us, out of my grandfather's loins, that is why it's bound to be a boy."

The next morning Leah asked him to come again, to her to sleep, and she will cook an extra good dinner. Jacob came. All went well. The next day however, Jacob went back to his second wife's place to sleep and eat.

Rachel saw a happy spark in Jacob's eyes and was immediately concerned. *Did my sister get him away from me? Did she catch my lover boy? I am his love, and nobody, and no one will take his whole attention away from me. I'll fix her!*

Openly she asked Jacob with a nonchalant tone, "Well, my beautiful hero, what makes you so happy?"

"My number one wife is pregnant, that is what makes me happy. Now none of the men around can say I am a nobody. I will have heirs, like arrows in the pocket of a hunter. This is good!"

Pregnant? My sister Leah is pregnant! And I am not, she did it first, that woman! How nasty of her!

Openly she said to Jacob while leaning her head on his chest and putting one arm across his waist, "My lovely hero, you will get me pregnant also, I know you can do it." With a hug and a kiss Jacob left for the fields, to the sheepherders, to the goats, the cows, and the farming. Rachel knew tonight he will come to her.

Two weeks later, Rachel was all excited, waiting for something to happen. She started developing a plan for a cradle and little blankets and swaddling clothes. But in the midst of all that excitement, her heart sank, there it was again, - nothing, no baby yet. She had to use the string with the little lambfur patches again. How Rachel hated those things! When Jacob inquired, she just sadly said "not yet." Jacob did not mind, he hoped he would have a child from Rachel someday.

Leah and Rachel tried to avoid each other, after all they were now enemies. Leah, because Rachel took her husband away. Rachel because Leah was pregnant and she was not. But Leah, when passing Rachel, tried to be civil and said a greeting. Rachel acted as if she just saw a pretty bird in the tree on the other side of the street and did not notice her sister. Deep down in their hearts both sisters suffered under the strain of common avoidance. Sometimes the maids Zilpah and Bilhah picked that up and tried to do tricks to each other like loosening a piece of laundry on the line so it would fall into the dirt. Or swiping a piece of firewood from the other or just making derogatory remarks. Leah then reminded Zilpah to cut it out, how shall their household function if one tries to make the other stumble? "We need cooperation around here. We have to stick together as a family. You know, one stick is easily broken, but two tied together does not brake that fast."

Some days later Leah felt nauseated in the morning, but she tried hard to eat her meals so that nobody would notice anything, as her mother suggested. However, she could not help her eyes from shining about the glad secret.

It was wintertime and the oranges were ripe. Leah called her maid Zilpah to fetch the baskets, they would go over to the nearby bluffs to the orange groves. Mother Laban also asked to bring her some oranges. So Leah and Zilpah walked together. Leah told Zilpah, "We will be busy in the future. We have to plant and raise flax and spin yarn, lots of yarn, because our family will enlarge. The baby that I am expecting needs a lot of swaddling clothes and blankets."

"O congratulations, Mistress Leah! May the God of Abraham and Isaac and Jacob bless you! Yes, now we have to be busy." Behind them they heard a voice: "Wait Leah, I want to come along." It was Denah, Leah's and Rachel's younger sister. The women stopped. "All right, little girl, walk along with us."

"You two look so happy," Denah said. "What is it?"

"A big secret," confided Leah to young Denah.

"What, what, tell me, I have to know."

Leah said nothing, just made a motion with her hand, indicating a full belly. Denah's eyes became all excited, a knowing smile crossed her face.

"So that was what Mother and you were whispering about."

"But Denah, you are not supposed to eavesdrop, don't you have any manners?"

"I did listen only a teensy-weensy little bit, and believe me, I did not know what you were talking about."

"It's all right, my little sister Denah, you would have soon heard anyway," said Leah.

Denah jumped up and down, she embraced her older sister and said, "I am so happy for you. Now Jacob will sleep in your house from now on."

"Sh, sh, little sister, don't talk like that, you are much too young to mix in."

And so, the three women climbed down the bluffs, and below was the orange grove.

"May I pick the fruits from the top, please, Leah? You are not supposed to climb trees in your condition."

"And you are too young to climb anyhow, your dress will tangle up and you will fall."

"No, I won't Leah, I am strong and can climb like a cat." So the orange picking went on until they had enough, for Denah, Leah, and Mother Laban. The three women were happy.

In the home, where Leah lived, there was a busy preparation time. The maid and Leah wove clothes for the baby to come. Then Jacob started putting wood together for a cradle stand. Time flew. Now that Leah was pregnant, all the other servants jumped when Leah spoke. Leah enjoyed the extra attention and she was totally happy, except when her husband still preferred to sleep and eat with Rachel. She still could not quite overcome that pain.

Now everyone knew about Leah's pregnancy. They knew her child would be the heir of the family fortune someday. This put Leah in a higher position socially. She did not have to threaten anyone with the whip. The servants jumped when she asked them to do a job. Leah was also very grateful to God. God had seen her trouble and helped her up. Being an unloved wife did not seem as hard anymore. She was carrying a new child in her womb. The first one of the clan. The child kicked, and it made her happy every time. She even enjoyed the occasional clumsiness that her extended abdomen caused her. All that was happiness for her. The months of waiting slowly came to an end.

The birthing time finally arrived. A midwife appeared. She prepared everything for the birth of the child. She had warm water ready on the fire place for washing the baby and the mother. She had cloth ready to wrap the infant. She waited. People and workers held their breath, there was less noise and roughhousing, because a critical, but necessary moment was here. People could never be really sure all would go well, and sometimes young, healthy mothers died during childbirth. Mother Laban wished that all would go well with her daughter. Father Laban drank a goblet of wine and drumbeat the wooden table when the minutes stretched into hours and still the baby was not there.

Leah, however, was confident. She knew a child that God had given her would also be born properly and live. She endured the labor pains quietly and stoically. The pain was great and all encompassing. The midwife felt her abdomen from time to time. Leah saw no change in the expression of her face, which made her think all must be normal. She realized she had to endure and endure. Leah was lying on her back on a mat which was on a wooden birthing chair. The chair had very short legs and the back was laid-back, with a stiff pillow under her head. Suddenly, she just had to breathe very heavily, she did not know why. It felt as if, down below, a rock was pressing against a brick wall. "What's that?" she exclaimed, "something is stuck, help!" But the midwife said:

"Do not worry, Leah, it's the head coming through. The end is near. Push! Push! Push more! Still more!" encouraged the midwife. Then Leah realized she had to push with all her available might, while grabbing the handles tightly of the birthing chair. Leah was used to heavy work and had strong muscles and now pushed with all her might.

"Slow down, not quite that hard," the midwife adomished. "I don't want you to rip. You are stronger than I thought." The head was now out, then came the shoulders and finally the rest of the baby. Even though the beginning was slow, it had turned turned into a regular spontaneous birth.

"A boy, a boy," cried the midwife. Word spread over the compound, everyone wished each other well. Mother Laban embraced her husband and they hurried over to Leah's quarters. The midwife, however, would not let anyone in just now, she was still busy with Leah. She rubbed down the infant hard and rough, which made him cry hard and strong and lustily. She made him ready for all to see and wrapped him tightly in linen.

Jacob was the first one allowed to hold the infant. He smiled and lifted him up high, "Yippee! A boy!" yelled Jacob. "What shall his name be?" he asked Leah.

"I think his name shall be Reuben," Leah breathed exhaustedly and feeling like a wrung-out dishrag.

"Reuben it is," called out Jacob. Just then the newborn started screaming, a loud, husky scream.

"My son is hungry," Jacob said with an authoritative voice.

"Sh, sh, Master Jacob, not so loud in the birthing room. You are upsetting mother and baby." The midwife took the baby from his arms, ushered him to go outside. "I am sorry, midwife, for being so loud." Then turning to his mother-in-law, he said, "I saw many lambs and calves being born and it left me cold, but ones' own male child got me all nervous." He then embraced Mrs. Laban and said "Thank you for your daughter."

Now more people came over to look at the, now screaming, child. A loud, healthy scream.

"My son is hungry," said Jacob, with a happy face to the folks that had come looking. "We have to talk quietly," Jacob said, "so mother and child can have peace." Red, dark-haired little Reuben seemed to know right away what he was expected to do, namely to suck, and suck he did, no trouble. Now the midwife shushed everybody away and demanded quietness, for the baby must drink without bother, and the young mother and the baby both must then sleep. Happiness and peace lay over the household. Even Rachel and Bilhah had come over. Even though she was angry at her sister and angry that she was not pregnant as yet, but such a new baby she must see, and thus overcome her contempt for her sister.

Will Jacob now sleep with me, since I was so good and had a male child for him? Jacob also had some soft feelings for Leah. *Maybe I should give in and be with her more often? But then, my father-in-law would be correct that I will get used to Leah eventually. No way will I give Laban the satisfaction of proving him right. I will stick to my intention and not love the wife he pushed me into marrying, just for Laban's sake I will be hard.* And after Jacob had made up his mind not to be loving or nice to Leah, for Laban's sake, then it was easy for him and it became his second nature toward his first wife. Sometimes when Jacob talked to Leah his tone of voice was harsh and she felt as if his words sliced into her heart, but she seldom told him so. She felt she had to be hard. But God saw that also.

And so one day after another passed. Young Reuben gained weight and was a joy to everyone, especially Leah. Leah could not help but notice that her husband still did not show love toward her; her sister Rachel was still more on his mind than she, even though she had given him the son. It hurt Leah deeply in her heart, but she thought of God and that comforted her. The baby was so cute. Every kiss that her husband did not give her, Leah placed on little Reuben.

~~~

Young Denah showed up again and asked to be taught how to help care for the baby, how to weave and tried her hand at spinning. Every girl had to know that. Mother Laban would not always let Denah go to her favored sister because Denah had to learn housekeeping at her father's place and help her mother with cooking and other chores. Her cousins and servants were such voracious eaters and seemingly could never get enough. It was fun for Denah to have a bit of free time to walk over to Leah's, help diaper the baby, cradle him and then sing to him to make him fall asleep. While there, she asked about the God of Abraham, how everything was in the olden days.

"What about the time when The Lord said to sacrifice Uncle Isaac? I would not have lain still on the altar, I would have fought to get off," Denah said.

"Well, you see, little Denah, Isaac knew that his father loved him very, very much, he would never hurt him. Maybe he was surprised too, and too amazed to fight his father. Abraham knew the birth of his son was a pure miracle, and God who created Isaac in the first place, could make him alive again or somehow do something."

"And then," Leah said, "a booming voice of the Lord was heard:

"Abraham, do not lay your hand on the boy. I have seen now that you are obedient. Over there in the bushes is a ram sheep stuck with his horns. Free it and that one you shall sacrifice to me."

Abraham dropped the knife in the sand and turned and looked, and yes, indeed there was the ram. A glad sigh escaped his mouth, followed by a joyous grin. As quickly as Abraham could, he untied Isaac. They embraced each other and laughed into each others eyes. Then Abraham proceeded toward the ram. Abraham cut the ram loose from the thorny bushes and led him to the altar site. He laid the sheep on top of the stones and tied it down, as he had before done to his son Isaac."

Fascinated, Denah asked,…"And then, what did Abraham do?"

"Then Abraham took his large butcher knife and with power and speed slammed it into the throat of the sheep. The ram made a painful cry. Blood spurted out of the wiggling sheep and ran down the rough altar stones. Slowly, as the blood drained out of the sheep, its movements became slower and slower, and it lay still. It was dead. Now Abraham had some gleaming coals in a clay pot and lit a fire with sticks and thus burned up the dead sheep. The smoke ascended up to the Lord, and God was pleased and Abraham and Isaac were happy."

"But why would the Lord make such a request, when He knew all along it would not become a fact?" asked Denah.

"You see," explained Leah, "the heathen nations around us are sometimes throwing their lovely little babies into the fire to sacrifice to some god, to gods that don't even exist, nor speak. It is not to be done. A mother and a father are suppose to love and cherish their children." And then Leah lifted up her "bundle of happiness" and kissed little Reuben.

"Maybe God wanted to see if Abraham loved the real God as much as the heathen their fake gods. I feel there must be a deeper meaning to this whole thing, but I do not know it as yet," said Leah.

"What did mother Sarah do when Abraham was supposed to sacrifice Isaac?" asked Denah.

"Oh, Abraham did not tell her. She would never have allowed it."

"Also, the Lord just wanted Abraham not to spoil little Isaac. Abraham adored his son Isaac. He could never spank him for anything. Isaac could do no wrong. The Lord wanted Abraham not to forget that Isaac is a special baby, a special son, the second one in a long line of people that surely will come. And this little Reuben that I carried in my womb will continue the tradition. But now go home, Denah, your mother will be waiting for you." So Denah went back to her Mother and told her what sister Leah had told her.

~~~

Leah became sad again that her husband spent so much time with Rachel, which allowed Rachel the opportunity to hear more about God than she. However, Leah felt that no matter how little she knew she would trust this God, and she knew she belonged. Her sister Rachel still was not pregnant.

Then one day Jacob walked over to Leah's place again. "How is my son doing? Let's see him," he said to Leah. Jacob took his son and looked into his face. Then little Reuben smiled to his father. Jacob smiled back and enjoyed the little guy. He gave him back to Leah.

"What are you cooking for dinner tonight?" he asked.

A little joy swept through Leah, and quickly she said, "lamb cuttlets."

"Ah, my favorite. I am tired and need a bit of sleep. The sun was so hot today and the sheep were so thirsty." He fell asleep, while Leah and Zilpah hurried to get the meal ready. Jacob ate, and watched Leah nurse little Reuben. Finally, all went to sleep. And then Jacob slept with his first wife again.

The next morning Leah prepared a rich, delicious breakfast for Jacob. He ate with glee and asked for seconds. After breakfast he said, the herds needed him, it was another hot day, hyenas might come around if the rivers dry out. "Bye, Leah, I must go." He left toward Rachel's home, picked up his gear and left. *If he wants something from me, he comes, but otherwise, it's always Rachel.* An unshed tear was created in her eye. But not for long, and sure enough, after nine months Leah was ready to deliver another child. She was happy. *Women must have many babies, then their husbands will love them. Jacob will love me for real this time.*

When her time came the midwife was there again, and this birth went faster as the first. Leah had found out that by opening her mouth and exhaling, no cry of pain comes out of her mouth. She wanted to be tough

57

and strong, not like some other women who scream so loud every man has to leave the premises. Finally, another baby boy was born. Wonderful! The child's hair was lighter than Reuben's. He was just a little bit shorter than her first child. This boy Leah named Simeon. Simeon was a forceful screamer. If he could not get his way he would turn crimson from crying. Leah had to rush to still him at her ample breasts. Simeon grew well. Little Reuben and Simeon played together even though Simeon could not talk as yet.

When Simeon was a toddler, Leah walked with Reuben and Simeon to the village well. There were some women also getting water. They talked a little. As Leah turned her head she saw little Simeon had climbed on the rim of the well. The well was about five feet across and about twenty feet deep. She wanted to scream but caught herself being afraid her child might get shocked and fall in. Suddenly all conversation had stopped, and every other woman stared at little Simeon, holding their breath, while Leah slowly and casually walked around the well until she was behind Simeon. Then she called him, "Come to Mommy, little Simeon, come to Mommy," and stretched out her arms. Little Simeon climbed down as slowly as he had climbed up and walked toward his mother. She grabbed him and held him tight. Common sighs of relief escaped from the other women's lips. Then Leah told Simeon in her most serious voice: "No, no, no climbing on well, no, no." She took him away from the well and packed him into her baby carrying cloth which was over her shoulders, and held Reuben tightly on her hand.

"Children," exclaimed an old village women, "they do the weirdest things. Your God of Abraham protected him. He is blessing you, Leah," said another woman.

"Yes, I guess, He is."

After some time Leah got pregnant again. The workload was increasing and she asked Jacob for some help. Jacob was orderly and did everything properly and got his wife another maid. When the baby was born she named him Levi. Now she had three little boys. *Now my husband will love me.* But he was still businesslike towards her, while she could tell his wife Rachel was the lover-girl to him. She could not understand it, that he did not love her: she cooked well, she sewed beautifully, she planted the garden properly, she weaved expertly, she even bore him three sons. *Should not all that make a man love his wife? Jacob is so busy and has hardly any time for his boys, either.*

The Dog

Laban could sell more wool and cattle due to Jacob's hard work. Now with extra money, he wanted to buy some special cloth imported from overseas. He saddled three camels, took a servant along to travel to the seashore. His route went in south-westerly direction from his home.

A large boat landed just when he arrived. It was moved by men with paddles and guided by a rudder. Tall, blond, broad-shouldered men emerged and a little different-looking dog. Laban had never before been at the ocean and it was all very interesting to him. He noticed especially that dog. It was multicolor in white, brown and some black and had long hair. The dogs in his neighborhood were pale with short hair and wild. These men spoke in a different language. They had some gold and copper pieces and obviously wanted to trade it for fresh fruit. It was interesting to see them dealing with local merchants in, mostly, sign language. Their dog, it must be a young animal, thought Laban, seemed to belong to one man. Then this man wanted the dog back in the boat. However, the dog ran away. Every time the man wanted to catch him he ran away. Finally, the man caught the dog and tied a rope around his neck and dragged him back toward the boat, but the dog put his little feet into the ground and tried to resist. Laban could see this dog did not want to go back into the boat. Then the man looked around at Laban, showed him five fingers, pointed to the dog and indicated he wanted to sell Laban the dog. Laban shook his head. *What would I do with such a dog?* He then raised his shoulders toward the man, indicating 'no use.' The man caught on. He saw some goats running around, nibbling at someone's vegetable stand. The stranger pointed to the dog and to the goats and said a word that sounded like 'sick it,' or seemed to have that meaning. Then the young dog ran over to the goats. He barked fiercely.

"Oh no," groaned the goatherder, "now that dog will kill my goats." But the dog just nabbed them in their hind legs. The goats immediately ran away. The stranger called "Chukko, Chukko, home, home," and the dog came running back to him.

Now Laban understood what the man had meant, why he wanted five pieces of silver for the dog. *It is a trained and domesticated dog.* Laban, being a crafty fellow, shook his head, and held up only three fingers. The man acted really upset, but finally, he accepted Laban's three coins and the man gave Laban the leash with the dog. Then the man showed Laban how to stroke the dog, praise him and give him some food. Then Laban followed his instructions. The dog made whining sounds and wiggled with his tail. He tried to lick Laban. Then Laban took that dog home with him.

The children, Reuben, Simeon and Levi ran towards the dog and tried to stroke him. Little Levi pulled his tail, and the dog Chukko made a deep threatening sound. "Don't do that, Levi, he is a working dog," said his grandfather.

Chukko grew and his hair grew still longer. In two years he was full-grown and had became an excellent cattle and farm dog. Laban had to just point his finger to the cattle in the wrong field and Chukko would run and not tear the animal apart, just bite them a little in their hind legs and bark fiercely, and the animal would run from Chukko wherever he chased it to.

Since Chukko had long hair, he seemed to suffer from heat in the summer or on hot days in fall or spring. He liked to rest under a shady tree when he wasn't used for a cattle drive. Chukko was also a very observant dog. If a stranger approached the compound he barked fiercely and showed all his teeth. Strangers got the impression that the dog was trying to tear them apart - until he was called back by someone from the homestead.

~~~

Once again Leah got pregnant. Time flew by so fast with three little boys making demands on her. The next baby was, again, a boy. This time Leah had run out of favored names. She asked Jacob about a name for him. Jacob said, "How about Judah? Judah seems such a futuristic and promising name as if big things will come his way." So this fourth baby was called Judah.

Leah was now very busily taking care of four little boys. Fortunately, she had her maids to help with their care and the housework. Sometimes Leah got tired of being sad all the time for not being loved. She forgot the feeling and just enjoyed her four little lovely boys. She enjoyed their laughter, their games, enjoyed seeing the strong little bodies climbing trees and hurling rocks. It was a terrific time nevertheless. When Father Jacob came home from the field at night, he looked in on his sons. They were all around him, climbing up on him and wanting things, "Dad, Dad, look at me. Dad see this rock. Dad, Simeon hit me. Dad, I will be as tall as you." Little Levi even promised his Father, "I will kill a lion for you when you are sooo old." Jacob enjoyed the attention his little boys gave him. But after awhile he departed to his wife Rachel's home where it was quiet, orderly and peaceful, just the right climate for sleeping.

Sometimes sadness came over Leah when she realized that nothing she did could make Jacob fall in love with her. She just needed some comfort. Then she went into her bedroom chamber and prayed to Jacob's God: "O Lord, I am like a dove in the cleft of the rock, in the secret place of the cliff. Let me see your face, let me hear your voice; for your voice is sweet, and your face is lovely." It helped her to talk to God. And with straight shoulders and her head held high she walked out of her bedroom chamber, ready to embrace another day.

So often it happened that something went wrong with the cattle and a servant called Jacob out into the night or interrupted his sleeping time and he, as the man in charge, had to correct the situation. Sometimes bulls were fighting with each other. This could not continue because such large cattle was too costly to loose or get injured. Then he and a servant had to shove a large board, prepared for this purpose, between the two bulls and thus force them apart. Such jobs needed a strong man like Jacob and other strong servants of Laban's.

Sometimes wolves came near the herds at night, their green eyes shining from the glow of the campfire in the darkness. That needed Jacob's attention. A good sleep in-between these nightly disturbances in the quietness and coziness of Rachel's silent abode was just what Jacob needed. Leah knew that and tried to be understanding. She knew that often her little boys would cry at night and thus disturb their father, but she could not help that.

In Rachel's home, there were no crying babies at night. There was peace, a dead peace to be sure, but uninterrupted. Over on the other side, behind the mulberry tree, there was a lone wife mourning for the empty bed, fighting the squabbles with the children alone. But that did not enter Jacob's mind. "Aoooo- Aoooo", - a lone wolf howling in the wilderness. *I hope Jaffer, the new servant on duty, is watching the sheep.* And then Jacob drifted off to sleep, in Rachel's arms. When Rachel knew he slept soundly, she would move away a bit, as not to disturb his needed rest.

~~~

Leah could never quite forget or overcome the fact that her husband Jacob did not love her. He came to her when his presence was needed to deliver food or grain or for disciplining the boys, but no more. No special kiss for Leah, no extra gentle touch, nothing. Nor did he sleep with her if he could help it. Sure, with two wives he had to switch his sleeping quarters from time to time, or else what would people say? His honor in the community was considered very important. Lately, Leah did not get pregnant anymore. *Very well, four children is a good number, and I enjoy them with all my heart. Serves Rachel right—no children—she took my husband away.* Rachel was upset and did not visit Leah too often, but she watched her little boys run all over the place with longing and often with teary eyes.

Leah, Zilpah, Rachel and Bilhah were doing all their work which was expected of women. It was flax harvesting season. Flax grew about one-and-a-half feet high. It bloomed bright blue with a small flower on top. A field of blooming blue flax was beautiful to look at. Flax would be planted like grain, close together. Then when the flax was ripe and the straw dry, it would be harvested like grain. The grains were ground in a mill between two large millstones. If that system was not available women would just put some handfuls of flax grain into a stone gourd and stomp it with a rock until it was all squashed and the oil would form. Then it would be poured through an old linen cloth - and you had linseed oil. The straw would be beaten and mangled in such a way that the outer rim would fall off and only the stringy part was left. Now the stringy flax fibers would be ready to be spun into yarn. Women and young girls had to sit for hours on their spinning wheels and spin and spin from early dawn to dusk and make miles of yarn. Those that had no elaborate spinning wheel would just roll the yarn onto a spindle. After supper, when it was too dark to do anything else, the women from the village would sometimes get together, sing and dance awhile, without men. One woman would play the tamborine and determine the beat. Rachel and Bilhah, and sometimes Zilpah, would join them. The fluid movements of their bodies helped them to loosen up after a long day of spinning or sewing.

Jacob however, if home, took care of his family's needs such as sewing a new saddle for a camel or stir-ups for a donkey. He had little time for leisure. Father Laban was getting older and did what was expected from him as a landowner. Towards the evening he was usually too tired to do additional work or play with the grandsons. He preferred to rest.

Leah did not often miss Jacob's love anymore because she had four little boys Reuben, Simeon, Levi and Judah to love, care for and teach. She praised God. God gave her comfort. She tried to be good and faithful to the husband and doing her duty as a mother. It was expected of her and she did it. Also, it was not her fault that she was given to her husband in that deceitful manner. That also gave Leah peace of mind.

The four little boys were playing with each other. They imitated their father. They used little stones as sheep, larger stones as cows, other stones as camels. They pushed little sticks in the ground as fences for their make-believe cattle. They imitated howling wolves or laughing hyenas. Then they would shoot their little arrows at the make-believe wolves. In between they fought like children do, and then Leah had to step in and create order again. She tried to be a judge when the boys were fighting. She did not want the freshest boy become a general bully and get away with it and become a tyrant.

The Rat

During a cool day in the fall, Leah stepped into her pantry. Flour, frying grease, jams, raisins, dates and other good things were stored there. Suddenly, she saw a fat rat scurrying away but not out the door. Leah quickly ran to her fireplace and grabbed a stout stick for the rat. She chased it around until she had it in a corner to kill it. But the rat did not want to be killed - and escaped into the only dark hole it could see: under Leah's skirts, climbing up on her. A blood curdling scream escaped Leah's mouth. She stepped backwards and hit her stomach where the rat held on to her dress. The rat got scared, saw a way out, let go and ran out the door. Leah stood very still. To feel any pain from a bite, she stroked up and down her dress - she felt nothing that hurt.

"Whew, that unclean beast!" A relieved sigh settled her composure again. Leah formed a new theorem: when dealing with a rat, don't corner it.

"Where is that Chukko dog?" Leah called out. "Reuben, where are you?" He came running to his mother.

"Go, call Chukko, and hunt that rat that ran out of my pantry!"

Chukko heard his name, came running and yapping happily, wiggling his tail. Reuben took him by the rope and went out hunting for the rat.

Later on Leah told everyone what had happened to her and most people laughed and found it so funny. Leah decided to use her new theorem also on people that were "rats" in her eyes, giving them leeway to escape.

The next day Leah had some disciplinary problems with the boys. When Jacob walked past her home in the morning, she told him about the boys and asked him to look into the matter.

"Leah, I am too busy right now. I really must go, maybe some other time," and Jacob left.

Awhile later Leah slung her youngest baby into her carrying cloth and went out to her garden to pick some herbs for her kitchen. On the way she had to pass Rachel's home. She could not help but overhear Jacob and Rachel's happy banter and laughter. She tried not to listen to their conversation. *There he tells me he is too busy to talk to the boys but not too busy to entertain my sister. I am angry. I must confront him!*

Just then she remembered her new theorem: when dealing with a "rat", don't corner it.

"No, I will not confront him now. Who am I? I am an intelligent woman and of proper age. I know how things have to be done, and if their father does not want to mix in, I will handle things myself. Really, I will!"

Bitter and energetically Leah kept picking her herbs. This time it was dill weeds, grape leaves and mustard seeds. She needed a lot of them for making cucumber pickles. She had her herbs nicely planted in rows and all plants had ripened and were ready to be harvested. The pickles would taste good. Leah enjoyed working, it was more fulfilling for her than pining over missing love. "Boys!" Leah called when she came back from the garden patch, "come here right now!" The little boys came meandering over to their mother. "Did I not tell you not to step on the land behind the shed? Zilpah sowed seeds there, and look what you did: all your footsteps going through it, even the dog's. You did not obey my order."

Then Leah took off her little leather strap and each boy received a slap on his behind, except Reuben who received two because he was the oldest and should have known better. "Now, run off, boys, and don't let me catch you again." They ran as fast as their little legs could transport them, back to play, somewhere else.

Fetishes

Grandfather Laban was the "big chief" of the tribe, the one who supposedly had all the money. When Egyptian or Edomite traders came by, the little boys came running and looking at their camels and their wares. They asked their grandfather to buy them this arrow and that rope and all the various things that little children like to have. Sometimes he would buy them something their little hearts longed for, like sugary dates, other times he would not. At one such occasion Laban saw two wooden statues, just good luck charms, called gods or idols. They were beautifully carved and artistically painted. The salesman said they are gods that will bring him good luck and safety. Leah and Rachel also were by the wagon, looking at the displays that were for sale. They also saw the statues. They thought those colorful statues would look good in their parent's house, give the room an air of elegance. Laban bought them. Mother Laban carried them into their home. When Jacob came home from the fields at night, Rachel told him about the two gods.

"There is only one God," said Jacob to her.

"I know, I know, Jacob, they are just to look good, just to enhance the drab living quarters. The merchant said they will bring them good luck."

"Nobody should pray to those wooden decorations, because the God of creation, the one who appeared to my grandfather Abraham, to my father Isaac and me in my dream is not a piece of wood."

Next time Jacob had some reason to go to Leah's home, the boys also told their father what nice things grandfather Laban had bought.

"Can we also have one of those things? Please, Father?"

"No, Simeon, Reuben, they are just wooden fakes, there is no god in them."

Later on the boys discussed those pretty colorful statues their grandfather had bought and that are supposed to bring good luck. Levi stood up as tall as his short little body could stretch and said, "I am not afraid of those gods." He took his knife out of his pocket, and announced, "Dad does not like them. I will throw my knife at those gods with great power, look at my strong muscles," he raised his arm to show his older brothers his muscled arm."

"Don't you dare, Levi," Leah called out because she had overheard the conversation. "Your grandfather paid a lot of golden dinars for those things."

"And I will kick them with my foot," exclaimed little Judah, and he hurried to run over to grandfather's place to do it.

"Stay right here, Judah, no running away, we will be eating supper soon."

~~~

Then came "school." The four young boys of Jacob had to learn how to shoot an arrow and a sling shot. Jacob had the older ones come to the field to him, gave them real arrows and a bow that he had made, showed them a rock as a target and "Now shoot!" Their little arms missed and the arrows and sling shots did not go very far. They lost interest. However, Jacob did not give in. They had to learn to shoot to defend their herds from wild animals or enemies. So Jacob had to drive them on with a stricter tone of voice. When they lost interest a few hard slaps on their behinds helped to restore their interest. They now had to target-shoot every day until they hit a specific target. The boys much rather played in the sand and had fun, but duty forced them to learn and practise. Tears did not count.

"I don't care if you cry, Levi and Judah," said their father. "You keep on shooting just the same," ordered their father. Reuben and Simeon were older and did not want to shed tears anymore, they tried to act like men. It did not matter if they finally were allowed to go home crying on Mother Leah's shoulder. She took her little boys in her arms, kissed them and explained to them that they have to learn to shoot straight and hard. They would otherwise be eaten by wild animals: lions, bears, wolves, hyenas.

"Now be real men, boys. Wipe off your baby tears and eat your dinner."

And slowly their little muscles grew and their targets were hit more often, until they showed off how well they could hit. But it was a long hard road to reach that goal. Father Jacob's strong arm and iron will forced them to become good marksmen.

Then came the time for butchering. The sheep they loved had to be killed for meat, fur and wool. The bones had to be boiled until all meat came off easily. Then soapstone was added to it and soap was made for the family. The little boys also tried their knives on the cadavers and tried to help cut them apart.

"Careful!" said their father, as he cut the meat apart, "get out of my way, or my knife will cut you." But the boys watched and learned to slice.

Renate M. Schulz

Rachel's Idea

Rachel watched all the activity in her sister Leah's house from the distance. She was very jealous. *Here I am, married for years already and no baby. What will people think? Isn't a good wife supposed to get pregnant?* Fortunately, her husband did not look down on her because of it. He loved her as always. He smiled to her and told her that he loved her, and that he loved her very much. He put his arm around her waist, he kissed her, he hugged her, he talked with her. He went to Leah only when duty required it. When he slept in Rachel's home he did not just demand his right, he tried to be orderly.

Suddenly, Rachel had a new idea: *That is it! Now I know what is wrong, why I don't get pregnant. My husband uses me just as a lovelady, to romance me. With my sister he does cold hard sex, nothing more. That is why she gets pregnant. I am sick of Jacob's love and romantic notions, I want cold, hard sex, nothing more, the way he does it with my sister, the kind that makes a child.*

"Jacob," Rachel said in a hard and determined tone to Jacob at night before bedtime. "It is your fault that I don't conceive. You romance me all the time; love does not get me pregnant. I want a cold, hard and effective union, the way you do it with my sister Leah. You are faking with me. I want a baby, and I want it now!"

Bilhah, Rachel's maid, woke up from her sleep when she heard that argument from a distance. She lay as still as a mouse, but her ears were wide open. She had to hear this one! Then she heard Jacob raising his voice to Rachel and shouting at her, and getting real angry.

"You think I am not a real man to you, don't you? Well, you are a stupid woman. I know more about regeneration than you think. The fault is your body. God has closed your body? You are barren!" Rachel, when she heard the word 'barren,' it sounded like a curse to her, held her hands over her ears. She just could not endure to hear such a word. Then Bilhah heard some more angry words from Jacob, but could not understand them all. Then she heard Jacob angrily storming out of the room, slamming the door. She heard him stomping over toward Leah's home.

Leah appreciated her husband's sudden appearance.

~~~

68

Bilhah, Rachel's maid, was shorter than Leah, Rachel and Zilpah. She was also slim and had light brown hair. Bilhah liked to wear nice clothes. Not that she had much as a maid, and most every piece had to be made at home. The yarn had to be spun first, then woven on a loom. However, she was usually happy. Her mistress had no children, not too much work to do. She could live a decent life and spend a good amount of time taking care of herself. Evenings she would wet her long hair with her fingers. Then she would braid it tightly. Then the next day or whenever she and Rachel went to the market or somewhere, Bilhah would open her long hair and it came out beautiful and wavy, attracting the looks of other women, and sometimes even men. Bilhah liked herself in that role, especially since her mistress Rachel was also beautiful. Bilhah vowed to herself that she would never want to be given in marriage to someone she did not like. However, she knew women did not have much choice; they were given to whomever her "master" gave them to. She hoped with all her heart she would never be given to some old, ugly, smelly, domineering despot. A man who would view her only as a "mule and childbearer". And if that happened anyhow, she would not allow him to beat her, she would beat back even if it caused her death. Bilhah actually got scared about her own determination, would she really go that far? Fortunately, being the maid of Rachel, perhaps for life, such fate would probably evade her. She considered herself lucky in a way.

Rachel still had her old nurse living with them. Her name was Deborah. She was rather old and getting weaker and needed some help. Deborah also tried to comfort Rachel about her lack of children. She also advised Bilhah how to behave to avoid trouble. And so time went on, and Bilhah's good life continued. Her mistress was still childless, and it did not bother Bilhah. It was not her problem.

"*Well,*" Rachel said to herself finally, "*what do people do when they have no child? They give their maid to their husband to sleep with, and then the offspring is the wife's baby. I can have children through Bilhah, I will show my sister! What grandmother Sarah did I can do also.*" Her mind was made up.

Bilhah heard the defiant monologue of her mistress and became scared. She curled up under her blanket and hid her head also. She knew Master Jacob will probably come to her now. She was scared and had never viewed Jacob as an sex object with her. Boooo! But then, she thought, she will get pregnant, have a baby to love and life will not be so boring, also it will raise her servant position somewhat.

~~~

Once again it was time for Rachel to bake bread. They were down to their last loaf. She started measuring out the flour.

"Bilhah, climb up and get me the bag of sourdough."

The sourdough was a little of leftover dough from the previous baking. It would turn sour in time and then, mixed into the fresh dough, would make the dough rise. Bilhah climbed the ladder to grab the skin of sourdough, but it was empty and the string ripped apart.

"Mistress Rachel, there is no sourdough, the bag is all empty and ripped open," she exclaimed. "Maybe mice or a cat have eaten it."

"What, no sourdough? Could you not watch? What are you good for?"

And on and on lamented Rachel.

"Jacob and the men are hungry, we must have bread today. Jacob is angry at me anyway. What will we do?"

And Rachel got real angry at Bilhah for not noticing it before. She yelled louder and louder. Bilhah was afraid she would get a beating with Rachel's leather strap.

Leah heard the commotion from the distance and sent her boy Reuben over to look what was going on.

"But not so obvious, you understand?"

"I know, Mother."

And he ran off. After awhile he came back and told her.

"Well, well, that serves Rachel right. Now Jacob will love me."

But then she also had enough common sense that the happiness of Jacob and the whole compound depended on food. Leah poured a generous amount of precious distilled strong wine into a container, gave it to Reuben to carry over to his aunt and tell her to put that into the dough instead of sourdough. It would rise in the oven. Rachel was all surprised. But she accepted the liquid and mixed it into her dough, as her nephew had told her from his mother. Sure enough, the loaves of bread rose beautifully in the oven. Just the taste was a little different. The situation was saved, the hungry men had their bread.

After a few days when Jacob's anger had subsided a little, Rachel approached Jacob and said, "Here, take my maid Bilhah," she grabbed Bilhah on the arm and shoved her over to him, "and sleep with her tonight or as long as it takes to get her pregnant. I want a child, even if it is from her."

Bilhah was a servant woman, sort of like a slave, and had no right to rebel, and where would she go if she said "no" and Rachel sent her away. Would a new master be better?

Jacob did not hesitate at all, a little diversion was always appreciated, especially with a neat well-dressed maid. Why not? It was the custom in those days, a way out? So Jacob took Bilhah to sleep with her in her room. Bilhah was a virgin yet, and the powerful man caused her some pain, but she was silent. Sure enough, Bilhah got pregnant very soon after. Nobody asked her if she agreed to this or not. If she was happy about it, fine; if not, it was her problem.

Rachel watched her every day to see if she would get her monthly cycle or develop morning sickness. Bilhah was not very happy. *Now I have to soon run around, getting a fat belly, maybe I will keep the weight, I will look like an old mama. Haw! Rachel wants the child, she shall have it. Why should I get my clothes dirty by some wetting infant, without a real husband of my very own? I hate being a maid. My hair, will I have time to tend it so it looks luscious? Other women on market day notice it and even guys try to grab it, but I won't let them. Let Rachel have the messy baby, I have housework to do...*

So Bilhah tried to comfort herself.

In time Rachel saw the symptoms of pregnancy in Bilhah. Bilhah was silent. Rachel was glad. She offered her good food to eat, made sure she did not lift anything too heavy, and had enough sleep, for she, Rachel, wanted that baby.

I will show my sister. What she has I can have too.

Then it was time for Bilhah's baby to be born. She was very much afraid of giving birth. She was slim in figure with narrow hips, and afraid she would die. Her mother had died when she was born. Rachel and the midwife, sat with her and they were ready and waiting. As the contractions got stronger Bilhah could not stand it anymore and started screaming and cursing Jacob. Jacob heard it and Leah's boys also. He took his sons and walked away with them, further out on the fields. "Boys don't belong near a childbearing room, let us go."

The midwife was not disturbed by such words of a childbearing woman. She knew from experience that the overwhelming pain can cause a woman to say things she would otherwise not say.

When the baby was born, Bilhah was weak and felt like a dishrag. She had lost a lot of blood and almost collapsed when she tried to get up. The midwife gave her lots of berry juice, told her to stay down, and fried some eggs for her. Rachel however, was happy and triumphant. She said, "God has judged my case, and He has also heard my voice and given me a son."

She let Bilhah nurse the boy, but she cuddled and held him. As people and children came to see the new baby, Rachel held him up for all to see. She was grateful to God. She called his name Dan. A few days later Rachel took little Dan outside and walked around with him, so that everyone could see that she has a child. Bilhah did not like to see her child in the arms of another one, but there was nothing she could do, except try to eat and drink enough, so her baby would have enough milk. Bilhah was slim and not a heavy eater. However, Rachel encouraged her to "Please eat more, so that my son will get filled up with breast milk."

Your son? Rachel? He is mine, mine.

As soon as baby Dan was fed, Rachel took him away from Bilhah. The baby became a blessing in spite of it.

After little Dan was weaned from the breast, Rachel decided she wanted another child. Again, she told Jacob to sleep with Bilhah. Bilhah had to submit to Jacob again. She felt used and was angry about it, and gave Jacob no friendly word or look. She stared straight ahead when Jacob impregnated her. Bilhah mustered up all her dislike and willpower, hoping she would then not conceive but it did not help. She became pregnant anyhow. Her nine month of waiting were mostly uneventful. The birth of the second child was a little easier. Deborah called it a spontaneous birth.

Then Rachel said: "With great wrestlings I have wrestled with my sister, and indeed I have prevailed." This little boy Rachel called Naphtali. Now the race is on! Rachel wanted as many children as her sister had.

"Two more children, Bilhah, to make it four. You can make it. You have good births and your children are good looking and healthy. Two more! Yes, I will keep up with my sister. If she has four, so I will have four. If she gets five, so I will get five, from you. And remember, no extra kissing or loving. Remember how badly it turned out for maid Hagar when she tried to weasel herself into her Master Abraham's love. Grandmother Sarah beat her until she had red streaks on her back - and Abraham did not do anything. She thought just because she could get pregnant and Sarah did not, she could rise. You remember that Bilhah!"

That old fat hippo, as if I cared for the master..., but Bilhah was wise to stay quiet. Bilhah could only sigh and mourn her fate.

Zilpah

It was late afternoon and time to go to the village well in order to have water for supper, washing the children and for next morning's breakfast. Leah sent Zilpah to the well to get water. It was getting dark and the only light was the fire on the cooking hearth and an oil lamp. The boys were dirty and had to get washed up for the night. Somehow, the rope that held the pail slipped out of Zilpah's hand. "Oh no, what am I going to do now? Everyone will curse me when they want to fetch their water." Zilpah looked into the deep well. "Yes, there is the rope swimming on the water level down below. Where is the end of the rope?" Her eyes searched in the semi-darkness. Finally, she saw it. The end had gotten stuck on a brick. "But how will I get it out?" Zilpah started crying quietly. Then she heard a man's voice, "What is it, beautiful maiden? Can I dry your tears?"

She looked up, there was a young man, tall and statuesque. He had a friendly face and a comforting tone in his voice. Zilpah told him about the slipped rope.

"I can help you there, do not worry. Just step back and let me handle it." After a little while the man handed the end of the rope to Zilpah. Zilpah was happy. She thanked the man and asked his name. "Joppa is my name. I work as a farmhand for a local landowner." Then his eyes rested on tall, broadchested Zilpah with naturally red cheeks, her dark hair neatly tied in braides, and said to her, "I hope you will come for water more often." Then he turned and left the well.

Zilpah had stayed by the well too long, this time, and Leah got impatient. *Where is that Zilpah? I am waiting, lazy maid...*Finally, Zilpah arrived with the water. "What did you do so long at the well?"

"I am sorry, Mistress Leah, I accidentally dropped the rope into the well."

"Then, how did you get it out, did you climb in? I hope not, you could drown or your skirts could get stuck somehow. Watch it better, next time."

With a red face Zilpah went to work helping with the washing of the boys and finishing the kitchen before total darkness set in.

"How did you retrieve the pail?" asked Leah again.

"Somebody helped me," Zilpah offered.

The next day Zilpah, again, took a little longer at the well than usual. But this time no accident happened. The 'someone' was there again.

"Will you drop the rope in the well again?" he asked with a smile on his face.

"Not this time, Joppa, but thanks a lot for getting it out yesterday. My mistress was really upset with me. I've got to hurry."

"Ah, a little kiss for all the trouble I had with you yesterday, is in order. Is it not?"

"Oh you, Joppa, thanks again, but I must run. I don't want to be beaten with the rope." And off she ran.

The next night Zilpah hurried to get the water real early, *just in case Joppa*...and sure enough, Joppa was there again.

"May I help you get the bucket, it is so heavy, and you could accidentally drop in the rope..."

"Oh, you teaser!" She smiled and their eyes met, they could not just run off, another little good-bye kiss had to be exchanged. The next night again, and again. Then it was a hug. Then it became a long hug and a longer kiss. *Oh no, there comes the neighbor's maid for water*...the two quickly separated as if nothing had happened and went about their work. Leah noticed that Zilpah always had a silent, but rather happy face after carrying water.

"What makes you so happy?"

"Oh nothing," she lied, "it is the fresh air, weaving and spinning all day makes me so stiff. I need the hike."

Then one day another person saw Joppa and Zilpah hugging and kissing behind the bushes by the well. The two talked together as how to build a life with each other. It would not be easy because Zilpah was a bond servant. Someone saw it and the person told Leah. So Leah now knew why Zilpah was always so happy carrying water. She confronted her maid.

"Who is that man you are always with at the well?"

Zilpah got all red in her face and embarrassed. With a small voice she said "Joppa."

"So, Joppa it is. What good will it do, you are working for me, for life."

"I have been thinking, sometimes a maid can be bought out. We two are in love! Joppa owns one cow already, and the best is the cow is pregnant, how lucky he is! Maybe he can redeem me, so we can get married?"

Leah knew how hard it was to watch others love each other and being loved, and no romantic love came her way, ever. She felt sorry for the maid. Jacob gave her what she needed in food and clothing. He talked with her whatever was necessary, but nothing more. Not, when she compared herself with her sister Rachel. Jacob used an authoritive tone with her, but with Rachel his voice turned quiet and casual. And often Jacob looked Rachel in the face and his eyes laughed. Not so with her. Leah could get so upset about that. She had to make herself tough. And here is Zilpah - in love! But a love she cannot have. Leah promised she would talk to Master Jacob about Zilpah and Joppa. There was the other, younger maid who could possibly be trained to take Zilpah's place, Leah mused. She was going to talk to her husband about that. But at least one thing Leah was glad about; Zilpah was not after her husband, one good point.

~~~

When Leah and Rachel met each other on the street or around the compound, Rachel showed off the two little boys with a triumphant look on her face toward her sister. Now she had two children also.

"My first two children are doing well, they are so strong and Naphtali is trying to walk already…"

*Her first two children?…*Leah felt as if Rachel tried to compete with her. *No way! She will not catch up, she has my husband's love and now she also wants the children, absolutely not!*

Then one day Rachel's maid Bilhah told Leah's maid Zilpah that Rachel really wants to catch up with her in babies. Zilpah discussed it with another maid. That maid told it to Leah. So, now Leah knew for sure that her guess had been right about Rachel.

The next day when the children were playing outside, Leah called Zilpah.

"Zilpah, come here! Rachel is trying to catch up with me with baby making, from Bilhah, of course. This cannot be. I want more children. It seems I cannot get pregnant anymore, but I want to have more children than my sister has. You will sleep with Master Jacob!"

Zilpah got a real shock and a worried look on her face. "What?" she exclaimed, "you promised to talk to Master Jacob about me." *Joppa, my Joppa, my love, what will I do?"*

But Leah did not see it or did not care. Then Zilpah took the gourd to go to the well and get the nightly water.

"No, Zilpah, you stay here, watch the boys. From now on I will get the water. You be ready for Master Jacob."

Now Zilpah looked really crushed. "But Mistress Leah, you promised…"

"Never mind, Zilpah, we will show Rachel who can have more children, she or I."

"Joppa has a cow already, the cow is pregnant, he wants to buy me out."

"Where would a mere servant get a cow from? I don't believe it," replied Leah.

"His master's cow gave birth to a really small and weak calf. Just then his only little son fell into the river. Joppa knows how to swim, he dropped the calf, ran and jumped into the deep water and swam over to where the little boy lay and rescued him. He shook the water out of his lungs and gave him back to his grateful parents. Then, his master said, 'I won't kill that newborn misfit of a calf, you may have it.' "

"That is a nice story, Zilpah, nevertheless you do as I say!"

Leah took the gourd out of Zilpah's hand and left for the village well herself.

Zilpah sat down, held her face in her hands and cried, tears trickling down between her fingers. Young Judah saw it and said:

"Don't cry, Zilpah, I love you." She gave him a hug and a kiss, and continued her evening chores.

When Leah came to the well she noticed the figure of a man behind the bushes. She stepped closer, since she was somewhat nearsighted, and yes, it was indeed the man Joppa. "Stay away from my maid," Leah called out to him. The man retreated wordlessly.

When Leah came home the children were in bed almost asleep. Leah waited awhile. Jacob was there delivering some more grain. She served him a cold drink and he thanked her.

"How are the sheep coming along?" asked Leah.

"Fine, Leah, just fine."

"How about the goats? Their milk is so sweet."

"The goats are fine, too. Are you also checking up on me like your father? Why don't you stay in your kitchen where you belong?"

That man! Can't he ever have a nice conversation with me? I better get to the point with him, before he disappears again.

"Jacob, I want you to sleep with my maid Zilpah."

"Whatever for? Aren't you satisfied with four children?"

"No, Jacob, I want more. Don't you know that a man has more honor when he has more healthy, good-looking children?"

"If you say so, why not? Where is she?"

So Leah stepped outside, grabbed Zilpah by the sleeve, walked her over to her husband. Jacob took her to Zilpah's sleeping quarters where he spent the night. Zilpah was very sad, she had to control herself to keep from crying.

Leah was angry about her husband sleeping with Zilpah, but still angrier at Rachel for trying to catch up with her.

That Rachel is a lot of trouble, we used to be friends. First she takes my husband away and his love that rightfully belongs to me, now she stoops so low as to further use my man for her purposes and outdo me with children. I will fix her!"

From now on Leah went to the well to get the water every day for awhile. Then when she noticed by careful observation that Zilpah seemed to have less appetite in the morning, and no monthly happening, she knew Zilpah must indeed be pregnant. But Zilpah did not look happy. And that sad face also told her mistress that the maid must be pregnant for sure. Then Leah let Zilpah go to the well again and fetch the water for the household.

On the third day Joppa appeared again. When all the other people had gotten their water and left, he exclaimed "Zilpah, my love, I missed you so, what happened?"

"The race is on. Rachel wants to catch up with Leah in children and I am the victim."

"Oh, no, Zilpah, it came to that?"

"Yes, Joppa, it did."

"One last hug and a kiss, Zilpah, my love."

"No, Joppa, not after I am impregnated by Master Jacob. They would consider it adultery and me a loose woman. You know what horrible things they could do to me! A goodbye kiss would only increase our love for each other, a love that must die."

Joppa was quite upset, he stamped his foot on the ground, "Why should Jacob have all the women he can get and I none?"

"Some day, Joppa, The Hero will come who was promised to Adam and Eve, the one to crush the head of the evil snake. He will do things right, only one man for one woman."

"I might be dead by then, Zilpah, what am I going to do?"

"Just the same, there is nothing you and I can do. So let's just do things right, so the Hero will like us when he comes. No good-bye, no kiss, no hug."

Zilpah lifted her container, turned, and left. Two salty tears spilled into the fresh drinking water.

As Zilpah came home to their yard, Master Jacob walked in her direction, driving fatted rams before him to get them ready for the market for the next morning, and young Reuben helping him.

Master Jacob saw Zilpah's red eyes and stopped. He pulled the cloth of her upper dress toward him, exposing her bare shoulder, looked into her red eyes and asked:

"Zilpah, you have been crying. What is it? Can I help you?" Zilpah looked away, down into the dirt as if there was some sudden interesting worm crawling in the sand.

"Nothing, Master Jacob, nothing. There was dust on the road, something came into my eyes."

Jacob quickly and gently stroked her soft cheek with the top of his hand as to not get her dirty, smiled, and said, "Women! Who can figure them out?" And they parted.

However, Leah had seen the scene from inside the house. Anger rose inside her. *That is all I need, Jacob loving still another.* When Zilpah came into the house, Leah told her firmly to stay away from Master Jacob.

"You are just the maid. And the child you carry from him is mine. Is that understood?"

"Yes, Mistress Leah."

Zilpah laid down in her bed and cried herself to sleep. She knew she could not do anything but submit. It did not fare well with grandmother Sarah's maid Hagar who tried to go against her mistress; she was beaten by her mistress and Abraham did not interfere at all. She knew the story. "Could not have Abraham given Hagar, when he divorced her, at least two donkeys, one to carry more water, one to carry pots and pans and a tent? After all, he had loved Ishmael and was very rich. You don't do that to your child, letting him starve from the lack of water. It was cruel. Also, Abraham had enough, he could afford to give the maid more." Zilpah had her ideas about that. No, Hagar could not prevail. However, God had stepped in and remedied the situation. Had Hagar not been in trouble, she would not have called to the real God of heaven. She knew her former Egyptian gods were nothing, just human inventions. So, God let this cruel act stand so He could help out. Hagar really felt loved by God after that. However, it still caused a bitter root to grow in the hearts of Ishmael and his children since. Zilpah understood that.

And so the days went by with summer and winter coming and going. Zilpah's time had come, the midwife was there, and Leah sat next to Zilpah holding her hand to comfort her during the birth. Jacob had already taken the children away, as usual, when birthing time came. He was not worried that anything could go wrong. However, hours came and went, the boys got hungry, Leah had to leave and check on the maid preparing dinner. Zilpah still had not given birth. Zilpah had a well-rounded figure, but was not really obese.

Jacob came home to eat and tried to go to Zilpah and see what was happening. He saw Zilpah lying there, sweaty and tired. He gave her a cup of water. Just then the midwife and Leah arrived.

"We will take over now, Master Jacob—," and the midwife pointed her finger to the door for him.   Jacob knew better than to go against an 'almighty' midwife. Leah also saw the cup and wrinkled her forehead. But she did not say anything, the time seemed too critical just now.   Leah figured since Zilpah is heavier than Bilhah, that may have slowed down the birth.   The pains became harder for Zilpah.   She started screaming, and weeping for her condition in-between, thinking of lost love Joppa.   The midwife and Leah tried to comfort her.   Leah knew, with a first child a woman seldom knows what to expect.   Then finally, finally, a somewhat pink but slightly limp baby boy was born. The midwife grabbed him by his feet, head hanging down, and carefully slapped him. Mucus dropped out of his mouth and loud healthy screams escaped from the little guy's mouth.

"There you go, little man," said the midwife, relieved. She secured the umbilical cord.   Then she cleaned up the fellow from the bowl of warm water that Leah gave her. Leah wrapped the baby tightly as was the custom and placed him on Zilpah's breast to nurse. He caught on right away.

"A boy, a boy!" called the midwife as she walked to the door. Master Jacob and the other boys came running and admired the new little guy. He was big-boned and heavy like his mother. Zilpah's son was a large baby. Leah named him Gad and said, "A troupe comes, we are multiplying. Good!"

The midwife advised that "even though the baby is sturdy, he had more mucus than other babies, and I want you to watch him closely and hold him up more. The mucus should soon disappear. Make sure to burp him well. If more mucus appears, we take this straw and suck it out of his nostrils. It is important." Leah and Zilpah watched the midwife demonstrating it.

Jacob felt God had blessed all his children and the family as such. Jacob did not think that he was in violation of the Lord's rules for having more than one wife. Leah, however, knew that God had given Adam only one wife. That is how she and the other wives knew it should be.   Leah talked to her mother about the first man that had two wives. His name was Lamech, who took two wives, Adah and Zilla.   He was a mean person. Leah did not think her husband should copy such a person. She thought of the Lord, and how good it must have been in the Garden of Eden when Adam and Eve could talk to the Lord personally and have their questions answered and be told exactly as to what was right or wrong.

Mother Laban agreed with Leah: a man ought to have only one wife! It would eliminate a lot of fighting and heartache. Leah told her mother that praying to the Lord helped her overcome sadness.—

Then the children came running in from outside and complained about hunger. Leah looked at the sun in the western sky and knew it was time to go home and start supper. She enjoyed visiting her mother once in awhile.

~~~

After Gad was weaned from the breast, Leah decided she ought to have another child. But somehow her body would not produce another pregnancy. *Maybe I am too overworked, maybe I should eat more, sleep more, but it does not go. Maybe I need a rest from bearing children. However, my sister wants to catch up with me, no way!*

Next time Leah saw Jacob she tried to have a conversation. She asked him questions about how the sheep, goats, cows and donkeys were doing. Also, if he needed anything in line of clothing. Jacob told her that Bilhah learned to weave and sew well and therefore, he does not need anything from her. Leah's heart was sad.

Then Leah suggested to him to sleep with Zilpah for a change once. Leah was his first wife and in the custom of the times, the "boss" over the other women. Jacob felt he had to obey his wife in that. At suppertime Leah took Zilpah aside and told her that she is to sleep with Jacob again and she won't allow her sister Rachel to catch up with her in babymaking. So when night came and all five children were sleeping in their quarters on straw mattresses, Jacob followed Zilpah to her sleeping quarters with Leah watching with tight lips. She hoped Jacob would not fall in love with Zilpah, like he seemed to after their first encounter. Jacob was friendly to Zilpah when they were alone.

"Relax, Zilpah, girlie, I won't hurt you, don't you have a good life under my roof? And your son Gad is strong, healthy and good looking. Enjoy our relationship."

"I am not allowed to, Master Jacob."

"I love all my wives, maids and children. I have a big heart."

"I am convinced about that, sir, if I may say so. However, I am only a maid and it behooves me to keep quiet."

Zilpah, as she talked to Jacob, became more courageous and continued:

"I would rather have my own husband, just him and me alone, the way the Lord started it out with our first two parents. Your father Isaac had only one wife all his life, so did Noah, your ancestor."

"But he had only three sons, Zilpah, we want more children," replied Jacob.

The next morning Jacob ate breakfast, went out to the fields to work the cattle, and Leah warned Zilpah to stay away from Jacob. After nine months Zilpah bore a second son. Leah named him Asher. She was so happy, now all the girls from the neighborhood would love her because she has six boys to marry off.

Bilhah's Plan

Rachel saw all the activity at her sister's house and was jealous of her children. She had only two, from the maid. She told her maid Bilhah that she will catch up with her sister in babies. "From you, Bilhah."

Bilhah was shocked. Next time Bilhah saw the younger maid of Leah she told her that Rachel will catch up with babymaking, and that she wants to have as many children as her sister Leah, or perhaps even more. The maid, again, told it to Zilpah. Zilpah told it to Leah. Now Leah saw that a race was on for real. When she heard it before, she could hardly believe it. *That Rachel!*

Bilhah did not want to be the victim of her mistress' wishes in regards to children. *No thank you, Rachel, not me. No more children for another woman. What am I going to do? There must be a way.* Bilhah was thinking and thinking. Finally, she had it; she would make Rachel jealous for Jacob's love. That ought to cure her mistress. Next time Jacob was in the house and Rachel also, and Bilhah nursed Naphtali, she started her plan. She kissed little Naphtali, stroked over his brown curly hair, lifted him up high until the little guy laughed and squeaked in pleasure. Jacob saw it. Then, turning to Jacob, Bilhah said:

"Isn't he a wonderful little darling? You and I make good babies."

Bilhah looked at Jacob's face and their eyes met. Jacob smiled.

"Here, Naphtali, want to make 'hi'hi' to Abba Daddy?" And Bilhah handed Jacob the baby to hold and stepped rather close to him while doing it. Rachel saw it and did not like it.

"Give me the baby, he's had enough entertainment; he needs to sleep now." Rachel took the baby from Jacob, carried him in the other room into his cradle, and told Bilhah to go get water from the well. Then Rachel carried the baby into his cradle and sang him to sleep.

At night when Rachel and Jacob went to sleep, Rachel made a face and told Jacob:

"I am not foolish enough to try and outdo Leah with children. If she wants a race, may she. But not with me. I won't play along in that 'game.' It is immature to do that."

Jacob remarked that Bilhah can be nice, sweet and motherly. He did not know that. He had the impression that she was as icy as the glacier on Mount Arrarat. And even though she bore two children already, she still kept her figure.

"Well, Jacob, obviously you spent a lot of time exploring her nature and her figure. I thought you were so busily working."

"Oh, Rachel, she is the mother of two of my children and an employee. I do have eyes in my head."

"Maybe you have your eyes where they don't belong."

"Now, don't you start that, Rachel. You know I love you."

Then Jacob fell asleep and snored.

However, another woman did not sleep. It was Bilhah. She kept very quiet and tried to get every word the two had been saying. She did not understand every word, but she knew by the tone of Jacob and Rachel's voices that her "little trick" had worked. She knew now that she would never have to be with Master Jacob again. Bilhah quietly stepped outside into the dark night and inhaled the cool night air, raised her arms high, swung around and was relieved and satisfied.

The next day however, Rachel told Bilhah not to spend so much time tending her hair. "It's a luxury, you have work to do." Bilhah knew why her mistress had said that and was pleased.

~~~

A few years passed with nothing extraordinary happening. The boys grew, the women did their child-tending, planting and housework. Jacob continued in his father-in-law's cattle business as the foreman. Now that every woman had some children, all seemed satisfied and there were fewer fights between the four mothers.

Leah's and Rachel's homes had become quite lively. Reuben, Simeon, Levi, Judah, Dan, Naphtali and Gad were running all over the place, playing, fighting, screaming, occasionally helping and at night, finally, it became peaceful and quiet. When they all slept, Leah could relax and take it easy. It was too dark to do any sewing. The grease lamp with the wick inside was also not bright enough for work. So, Leah tiptoed out of the children's sleeping quarters and looked at the stars and the night shadows surrounding her home. Lightning bugs flew around, but when she tried to catch one with her hand it was gone, she was not fast enough. The boys were able to catch some. There were a lot of night noises from the grasshoppers with their chirp, chirp, chirp sounds. Leah looked at the stars in their infinite distance and wondered about them. *Is God where the stars are?* Then she heard the hoot, hoot, hoot of a night owl. Suddenly she saw a low-flying bat coming right at her. She quickly lowered her head and stepped into her house and closed the door. Old women always warned, "When the bats are flying, women must go inside because bats want to land on womens' hair." Leah did not believe it, but she figured, it is better to be safe than sorry. "Good night, world," she said, laid down on her bedroll and fell asleep.

Masterboy?

The next day was bread baking time, a big job. Leah called in young Judah and Levi to go to the shed and get firewood. They were playing nicely and did not want to interrupt their play, but with a frown on their faces left anyhow. Disobedience was not tolerated. Then the two saw young Naphtali (son of Bilhah).

"Hey, Naphtali," Levi said with an air of importance. "Go and get firewood for Mother and bring it to us. Right now!" Naphtali did not want to go. Then Levi gave him a kick in the butt and ordered, "You go!"

"Why should I always do the work while you two are doing nothing?" whined Naphtali.

"Because we are from the first wife of my father, we are the masterkids, you are from the servant woman."

Then Judah added his own comments, "servant boy, servant boy, go." Naphtali was younger and smaller than Judah and was afraid those two bigger boys would be stronger than he, so he obeyed. Also, his tricky older brother Dan was away helping Father. His "mother" Rachel with his birthmother Bilhah had gone to the market, no one to stick to his side. So, Naphtali obediently got the firewood, two large piles of it and put them in front of Levi and Judah. They picked them up and carried them in to their mother.

A few days later Judah was ordered by his mother to rinse the baby's fur-wrap in the little stream and bring it right back. The baby Asher (from maid Zilpah) had it soiled, it smelled. Judah grabbed it carefully with two fingers, held his arm stretched out far away from his body and thus walked toward the stream. Then he spotted Naphtali.

"Hey, Naphtali, here take the baby's fur-wrap and rinse it in the water, right now!" Naphtali wrinkled his nose and tried to run away.

"I am not your servant. Why should I always do your dirty bidding?"

"You are from the servant woman, I am the masterboy, you must obey me. Go, or else..." Judah yelled. However, Judah had spoken too loud. Father Jacob happened to walk by and had overheard it. He reprimanded him.

"Judah, you are not a 'masterboy'. Remember that. It does not matter to me who your mother is, you are all alike to me. One is as good as the other. If you are given a job, you do it. No more of this idea of one being better than the other. Understand?" Then Father Jacob let his fingers comb through the brown wavy hair of young Naphtali. "You go and play now." Naphtali made a happy sigh and ran off to play. Then Judah, still holding the dirty fur-wrap with his two fingers, walked to the little stream himself. He dipped it into the water and swung it around and around until all stool had rinsed away. Then he swung the fur piece with one hand in large circles around over his head, just like a dog shakes himself after a bath. All water droplets flew out. Almost dry, Judah took it back to his mother who thanked him for a job well done.

"Mother," asked Judah, "are we boys all alike? Is one as important as the other even if he is born from a maid?"

Leah wondered where that question came from but she answered him.

"Yes, my dear boy, you are all equally important to me, to Father and also to the Lord in the heavens. Just be good boys." Then Judah told it to his brothers Levi, Reuben and Simeon.

Later on, when Naphtali saw Judah alone, he made a triumphant face to him and added, "My big brother Dan can beat you up."

"No, he can't because I am bigger," said Judah. "And if he tries, it's because he fights dirty. He acts like that poisonous snake in the grass that bit the horse from behind."

"We are all alike, said Father, and that is it," insisted Naphtali, "and if…"

"Naphtali! come in here, right now," called Rachel with a determined voice from her house. She was afraid a fight might start again. *It is good that my Jacob finally told the boys of my sister's that all are equal. He is too busy and has little time to teach them what is right and wrong. My "sons" will not be slaves to Leah's.*

~~~

Jacob and his older boys, Reuben, Simeon and Levi, were helping their father with the cattle. Every night they drove the sheep into a stone enclosure. There were very many rocks laying around. Large stones were placed in a circle. Smaller stones were laid over these until it was a good enclosure, high enough that no wolves dared to jump it. But someone had to still stay around the pen at night just in case a lion or panther tried to jump over the stone wall. Sometimes they had their cattle farther out on flat land with not too many rocks. Then they built a thorn fence instead. Sometimes there were caves where they drove their cattle and young lambs into at night. The cattle herders and Jacob, with his older sons, would make a fire at night and watch. If the green eyes of a nightly marauder appeared in the black of night, and got too close to them, the shepherd would shoot an arrow in that direction. If a howling sound was heard it meant that the animal got hit and there would be peace once again. The man would retrieve his precious arrow in the morning.

Since sheep eat grass pretty low to the ground, and then the bright, hot Middle Eastern sun would burn the ground, the grazing fields can turn into a desert in a short time. So Jacob had to drive the sheep from place to place as not to overgraze the pastures. The dog Chukko was a great help in rounding up sheep and driving them on to where Jacob or Laban wanted them to go. Wilderness dogs from the area could not be trained like that.

The Lion

Jacob and a male servant were guarding cattle and working on a fence. Afterwards Jacob and the servant were lifting more stones on top of a stone enclosure to make it higher, for future use. On top they put some more dry thorn bushes to protect the sheep at night from marauding animals that may try to jump the stone wall.

Suddenly his servant Josep let out a curse, "By Moloch! Master Jacob, look at this."

"Don't you swear by Moloch, the idol. In our family we believe and worship the real God who appeared to my grandfather, whose name is Jahweh."

"All right, Master Jacob, but still look at this," and he pointed to the ground. Jacob walked over. And there in the sand were the tracks of a giant cat.

"This is no oversize housecat, Josep, these are the tracks of a lion. This is serious and so close to our cattle. How did this lion get there? Must be a loner who got pushed away from his pride."

"Shall we follow the tracks where they lead, Master Jacob?"

"Yes, let's, for a little ways."

So they both followed the tracks that went around some boulders, and lo and behold! There lay a young pregnant cow, dead, all ripped apart, pieces of flesh already missing. Both men shuddered.

"This is devastating," said Jacob. "We have to do something about this. That lion needs another cow every three to four days, and eventually he will even get one of our children. You Josep, stay here and watch the cows, don't let them get away far, while I run to the village and get help."

"And what shall I do here all alone, Master Jacob?"

"You just be a man and do your job. The lion is full right now, he will probably be going to sleep."

Jacob ran home fast. He told his father-in-law Laban about the lion and the loss of a prized cow, even pregnant. Laban sent out messengers to tell all the neighbors. Reuben also was sent out to tell others in the neighborhood. They were all to meet at Laban's place to come up with a plan of action. One after another of the neighbors appeared with some of their farmhands.

The men brought along bows, arrows, a few long spears, swords and slingshots. Then came Rabam, the village leader, and said,

"We have to have a plan of action. And since this happened to Laban's cow and near his land, he has to develop the plan of action and we can help him."

By now the whole town was aware of the lion threat. All the mothers, including mother Leah, warned their children not to go out at night, because the lion will get them. The little boys of Jacob took their little knives and tried to kill an imaginary lion. They took their little bows and arrows and started target shooting.

Laban stood and made his plan known.

"We will take Chukko the dog. He is smart and knows how to track silently." Chukko heard his name and started running towards Laban, jumping up and down on him, yelping loudly, knowing that something exciting is going to happen and he will be in on it. But Laban held Chukko's mouth tight and ordered him to be quiet. Chukko wiggled his tail hard and shut up, and his ears pointing up, trying to understand what was going on.

Laban told the men to form two groups. Each group must have every kind of weapon.

"First we let Chukko go ahead and smell the tracks of the lion. My group will follow. The other group will go around and approach from another side, silently, no talking, only gesturing."

"When we see the lion we must shoot it with bows and arrows and slingshots. If it is hit, it will be wild and angry and attack us. Then the man with the spear, whoever is nearest, will poke the spear into the lion, all the way through, right into the ground, while the others hold their knives and axes ready. The lion would, of course, strike back and curl up and hit his attacker with his legs. Then the spearer has to keep the spear firmly pressed down into the ground, hopefully there is sand there and not rocks. Then the spearer will jump in circles round and round, avoiding the legs of the lion until the lion's strength is used up and it dies."

"If the lion hears or smells us coming," continued Laban, "and runs away from us, we will shoot arrows and slingshots after it. Then Shuba, the wife of Armat, will make a poison, and we will poison the cadaver of the cow, hoping the lion will come back to it."

Jacob saw a special smoke cloud going up in the village and asked his father-in-law what it means. Laban told him that some old grandfather is sacrificing to his god to give the men a good hunt and protection.

89

"That won't work," said Jacob. "Only the God Jahweh, in whom I believe, can help us," corrected Jacob. The men were afraid, but it behooved them to act brave.

When Jacob was ready with his bow and arrow and a sharp knife he said 'Good-bye' to Leah and Rachel. "So this is it, wish me good luck."

"Yes, Jacob, may the God Jahweh be with you and our men," answered Leah.

"Can I go along, Dad?" asked Reuben.

"No, my son. You, Simeon, Levi and Judah will go out and guard the sheep and the cows where Josep and I were working. And don't you dare lose any of them. I want a good job done. Be quiet, no fighting, no undue noise. You know cows spook easily from a sudden noise."

"Yes, Father, we will." Reuben, as the oldest, gave everyone of is brothers a staff and a skin of water. Leah gave each one a piece of bread, and off they went.

Then the hunting party separated into two groups. Laban's party with Jacob in it took the lead and stepping tenderly and noiselessly as possible to the field with Chukko in front, following the tracks of the lion. Everyone was tense and frightened, but no one let on. After all, they are not scared women, now they have to prove their prowess as men. Leah sent a young servant after the group with a water skin, for it was a hot day.

Chukko smelled out the tracks and all followed silently. Suddenly Chukko stopped and the hair on his back stood up. The group of men stopped also. Laban waved to the other group with his arm and pointed. They knew now that the lion is very close. Greatest silence was necessary. Everyone was tense.

Chukko went around another boulder - and there slept the lion in the distance. The men approached a bit closer, the lion opened his eyes - and the arrows started flying and the slings were shot. One seemed to have hit the lion, for now he jumped up and howled and jumped toward the attackers and Chukko the dog.

Laban yelled "Chukko, sick it!" The lion hit Chukko so hard, he flew eight feet to the side, and turned to the men, striking out with its paw. A young man's belly was sliced open, blood spurted out of him and he collapsed. Quickly another man handed Jacob the long 7-foot spear. Jacob immediately thrust it into the lion that was just by him. He thrust it hard, all the way, with force, right through it, right into the ground. The lion did curl up and tried to right himself and tried to hit Jacob with his paws, but Jacob kept up the weight and jumped round and round, avoiding the paws of the lion. The men had jumped back as to not to get in the way of circling Jacob. The lion's roars grew quieter, and his movements slower, blood squirted out all over the ground and on Jacob. Finally, the lion lay still. Jacob kept up the pressure of the spear in the ground that had gone through the lion's body. Now Laban jumped forward and with an axe severed the head of the lion. The fight was over. Everyone made a sigh of relief. Chukko the dog barked happily and tried to get a bite out of his enemy, his well-deserved reward. Laban stroked his fur, Chukko beat his tail happily. Miraculously, Chukko was not hurt.

But on the ground lay the young man, screaming, with the belly bleeding and open. Laban turned to him and examined the wound.

"Well, it is not all the way in, the intestines are not ripped open, it could possibly heal."

"Please, Master Laban, do something," he whined, "I don't want to die. My grandfather sacrificed to the gods and it did not work, now I must die."

And the young man cried loudly in pain and agony.

"Stop whining, and act like a man," said Jacob. "Now you see that the gods don't help. Only our God Jahweh can help."

In the meantime some men cut two branches from a tree, tied some of their clothes around them and made a crude bed where they laid him on. In the middle they left an opening. They laid the young man on his belly as to not touch the wound and let the blood, "the spirit of the lion" flow out. The young man who carried the water gave him something to drink. And so the men started walking home. Others skinned the rest of the lion.

The young man said to Jacob, "If I don't die I want to believe in your God, and then please let me work for you, I'd like to be your servant."

When everything was under control again, all men started walking home. They could not wait to tell their dangerous adventure to their women and old men at home. And Master Laban was glad he had a good dog like Chukko. The men admired Chukko, but this kind of dog was not available in that country. It was a northern dog.

Finally Jacob walked home, sweaty, dirty and tense. Rachel received him happily. But Jacob was drained, he just had to go and lie down for awhile. Fighting that lion had taken something out of him; he was totally stressed out and wanted a rest.

"Get me water, Rachel, and make it quick, and I want to sleep and hear no sound out of Dan and Naphtali, you understand?!" He used a dictatorial and demanding tone. Rachel was not used to that tone and looked defiant but knew that a man who just killed a lion must be excused. She hurried over to Bilhah and ordered her to make the boys silent. But they just got turned on by all the commotion and did not keep silent and imitated with loud yells how they were killing an imaginary lion. So she took her leather thong that she carried on her belt and gave each one a slap. Now they cried even more. Then Bilhah jumped in, grabbed them, held her hands over their mouths and dragged them outside and away, whispering to them.

Rachel handed Jacob a gourd of water. He did not bother with a cup, just gulped it down and drank. Then he lifted the rest of the water and poured it over his sweaty hair. "More water," Jacob demanded. Rachel handed him another filled water gourd, and another until he felt clean. Then Jacob managed to take a short nap until it got really dark. Then he got up, ate supper and left for the cattle and sheep herds. Jacob was thankful to his God.

In the distance he saw green eyes, the wild dogs who had smelled out the lion's cadaver wanted to have their share. Jacob chased them away and threw a rock toward them. *"Beasts! I have no peace, neither day nor night."*

The next day Laban discussed the lion situation with Jacob.

"So, son, you did not see or hear a thing, nor your servant?"

"No, Father Laban, the lion must have come against the wind, and jumped the cow and broke her neck so fast, she did not have time to cry out. Too bad."

"Yes, too bad Jacob. And to think the cow was pregnant, what a loss! But it is bearable, your wives still have an inheritance to draw from…"

"Now, don't rub it in, Father Laban, it could have happened to anyone." Jacob went back to work. "That Laban; he does not appreciate me. Now he blames me for the lion."

~~~

On the next cattle drive, young Judah came along. It was his first real sheep drive out in the far fields. He was all excited and drove the sheep along with a loud voice. Suddenly, a ram with strong horns did not seem to like this newcomer with all that noise, he jumped at Judah. Young Judah fell down, and the ram punched his horns into him again and again, while Judah screamed. His older brother Reuben yelled back.

"Lie still, lie still, act dead." Judah fell silent, curled up and lay still. After three more punches the ram seemed to have calmed down. He stomped his front foot on the ground three times and waited, and then triumphantly left for his ewes and their lambs. After awhile Judah opened his eyes, carefully looked around, and lifted his hurting body off the ground, trying to walk home to Mother Leah.

"Never mind, Judah, be a man, you will stay right here and do your job, we don't need weaklings around here," said Reuben. So, laboriously and slowly Judah took his shepherd's cane and tried to catch up with the sheep, carefully trying to keep a distance between himself and that ram. But at night he was allowed to go home to his mother.

"Mom, Mom, my Mom, where are you?"

Leah heard the call and ran inside to see what the trouble was. Then Judah threw his arms around his mother and started crying and big tears ran down his cheeks.

"What is it, my son?"

Then he told her the story about the vicious ram and how much he is still hurting.

"Let's see your body?" She lifted his fur vest, and yes, he had black and blue spots all over him. So Leah took a bowl of water and added some boiled chamomile to it and washed him off. She gave him food and special juice to drink, from elderberries and mixed with wine. This juice was reserved only for sicknesses. She kissed him and sent him to bed. The next day Judah felt much better.

"Good day, Mother, I am going back to sheep herding, I am a man, I can take it."

"Yes, my son, I know you can." Leah was proud of her brave boy.

~~~

Often the children were fighting each other. So Mother Leah had to step in and pull them apart. "You have to be good boys and love each other," she demanded.

"Why, Mother? Asher scratched me."

"Because he took my arrow away," exclaimed Dan. "Father gave it to me, therefore it is mine."

"I want one too, chimed in little Asher.

"Zilpah, take care of your boys, they fight too much. I have other things to do." Zilpah had noticed the words "your boys." It made her happy. The relationship between Leah and Zilpah had improved, now that Leah had enough children and Rachel had given up the race for more. Time went by, the boys loved each other and fought each other like all children do.

The older four sons, Reuben, Simon, Levi and Judah were working out in the fields since they were old enough by now.

The Mandrake

One day during the wheat harvest Reuben found a strange plant far out in the fields. He looked at it carefully. He recognized the plant, because he had heard about this plant. It was somewhat poisonous, but is supposed to have great special powers. If a brew is cooked properly from this plant, and given to a man to drink, that man falls in love with his woman. He got all excited, *This is for my mother, my poor mother, who is never really loved by father. He always talks with her in a rough voice, and to us also. I don't like Father.* He carefully dug out the plant with the roots, wrapped it in a fur and took it home. As he passed the home of Rachel, she saw that he was carrying something and trying to hug it carefully.

"What do you have there, Reuben? Let me see it."

He tried to walk off and hide it, but Rachel managed to see it anyhow.

"A mandrake!" she exclaimed. "A mandrake, for love. I want it. Please give it to me."

Leah saw it from inside her house and walked out to see what was going on. Zilpah and Bilhah also saw it.

"Please give me some of your son's mandrakes."

Then Leah started telling her:

"First, you take my husband away, all the love, kissing and hugging you steal away from me, and now you even want my son's mandrakes, my son's, mind you. How dare you?"

When Rachel saw that this approach would not work, she turned to diplomacy. She suggested a trade.

"You give me the mandrakes, all of them, and in exchange I allow you to have Jacob this night."

"Why all of them? Rachel, you are getting fresh!"

Then Rachel's eyes started to fill with tears and she whispered.

"I need them, all of them for him and me."

Leah suddenly understood, Rachel wanted to drink the brew herself to get pregnant. A soft spot opened up in Leah's heart and she gave Rachel the whole plant, roots, leaves and all.

"Don't forget the trade, Sister…"

Now Leah had to prepare a larger supper for this night. She warned all her boys to be well behaved for Father would be there. Now Leah had to watch out as to when Jacob would come home from the field at night, so that out of habit, he would not wander over to Rachel's place. Leah kept watching for his return. As soon as Jacob came near their compound, Leah went out to meet him and informed him that this night he has to stay at her home, for the trade with the mandrakes. Jacob, as a man used to several women, had to obey his wife number one, it was the custom, he dare not go against it. At least not on his father-in-law's yard.

And God listened to a rejected wife's plea. Jacob stayed only one night, the price of the mandrakes. Leah's heart was sad again, just one night. *He just does not love me. No matter how good I am, he does not regard me precious. Yes, he feeds me and clothes me and the children, does his duty, yes, but not an ounce more.* Tears filled her eyes again.

However, only a couple of weeks later, Leah was rewarded again with another pregnancy. She thought of God. Faith in His presence had established itself in those years of marital loneliness. Leah saw in her compliance to Rachel's wish for those mandrakes a good deed for which God rewarded her with a child. Rachel had hoped the mandrakes would get her pregnant, that is why she wanted them. Husbands were happy when their wives were fruitful. The earth was not as crowded as yet, and many hands were good for helping at the farms.

When the baby was born it was a boy again. She named him Issachar. Now she had five boys, she was glad. She was also very busy. Taking care and raising all of those kept her mind away from Jacob and she was liked and loved by her boys. Often they talked and laughed together. Leah was getting tired of always mourning after unfulfilled love. She needed some laughter, some fun, and these kids were just the right thing for her. She enjoyed them all, even the ones from Zilpah.

Once again Jacob visited Leah in connection with a grain delivery for the growing family. Once again Leah conceived. After the due time she had another little baby boy. She was grateful to God again. And again, she thought and told Zilpah, "God has endowed me with a good family, now my husband will dwell with me, because I have borne him six sons." His name was Zebulon. She was still thinking, as most people did, that goodness produces babies, and God rewards her for her virtues.

Renate M. Schulz

The First Girl Dinah

Sometime later God gave Leah another pregnancy. She and Jacob were discussing another boy's name. His name should be Enoch, like that very god-fearing ancestor who did not have to taste normal human death but was just taken away by God. They hoped he would be a good son. The birth was a bit slow but otherwise normal. However, when the baby emerged from the womb it was a girl. A girl, after all those boys! Leah was overwhelmed. She called her Dinah. It was supposed to be in remembrance of her younger sister Denah. Now Leah was content and happy.

"I have a daughter, everybody look!" And indeed, after all those boys a girl was an exciting event. Even Father Jacob had to admire her face. He counted her little fingers and toes, tipped with his large finger on her tiny nose, made faces to her, and Dinah looked wide-eyed into this new world of hers. Then she started screaming with high tones, unlike her brothers. The midwife took the baby and handed her to Leah, who started to nurse her. Even the boys and Rachel all came to pay tribute to this wonder of a little girl. Everybody wanted to hold her. "You will spoil her," admonished the midwife.

"To whom will we marry her to?" asked Father Jacob.

"Never mind, my lord," said Leah. "Let us wait, let's give the poor thing a chance to grow. Maybe she will make up her own mind. Women are smarter than men give them credit for."

Leah did not recover really fast after this delivery, she needed more bedrest. However, with Zilpah and other maidservants around, she could afford to heal properly while taking it easy.

Education About Noah

All this time Jacob was still a regular employee of Master Laban. Jacob worked hard. He slept little, kept a close watch of Laban's sheep and goats. Leah and Zilpah as well as Bilhah and Rachel contributed their part to the running of the large family group. They had to work every minute of the day because once the sun went down it was pitch black outside. The only lights were the stars above or the moon and the little fires of the sheepherders. Inside the huts a small lamp by the hearth, was too small to allow much work. Even old Deborah tried her hand on twisting yarn on the spindle in the dark, just by feeling, until her head fell forward in sleep. Then Rachel would gently take her by the shoulders and lead her to her sleeping straw sack. Deborah was old, her bones often hurt. Rachel made sure her sack was stuffed full and soft with straw and hay. Then came that long night. Whoever did not eat enough during the evening meal had to stay hungry at night. Food was always somewhat scarce with so many children. Leftovers were put away for the night. Swiping food in-between was considered stealing and could be punished. The family members would often talk and tell stories at night, or sometimes just go to bed and listen to the wind or rain until sleep overpowered them.

One time Leah had honey and dates put aside to bake cakes for the family and some for her parents also. Gad, Asher, Issachar and Zebulon, the four youngest of the boys, found out about the stash. They were hungry for sweets. So when Zilpah had gone to the village well to bring water and Mother Leah had taken little Dinah to her grandmother for a visit, the four boys approached the sweets. Each boy took one date. The dates were delicious and absolutely delightful. But one each was really not enough, they had to have at least two more each to make the taste stick. Now twelve pieces were missing. Then Issachar remembered that it would be his turn to shepherd the goats this night to relieve Judah and that calls for some extra food. So he took two more pieces. Gad, who always liked to dare and advance his cause, said that he also has to relieve Levi this night to guard the sheep and the goats, so it would be only fair if he also had another two pieces to stay awake. Finally, they closed that jar and left.

When Mother Leah came home, she put baby Dinah to sleep, and prepared to bake those sweet cakes. As she went to the jar, there was only very little left, not enough to bake for such a large family. *What happened here? I had enough to bake and most of it is gone!* She asked Zilpah who just came back with the water. No, Zilpah did not take any. "The cat, perhaps?"

"Cannot be the cat, it would not be smart enough to properly close the lid. Where are the boys?" Leah stuck out her head and called the boys. No answer. She took the metal bell and rang it loud. Finally, all four came traipsing in, one after another.

"You called us, Mother, what is it?" asked Issachar in his slow way of talking.

"Where are the dates and the honey?"

"Dates and honey?" They looked at each other with knowing eyes. "Don't know, why. Is something missing?"

Mother Leah saw some honey spots on Zebulon's skin.

"You took them, you all stole them, you liars! Now I cannot bake. Now I will bake only for Father, Zilpah, me and Grandfather and Grandmother, and you get nothing."

Then she took the leather strap from a peg in the wall and started whipping all four of them.

"That is what you get for lying. Now get out of my sight or I beat you more." They quickly disappeared but did not cry. They knew they had it coming.

In the evening when Jacob came home for supper, she walked over to Rachel's house and asked him to come out. Then she told him about the stealing and lying boys and what he thinks should be done.

"I will think about it," he answered. She left for her home.

A few days later, when the weather seemed to stay clear, Jacob told Leah, Rachel, Bilhah and Zilpah that everybody has to come out to the fields where the flocks are toward the evening for a grand picnic and a family meeting. Everyone was excited, and preparations were made. Then they all hiked to their father and their older brothers where they watched the herds that day.

They all ate their picnic supper with great appetite until all was gone. Then when all the cattle was secured for the night, Jacob asked all the people to sit down by the campfire. Jacob then told everyone about the boys stealing honey and dates and lying about it also. The four little defendants were glad the sun was going down so no one would see their shamed faces. Father Jacob was going to give them a speech, a long speech.

"We live here around Haran in the province of Aram. What do you see to the north where the sun never shines? And toward the east?" "Mountains," the younger boys replied.

"Yes, that is right. Do you know the name of those mountains? They are called Ararrat Mountains. Do you know what is high up on those mountains? Noah's ark."

"Can we go and see it?" asked young Zebulon.

"Silent boy, when I talk you be quiet or else here hangs my strap," and Jacob's hand stroked the leather strap hanging from his waist. This made everyone fall silent.

"Do you children know that almost 400 years ago our Ancestor Noah was in that ark with his wife, three sons and their wives? Do you know why they had to go there? Because the people around them were so bad. Stealing, lying," he pointed knowingly toward the four perpetrators, who bowed their heads ashamedly, "murdering, cheating, playing games when they were supposed to be watching the herds." Now even the older boys including Dan and Naphtali sunk their heads. "They did not want to be good. They did not want to be truthful. And what happened to them? God let a big flood come and a strong rain and drowned them all. That is what they got for being evil. However, the Lord promised to give them no more big floods, maybe just little floods from a rising river or so, which does not count. However, when the flood was over our ancestor Noah built a large altar to the Lord out of large stones and killed and sacrificed a sheep on it, to please the Lord. So the smoke from it would go up to the sky where the Lord lives, somewhere up there," Jacob said, pointing his finger up to the sky. "The Lord would smell the smoke and be pleased with him and his family. Thus Noah thanked the Lord for saving their life in the flood and the life of the animals."

"Then the Lord said to Noah, 'From now on, if somebody sheds man's blood, his blood shall also be shed by man.' "

Now Levi raised his arm and asked for an explanation, for he loved rules. So, Father Jacob explained that when Cain had murdered his brother Abel, he was afraid that other people that were born after him would try to kill him also for that. So the Lord granted Cain the favor, made a sign on his body, and now everyone who was born after him would know that this is evil Cain, and to leave him alone. But Cain had to go away from Adam and Eve, he did not want to be around them anymore. Adam, Eve and their third son, Seth, were satisfied that he had gone away. However, now everyone thought they can just kill whomever angers them, and they will stay alive, just like Cain, no particular punishment will come upon them. And so mankind became bad and got worse, so bad that the Lord decided that there is no hope for them. He wanted to kill them all in a large flood."

Then Levi asked another question, "How do we know what is good and what is bad?"

"Common sense and your conscience will tell you what is good and what is bad, listen to it. However, some day the Great Hero will come that the Lord in heaven will send to us on earth, and He will give us the laws and regulations."

After that they were all talking and discussing as to what they will do when that Hero comes. Then they packed up their things and the mothers, maids and children went home again, and the older boys back to their herds.

That ought to give my boys something to think about. I just don't have enough time to teach them. Let Leah or Rachel do it. So thought Jacob.

Rachel's First Child

Sometime after the family meeting Jacob came home again to his wife Rachel. Out of habit, Jacob went to sleep with Rachel in an intimate way. He did not expect anything from it, just personal satisfaction. Rachel let him have his way, as usual. It did not mean anything to her anymore, she promptly fell asleep. And life continued its normal way. She had given up hope that this could give her a baby, although the sadness of it was always with her, more or less. Sex did not matter for her anymore.

Then some weeks later Rachel felt kind of ill although she could not remember what spoiled food she could have eaten. *I am getting old,* she thought with a sigh. However, when her monthly time came, it was not there. The moon took another turn in the sky and still nothing happened. It was as if a lightning hit her soul. Never in all her years has this happened to her. *Could it? Could it not? No, it would be too good to be true. And yet, and yet...I am all excited, this cannot be.* She walked around as if delirious, and did her housework with a song in her mouth.

My, my, thought Bilhah the maid, *what is happening to Rachel?* She watched her closely, she knew eventually she would find out, she dared not ask.

When the moon turned again and still the old way did not come back, she was sure and walked out into the nearby field where Jacob was mending a fence. He looked up and wondered what extraordinary circumstance happened to cause his wife to come into the fields.

"Jacob, she said, guess what?"

"What is it, Rachel? It must be something good, judging by your face."

"It is, Jacob. I am pregnant!"

"No, Rachel, you could be mistaken," but Jacob started laughing nevertheless. He looked at her midsection. She tightened her skirt and it showed a tiny enlargement.

Jacob was so happy, he embraced her and kissed her and swung her around once, but immediately released her with shock.

"Oh no, I did not hurt you and the baby?"

"No, Jacob, I feel fine. Shall I tell my mother?"

"Just wait another moon until you feel the baby's movements, and then let the 'thunderbolt strike.'"

Rachel went home happily, walking like on air. She started drinking more milk, eating more food, for the little one would need more. But it was

101

hard for her to wait another month. Finally the day came, she felt movement in her womb. She put on a nice dress and hiked over to her mother's house.

"God bless you, Mother," she said. Then she stood in front of her, wrapped her skirt tightly around her figure so that it would show a protruding belly. The mother saw it and first was worried that her daughter could be sick, but looking at her happy face - she realized the reason. She started to laugh and embraced her daughter, two women loving each other in joy and gladness. Then the mother asked her details as to when it happened and how she feels. She served her some food. When Father Laban came by they told him about Rachel's pregnancy and he was also overjoyed. Now everyone on the compound, including Leah and the boys, heard about it. Leah was not angry. She had enough children of her own to love, enjoy and to take care for.

Finally, the nine months were over and all was ready for the birth. Rachel had wanted to have a child herself so long and was not afraid of the birth pains. She wanted to show the maids that she is tough; she won't scream. Rachel had Deborah, her old nursemaid, with her also. She held her hand and comforted her and assured her that the Lord will bring the birth around just fine. Rachel managed to be silent and happy at the same time. Jacob was tense, yes, but he was confident things would work out all right, he had seen many births before.

Rachel felt that the pains were stronger than she had thought, but she managed to be brave. Finally, the hardest part came, the head. Rachel thought she would burst in half, but she did not. And immediately a loud cry emanated from the mouth of a little red new, wiggly human being.

"A boy, a boy," called out Deborah, the midwife.

Now the normal clean-up-the-baby routine started. Then Jacob entered and whoever was around to look at Rachel's first new baby.

She and Jacob were grateful to God for this precious gift of a male child.

Jacob walked out into the fields where he was alone and in a loud voice thanked his God for this child.

Jacob and Rachel gave the baby the previously chosen name of Joseph.

Rachel said: "God has taken away my reproach."

Then Rachel made a wish to the Lord. She wanted another child. Just one single, only child was not enough for her. She wanted two. The Lord had heard her wish. Would He do it?

Joseph grew and was healthy and happy. He learned to talk rather early and was very bright. Jacob enjoyed his presence immensely.

The other sons of Jacob all looked at their new brother, from their father's love wife. He looked smooth, and his skin unruffled from the birth. They hated to say it, but he was good looking. His skin was rather dark, just like his mother's.

"Don't get so close to him, boys," said Rachel. "I noticed some of you have a runny nose, you will make him sick." When the boys had left the room, Simeon remarked, "Hey, Naphtali, she meant you, and you, Dan. You live near her home." He pointed to them with his finger and added with a sarcastic smirk, "The 'prince' will get sick, better watch it."

Whenever Jacob was home, he held little Joseph and cradled him in his arms. He got so attached to him, and could not see enough of him. Fancy maid Bilhah now had more work to do and worried about her own comfort. But on the other hand, her mistress was now pre-occupied with her own son and she could now more enjoy her own two children Dan and Naphtali. Bilhah always looked at the good side of things and what profit for herself a certain happening could mean.

~~~

Father Jacob spent much time with little Joseph, then Leah reminded him about the shooting lessons of his other young sons.

Then Father Jacob asked big brother Reuben how the teaching is coming along with the younger boys. Do they practice target shooting? Are they hitting anything? Now Reuben as the oldest was "in charge" and he was going to make sure of it. He called Naphtali, Issachar and Zebulon and asked them to perform for him. But the boys just made faces to him.

"You are not our father."

"What do you dare say to me? I am your big brother and 'in charge,' you show me how you shoot." Especially Naphtali from Bilhah was rebellious. A hard slap at his cheek solved that problem. Zebulon also took up his arrow and tried to prove his marksmanship. Issachar was slow, he moved only when he had to.

"Come on, come on, little brother, go shoot or I kick you." That brought him finally to his senses. The boys missed most of the times as yet. But Reuben did not let up, they had to try again and again under their brother's supervision. Life was not easy and they needed to hit a target or else become a victim of wild animals or enemies. Reuben reminded them about the lion a few years back and how important it was that they become good marksmen, good shepherds and learning how to count sheep, goats and camels. He told them that if he is ever absent, Simeon will be in charge. He reminded them that Simeon is even tougher, they had better be aware of that. "And, I don't care what your little hearts are feeling. You just do your job." Reuben raised his fist as a threat and his younger brothers got the point.

One day the younger boys were playing hide-and-seek in their spare time. Naphtali was seeking, the others were hiding. One after another was found, but Zebulon was not found. They looked in the yard, behind the house, in back of the yard, they called his name, he was gone. After awhile Leah called for dinner, everyone came home. Rachel also called for dinner, and her two boys from Bilhah came running.

"Where is Zebulon?" asked Leah.

Issachar, Gad and Asher looked at each other and said "we don't know."

"What, you don't know where your brother is? When did you last see him?"

So Gad explained, "We were playing hide-and-seek and we could not find him, and then we forgot to look for him."

Immediately Leah ran to Rachel's house because she thought Jacob might be there, and he was.

"Zebulon is missing." And she told her husband what the children had been doing. Jacob put down his spoon and announced that they have to go looking for him immediately. He called all available men together. Laban's other farmhands and Jacob lit torches and went looking for Zebulon, calling his name. Leah was very much upset and scolded the boys, but they insisted they forgot. They also asked the boys Dan and Naphtali, but they had not seen him either. Then they ran over to the big boys that tended the herds. It was Reuben and Judah's turn to help out. But they had not seen him either. Then Father Jacob took a camel from Laban and rode out toward the main road because a group of traveling salespeople had been in town. They might have kidnapped him. But they assured Jacob that they did not capture or buy a little boy. Jacob was quite upset and walked into Rachel's home again discussing the matter. It was pitch dark by now and still no Zebulon in sight.

"Could an animal have gotten him? Isn't the Lord on my side?" thought Jacob. Just then little Joseph in the bedchamber started to cry and Rachel went to get him. She stumbled over something and almost fell down. She looked and felt in the darkness, there were two little feet sticking out from under the bed. She yelled, "I got him, I found Zebulon."

Jacob raced over there, pulled him out. Yes, it was him.

"Hey, what were you doing under that bed?" Zebulon rubbed his eyes and tried to figure out where he was, then it dawned on him.

"We were playing hide-and-seek and I was hiding really good, I had fallen asleep. I am hungry." Jacob took him over to his wife Leah who embraced and kissed him. Jacob was also happy and shook his head at the most impossible things that children can do.

The seasons came and went, the children grew. Leah now had lots of people to bake bread for, together with the maids and workers. It was a huge job. She needed a lot of grain. Husband Jacob would measure out the grain for her, after the workers, she and the boys had threshed it. They would find a flat piece of ground with hard stamped-down earth and laid the grain stalks on it. Or if a large flat rock was available that would also serve the purpose. Then the men would take a long stick about two inches thick and attach a leather loop to the end. Then they would attach another shorter stout stick to it. With this thing called flail, the men would beat on the dried straw. That would knock the grain seeds out of the straw. Then they would remove the straw, sweep up the grain and the chaff in containers. This was harvest, a happy occasion. It was hard work, but everyone was in a good mood when the Lord had granted fitting weather for such a successful harvest. In order to separate the heavy grain from the light, strawy chaff they waited for a windy day. They would pour the mixture slowly from a high held container into another, lower one. The wind would then blow the chaff away, while the heavy grain fell into the lower bucket. If there was no wind and mothers needed the grain for baking bread, they would just have to blow by mouth. Some farmers had large sieves and shook the chaff out of the grains, called winnowing.

When the grain kernels were clean, the job for the women started: the grinding or crushing of the grain. Then Leah called all her younger children together to go out for a hike with a donkey to collect more grinding stones. The little boys and young Dinah went along. The sky was blue, the sun was warm, it was a happy time. A grinding stone had to have the shape of a bowel. And time and again one of the children exclaimed excitedly that he found just the right rock. Mother Leah looked it over, sometimes she took it, sometimes not. Then they also had to find another rock that was round with which to actually crush the grains. It was hard work. When done the women had whole grain wheat and whole grain barley. It was rough but very healthy. In some areas they would have deep hardwood buckets to pound and crush the grain with a long-handled pestle, so the women did not need to bend down. Nobody was bored or unemployed, even children had to help wherever they were needed.

The family also had some chickens. However, they were difficult to keep because they lacked good fencing. Jacob had built the women a large cage out of wood and wood railings. At night the chickens had to be chased into the small cage. Since Chukko the dog was around, he would help to rein them in at night. He also would sniff out little animals such as weasels and foxes that were preying on the chickens. Weasels tried to silently squeeze through the railings at night when the chickens were sleeping. They would sidle up to a chicken and quickly bite a small hole into their neck and immediately suck the blood. Sometimes the job was done so fast the chicken had no time to wake up and screech in alarm. Then a weasel could kill more than one chicken. Zilpah still loved to tend the chickens. It gave them fresh eggs and a change from their other meats. Hawks also sailed the skies spying on the chicklets. It was a constant battle to keep them alive.

Now that Rachel had a baby boy she was satisfied and not so very eagerly guarding her husband from her sister anymore. This made for a more relaxed atmosphere on the Laban compound.

Mother Laban

One day Denah, the youngest daughter of grandmother Laban, came over to Leah and told her that their mother does not feel good. So Leah and Rachel rushed over. There lay their mother, on her sleeping mat, looking rather pale. Denah had boiled her a tea, but she did not feel like drinking much. They greeted their mother, sat by her side, held her hands and asked her what hurts. Mother Laban touched her right side and told them that sometimes the pain is really strong. The girls kissed her. They knew there was not much they could do, after all, Mother Laban was old. Mother Laban was also sad, because her husband Mr. Laban, had taken another younger wife and she could never quite accept that fact. And even though the new wife with the children did her nothing especially evil, it was a crowded and bad situation, but what was she to do? She had no rights. And she was ill besides.

Denah had also been given to marriage some time ago. Her husband did not live too far away, and since she had no child as yet she could visit her mother more often and help take care of her. Then the daughters Leah and Rachel said their good-byes to their mother. Leah, who had gone through some troubled times herself, encouraged her mother to trust in God, the true God, the one who spoke to Noah and their ancestors, and to Abraham, Isaac and Jacob. Then they left. A day and a half later Mother Laban had departed this life. All the women came together, even neighbors and started a loud death wail, lamenting and crying, as was the custom. Then Mother Laban was buried. Leah cried and the older boys (cousins of Leah, Rachel and Denah) were sad also.

Leah had to explain to the younger children, when they asked her, why grandmother was in a deep hollow in the ground. Then Leah told them that grandmother's body was old and worn out, like a broken sandal.

"What do you do with a broken sandal when it cannot be fixed?"

"You throw it away, burn it up in the fire."

"Yes," said Leah, "that is why we have to bury grandmother, in a deep hollow in the ground, her body cannot be fixed anymore."

"Will she come back?"

"No, never. But, maybe some day, when the Big Hero comes that the Lord will send...Let us just wait and see what He will do." That inconclusive answer satisfied the younger children.

Then Asher (son of Zilpah) said, "When the Hero comes I will bake bread for him, so He can eat lots of it, and I bake it just nice and brown."

"And I will eat it too," said chubby Issachar, "and sit at his table."

"You are not," replied Asher, "If I bake the bread, I sit by His side."
His fist was moving in Issachar's direction. Issachar, being younger but
heavier, would not accept a punch and a new fight had started, while the
other children were taking sides. Leah yelled at them, took off her leather
strap and worked it on the children, and immediately peace reigned again on
this solemn funeral day. When Father Jacob was around, the children were
more careful because his slaps were harder and left red streaks on their
bodies. When Mother Leah slapped them they screamed loudly so she
would think they were hurt badly, even if it was not so.

Ancestor Cain

It was very important that a girl be a virgin when getting married. If a girl was not a virgin, she was considered a lesser quality woman. If the man married her in good faith and found out later she was not a virgin, it was considered cheating and she could get a punishment or the marriage could be annulled. Men were given more freedom. Therefore, Leah, Zilpah, Rachel and Bilhah each told their boys to go for a pure woman for marriage, one who is a virgin. Leah also taught that to her daughter Dinah.

Jacob saw that his children needed more spiritual training than what his wives could give them. He did not have much time for it. But if they asked him specific questions he would answer. Then one cool winter day, when they were sitting around their fire in Leah's larger home, the sheep were fenced in tightly and all seemed in order, inquisitive Joseph asked a new question. He always came up with the weirdest ideas.

"Father, you told us the first two people the Lord created were Adam and Eve."

"Right, son, it was so."

"Then," said Joseph, "came Cain and Abel. Abel was killed. Then Seth was born. Where did Cain get his wife from and how was all that?"

"Oh, you nosy children, common sense."

"Please, Father, tell us before you forget, you are so old."

"Hey, children, who says I am old and forgetful?"

Jacob made a deep sigh, he knew this would be a long story. He asked Leah for a pitcher of water, and cautioned young Joseph that this story is not important enough to remember or waste expensive papyrus on, but since they were asking...Then he proceeded:

"Cain was sure more children would be born to his parents, and everyone will remember that he killed Abel. Everyone will hate him. They might try to kill him also. So he had asked the Lord to protect him. Wasn't that low of Cain? He was not afraid to kill someone else, but was too afraid for himself?"

"Yes," cried the children, "bad, bad Cain."

Jacob continued. "The Lord did make a sign on him."

"What kind of sign?"

"A red large spot on his forehead. Adam and Eve did not want him around. Eve also was pregnant and she was afraid of Cain and the safety for the new child. So Cain was told to leave."

"Go far away and never come back. We don't want to see you anymore," said Adam to Cain.

"So Cain left and walked east, always east. He was all alone, no other human being was there, only animals, bushes, flowers, trees and more animals. Then, when Cain found a very large grassy meadow, all flat land, he thought he would stay there. It was near a large river. Cain was still afraid. So he found a lot of large rocks and rolled them into a circle and piled the stones on top of each other. When night came he would crawl into that stone den to sleep. He pulled thorny branches carefully in front of that hole. Then he found some flat rocks and tied wooden handles on it to make stone axes for chopping wood. He was busy but very much alone. He ate berries, dug roots and ate plants for food. When it got cooler in the season he killed a deer with his ax and wore its fur for warmth."

"The seasons of the years came and went. Then one day Cain could not stand the loneliness anymore. He said to himself:

'I wonder how my parents are doing? I will go there and take a look.' He walked west and always west, being careful to have his stone ax handy and an extra one in case the first one breaks. Finally, he came to the area where he used to live with his parents. He recognized the mountains and river spots. He stood still and listened."

'Anything dangerous that I can hear?' "He stepped closer. He stood still again. He saw animals walking in that fashion, a few steps, then standing still and watching and listening, then proceeding again. Cain walked further. In the distance he heard voices."

'People, how wonderful, real people! There are men and women, the women looks like Eve, my mother, with long wavy hair.'

"The men looked like his father Adam and his dead brother Abel. A bothersome thought came over him when he thought about Abel."

"Cain climbed a thick-leaved tree to better observe them. He saw more women, they were so beautiful. He never saw such a sight of beauty before. They looked miraculous to him. He listened. He heard Eve call them girls and the male people they called boys. He knew the word boys. But when he left, years ago, there was no girl born as yet."

"When it was getting dark his mother had cooked a meal and they all came to eat. They also ate nuts roasted over a fire. Cain got hungry smelling that aroma. *'I wish I had a woman to cook me such good food, my stuff never smells so delicious.'* "

"Cain saw another man there, still young but also one who leaned back and had girls serve him. They called him Seth. *'That must be my younger brother. He looks like Abel but taller.'* "

"When all had gone to sleep Cain descended from the tree, and slowly and quietly, like a mouse, walked back east again to find a shelter to sleep and find some berries and dig some roots for supper. He also found a tree full of ripe bananas. The next day Cain again went to look for those people. He climbed that tree again."

"Then he heard Eve telling a pretty girl what to do and how to do something. He could not understand what it was. But that girl got real angry at her mother and they fought. Then Seth got up and told her in a rough voice to obey her mother and behave herself. She made a pouty face and did it, finally."

'Yes, that is the way to keep her in line. But how beautiful she is! That long, wavy hair, those sharp eyes, that curvy figure, what a sight! I wish I had her. Would she go with me or would she turn back if I asked her? I bet she would go with me because she does not seem to like her mother and father. I ought to get her somehow. But will they allow her to go with me? I doubt it. They don't even want me around here.'

"In the evening of that day, that girl and another went to the nearby river to wash themselves, they left their fur clothes at the edge of the water. Cain had slid down from his tree and now watched hidden behind some thick bushes. The two girls splashed water on each other, swam with fluid movements, and they laughed and kicked. After some time the other girl stepped out of the river, slipped into her fur covering and left. The girl he desired was still in the water. Just when the other girl had gone home, this girl stepped out of the river. Cain waited until she was dressed, ran up to her, grabbed her around the waist, flung her over his shoulder and ran east. She screamed. Cain held one hand over her mouth and kept running east. By that time the others from the campground had heard the commotion and the men, including Seth, ran after him. But Cain kept running and running. They almost caught him, but then they recognized him by the red spot on his forehead. Then Adam said, 'Let him go, it is Cain, the evil one, we are not allowed to kill him. That girl is often so nasty, she deserves Cain.' "

"After Cain was a good distance away and safe, he put the girl down. She was angry at him and spit him in the face."

'Hold it, my beautiful woman, go easy here, you see I am stronger than you. I like you, I want you, I won't do you any harm, just obey me. Your mother does not like you anyway, I heard you talking to her. So come with me, please.'

"The girl looked at Cain from head to toe, she saw his smile. She waited. Cain stroked her gently on all her curves. She liked it, and said,

'All right, I will go with you. Where will you lead me to? I know I am beautiful. You better have a beautiful place for me to stay to fit my looks or else...'

'I have a cave house toward the rising of the sun.'

'A cave house? That sounds dark, humid and gloomy to me. I want a house in the middle of a large pasture out of white and colored marble. Do you know what that is? You seem so arcane.'

'Do not worry, my fair maiden. I will build you whatever you want. Just stay with me.'

'Very well, then, she said condescendingly. I will try it.'

"And they left together. So far goes the story," said Jacob.

"Thank you, Father, for telling us. Were they living a good life?"

"No, children, they were not. And Adam and Seth made up their mind to be watchful for them in the future."

Then Jacob told all his children to go home, time to sleep and "obey your mothers."

Jacob's Business

Jacob looked over his large family and was reminded of his parents way back in the south country. He had not seen his beloved mother for a long time. *How might my mother be? How might she feel? How will she get along with those weird daughters-in-law? How might my father be? I received The Blessing. This also means I have to support them in their old age. I ought to go home. But how? I have to talk to Laban about that. I ought to get payment for all my hard work. What should my payment be? I have to make up my mind beforehand, and then ask for a little more in case he wants to give me less. Laban is sneaky, and I have to be careful.*

Then Jacob, when he was finished thinking about all this, sought a convenient time to talk to Laban. He did not tell and discuss it with his two wives. So, some time after the funeral, Jacob met Laban and told him his wish to go home to his family. His father and mother are old, he ought to be there. To Laban, this made sense. He asked him what he wants for his wages, for his work. Jacob told him he does not want any gold or silver, just all the sheep and goats that are brown or multicolor. Every sheep or goat that is born to Laban's cattle and is brown or multicolor should be Jacob's. To Laban that seemed reasonable, so far. White wool would bring in more money.

Then Jacob separated the goats and sheep by color. The white ones stayed with Laban, the colored ones went to Jacob. Now Jacob had two little herds of goats and sheep already, a good beginning. He also purchased a few donkeys. His oldest son Reuben was already an older teenager and considered a man; Simeon, Levi and Judah not far behind. Jacob ordered his sons to be in charge of his herds and to drive them further south, three daytrips apart from Laban's herds, so that there would not be a mix-up. Jacob remembered what his father Isaac had told him about the mix-up of cattle between Abraham's and Lot's servants and the fights that followed. Jacob warned his young sons about that.

"Yes, yes, Father, we know, we know," they answered rather haughtily.

Mother Leah gave them loaves of freshly baked bread, skins of fresh water and their blankets. They also received a large earthenware pot with pickled cucumbers and cabbage. They loaded their provisions on carts pulled by donkeys. Leah kissed her sons, Bilhah kissed her Dan. Judah and Dan were allowed to go along, even though they were young. The young men drove their herds on with shouts and slowly departed. Leah ran after them and reminded them to be good boys and not to forget the Lord their God.

Leah added, while following them a bit, "Don't forget your morals, no running after a whore. And go only after orderly, God-fearing women should you see any. And stay warm, dress up at night. And do watch over Judah, who is still so young. Judah, however felt big and tall: *Why does Mother always treat me like a baby? What if the heathen girl is beautiful and likes me? Besides, I don't care for women. Mother is too scared, but I am sure, she means well. I will just smile and wave to her, then she will not give me any more orders.*

These older boys were eager to go on their own, eager to get away from the guarding and watchful eyes of their father, out and away into freedom. They had some servant men along also. Reuben was the chieftain, what he said had to be done. So, slowly the boys with their two herds disappeared and left behind them a cloud of dust, while the women, Jacob and Father Laban, with his younger wife and children watched.

It was the first real good-bye of Leah's and the maid's children. Tears came into their eyes. Leah embraced Bilhah and both cried a little, but then they dried their tears.

"At least they are strong, healthy, smart boys, we should really be happy," said Leah. And they all went back to work. The boys that were left behind now felt happy also, for now they were going to be the big chiefs next in line.

Then Laban counted his sheep and goats. He asked Jacob to get a certain number ready for market.

"So many?" asked Jacob.

"Yes, Jacob, I like to sell them. Remember the expensive cow that the lion killed under your unwatchful eyes? And altogether there were 15 sheep and seven goats that got lost or killed while under your supervision during the years? I cannot always afford all those losses. You have to tighten your belt and your four women and their twelve children also."

"Father Laban, don't you remember that I had made up for that? The Lord has blessed you richly while I worked for you. You had just a small herd when I came, Rachel could take care of it, and look at it now, how rich you became because of me."

When Leah heard her husband arguing back and forth with her father, she felt awkward. She left their vicinity and found some gardenwork to do. She did not want to be involved. She felt she ought to like her father for marrying her off. But on the other hand, when her sister Denah got married and Leah wanted to wear her golden foot bracelets, they were gone. Mother said Father had sold them. So she had to go to the wedding like a poor woman. Rachel's foot bracelets were also missing. Then Father promised Leah some 16 measures of Egyptian linen, and when she got them they were only 12, barely enough for a fancy gown. When she asked him about it, Father had replied that was to make up for losses incurred. So, her father was not that good-natured after all. Jacob gave Leah whatever he could, all except love. *Well, I can love his children, that is better than nothing. At least they love me back, we can talk and have fun together.*

Leah had to go back into the courtyard and continue spinning yarn. She watched the mice and worms. They all seemed to be digging in deeper into the ground than other years. That means there will be a colder winter than usual. She looked at the mountains in the distance, it was a very warm summer, and the snow on top had melted down quite a bit. *I would like for us to go to Noah's ark, but it is too far away.* She wished to go traveling once, and was rather envious of the birds that could fly where they wanted to. Leah made a little song for herself that she sang or whistled when she felt like wandering:

Take me along, little bird in the air.
Let me see the world so fair,
the other side of the mountain,
to drink from another fountain.
Pick the Rose of Sharon,
test the desert barren.
Take me along, little bird.

I see the deer walk in the bush,
see the crane stilting the rush.
There! - the lion downs the deer,
causing shock and mortal fear.
Lord, bring back your Garden Eden,
only you can give us freedom.

~~~

Whenever Jacob was home little Joseph was by his side. Joseph asked many questions and Jacob never tired answering them. Leah noticed that Jacob loved Joseph more than the other boys, almost more even than her daughter Dinah. Although he seemed to love her too.

Joseph saw a caravan coming along with salesmen and their wares. Now this was always exciting. Everyone came running, except the adult women who did not want to appear too eager. Little Joseph was there also. There were signs written on clothes and parchment that the traders had. Joseph looked at those signs and studied them. Then he asked his father what they meant. Jacob told him that they represent words in the Egyptian language. He pointed to some and told Joseph what they mean. Little Joseph repeated the words and looked at the signs. He even asked the tradesmen about more signs and their meanings. He remembered them very well and could understand them and saw others that were similar. So Joseph figured they meant related words, and it was so. Joseph was so happy about that, he exclaimed.

"Father, Mother, everybody, look, I can read!" Then he took a stick and drew those same signs into the sand until they looked true to form. Then Joseph started begging his father.

"Abba (Daddy), buy me parchment, please, please, I want to write." "You are too young, and parchment is very expensive, it takes very long to make."

"Please, Abba Father, please, just a tiny little piece, please." And Father Jacob bought a small piece of parchment for his son Joseph, not larger than his hand. He told him to write down the words and signs he could identify today. He figured he would forget them in a few days. Joseph treasured that little piece of parchment. He took a cold black piece of coal from the fire and wrote them down, and wiped them off, and wrote them again, until they looked more like he had seen them with the traders. He wanted more parchment, but Father told him to wait. Joseph hid the parchment in an old clay jar that he begged from Zilpah. Zilpah was in charge of making clay jars because her father had been a potter. Joseph did not loose interest in his piece of parchment, instead he treasured it and was determined to get more. Joseph felt he would get from his father whatever he wanted, he just had to be moderate in asking for it, then gradually increasing his wishes.

And so the summer months passed. The winter was really a little colder than previous winters. The mothers had to take sheep and goat fur, sew it together, to make jackets, leggings and hats for their children and Jacob. Jacob took the fur fleeces from his own herd that his older sons were guarding. Laban would not have looked friendly on him had he taken from Laban's animals. Laban's new wife was also very watchful that nothing would get away from her and her children.

But still Jacob was very efficient and a good shepherd, and God blessed his efforts. He worked hard, often day and night as necessary. The herds were doing well and multiplying.

But now Jacob had to start working for his own family, as per his contract with Laban. He would get the dark sheep and goats, Laban would get the white ones.

Jacob sliced off green stems from willow trees. Then he cut off the rind here and there in artistic patterns to make them look colorful. Then he stuck those long sticks in the ground near the watering troughs. He stuck them in the ground so as to create a row of fences. Then when the herds came in, the dark sheep were driven toward the fenced-in area to the water troughs. Laban's white sheep were also driven toward the watering troughs at the same time. This way both groups had to meet there at the water. That way they had no choice but to mate with each other. The decorated willow sticks looked small, bendable and unobtrusive. A stout fence would have been too obvious. Jacob knew that the dark color is more prevalent than the white, and that now there would be more speckled kids born than white ones, for him. And so it was. There were a lot more speckled kids and lambs born than white ones. As per agreement, the dark and speckled ones were Jacob's.

The Lord showed Jacob in a dream that He is really the one that is blessing his labors, not those manipulations with the sticks. He quietly told that to Rachel and Leah, what the Lord had told him in a dream, and urged them to be silent about it.

Chukko

Laban and some men were talking when they heard some screams in the distance. A maid was screaming at the goats who had invaded the vegetable garden. She tried to chase them out. Then Laban told his dog Chukko, who sat watchfully by his side, "Chukko, go sick the goats!"

Chukko slowly and laboriously stood up and walked and then started running toward the goats. He knew they were not supposed to go into that enclosure. He was a smart dog. There was no other dog like that around. When the goats saw the dog coming and growling at them, they ran and jumped away as fast as they could.

Chukko walked back to his master, but slowly. Laban stroked his fur and said, "Good dog, good dog." Chukko laid himself down heavily at Laban's feet, beat the ground with his tail and rested. Laban was wondering about Chukko. He was so slow lately.

"That dog must be getting old," Laban told his friends. "The heat is also bothering him with that thick fur of his.

"Hey, Rusha, bring Chukko some water," called Laban. Rusha was the new maid Laban had hired when his first wife had gotten sick and needed a caretaker. Rusha came and brought the water, Chukko licked some, but not too much.

The next morning Rusha brought some milk and leftover kitchen food to Chukko's dog house. But Chukko did not come out. She bent down to see if he is in there. Yes, there he lay, but still, with glazed eyes and stiff.

"Chukko died," she screamed.

The children came running and looking. "Aw, poor dog, poor Chukko, poor Chukko is dead," said Zebulon, the youngest of the boys. They were sad. Then they all ran to grandfather Laban and told him about Chukko.

"Well, kids, go tell Amro, the new slave, to dig him in behind the compound where the large rocks are, and don't bother me about that."

"Buy us a new dog," Asher told grandfather. "Won't go, child. Such dogs are not from around here." Amro found a shovel, he put dead Chukko on an old fur and pulled him over to the burial spot where he dug a deep hole. The children watched. They picked flowers and threw them on top of dead Chukko. Then Amro filled up the hole with dirt. "Good bye, Chukko, old friend, good bye." Little Dinah shed a tear and all went home sad. There was never such a good dog as Chukko.

Gad and Asher, whose mother was Zilpah, were tall and strong for their age. They decided to walk out toward the forest and catch themselves a wild dog and bring it home. They walked slowly and looked around. Then they stood still and listened. They heard something, like a whine. Silently they tiptoed over to the sound. There was a large tree with a hollow on the bottom. They walked closer and their hearts beat excitedly; young wild puppies. No mother dog around. Gad grabbed the largest one and stuck him in his sack. Then they walked home with it. They had not gone very far, when the mother of the pups came racing after them, barking fiercely. The boys got scared and quickly jumped on a tree to escape the sharp fangs of the mother dog. The puppy stayed below and the mother smelled him, checked him out and carried him in her mouth back into her den. When Gad and Asher heard loud sucking noises, they saw their opportunity to escape. They slid from the tree and ran as fast as they could, each picking up a stick they found, just in case..."Well, brother Asher, how did you like our first hunt?" They laughed.

And so time went on, Jacob's herds grew in number and strength, while Laban's did not multiply that much. Laban saw that and changed the rules. But still Jacob's herds increased more than Laban's. Laban was getting more and more unfriendly toward his son-in-law. Something had to give. Jacob wanted out and worked toward departure for his home country.

Old father Laban noticed that some wild dogs had a color change lately. Their hair got lighter and some of them had black ears and black eye patches. They also did not seem quite as shy as the wild dogs before. He knew his dog Chukko must have sired those when he ran loose during dog mating season. Laban wondered if those newly colored dogs could be caught and bred to replace smart Chukko. He planned to try it and see if any of them could become working cow dogs. The puppies sired by Chukko were smaller than their father was. Jacob also caught a couple of those half wild dogs to try his luck with breeding.

Jacob's Departure

Jacob had to now seriously make a plan on how to proceed, how to get himself freed from his uncle's service. *Would he let me? Can Laban afford to loose me?*

He had to proceed with utmost caution. In a society where people's houses were small and crowded, everyone knew pretty much what everyone else was doing, he did not want his departure publicized and discussed in the village. He had to be careful. So Jacob decided to execute his plan on a festive day, like sheep shearing day. Sheep shearers are hired, the women must cook plenty of good food. The sheep are driven into corrals, and one sheep after another gets its thick winter fur sheared off. The fleeces will bring in money and everyone will be happy and pre-occupied. This day Jacob chose for his move.

Jacob was working in the outer fields and sent a messenger to his two wives Leah and Rachel to come out to him, alone. They came, wondering what he may have to say. Then Jacob told them his plan.

"We are leaving, and moving home to my father and mother, home south."

"But Jacob," said Rachel, "where will we live in the meantime?"

"Do not interrupt me, please, I have it all figured out. I have a lot of goods accumulated, and this is going to be a big move. But the main thing is you must not talk about it. Do you understand? You two women are the only ones that know about this, and the Lord. I want no leaks."

Then Leah as well as Rachel were interested. They told their common husband that their father really did not treat them well lately and did not give them what he ought to, but the Lord made Jacob rich, and why not leave?

"Let us go," said Leah and also Rachel.

The two women, now friends again, walked briskly home and started packing. Zilpah and Bilhah asked about this.

"Where are we going?"

"Oh—, we are just going to our cattle." Both women, each in her home, threw their clothes in bags and rolled up all the sleeping mats and blankets. They gave their children some bread to eat and ordered them to get their personal belongings into their little nets, fast. "Father will come. You must all be ready and waiting for him."

Then Jacob came and loaded all his possessions, his children and wives and maids on camels and donkeys. It did not take very long. Leah and

Rachel had their goods packed already. Flour and grain bags, cooking utensils and sooty pots had all been hastily thrown into wooden boxes. Leah, Rachel, Zilpah and Bilhah packed behind closed doors. Some nosy neighbors asked Leah what they are doing in such hurry. She explained to them, "We are joining our herds. The herds need fresh grazing grounds again.   Our young sons and their cattle herders need our help and supervision."   Rachel said the same sentence to Bilhah and the children. They did not say good-bye to any of the neighbors.

Rachel was a little scared to leave everything behind and hoped for good luck and safety. Where would they sleep? Where would they go? Would any bandits grab them? She knew she was beautiful, and she knew that grandmother Sarah and even her mother-in-law were liked by foreign dignitaries once. She planned to throw a large veil on herself once they got going. Also, what would they eat? The four women had never made a trip like that. To Jacob it was not strange, because his father and grandfather used to travel around as nomads. He knew how to pack and move.

Rachel wanted some extra good-luck assurances and snuck back into the house of her father Laban, who was not home, nor were his wife and children. They were all with the sheep shearers, far out in the country. It fitted her just fine, nobody home in father's house, not even a maid left behind.   She took the two elaborately painted idols that her father had bought years ago, wrapped them in old clothes and quickly carried them to her camel and hid them in the camel's traveling bags, and sat on the camel. She did not say anything to her husband, she was sure he would not like it, since he knew the real God. She did not tell her sister Leah either. Who knows what she might say?   Leah was kind of trusting God only, for success.   But Rachel thought a little good-luck piece cannot hurt, besides this way she would not be so homesick.

The whole caravan left within hours. People around them wondered about all that sudden activity, but the headwomen, Leah and Rachel, carried a nonchalant face and did not specify anything, except that their cattle needed fresh grazing grounds and all hands are needed to help.

The camels walked fast with long strides. Soon they arrived at the place where Jacob's sons had their sheep, goats, cows and donkeys. The sons Reuben, Simeon, Levi, Judah and their servants were wondering why Father, their mothers and siblings were suddenly visiting them. Reuben stepped up to them and waited for his father to give a reason.

"Boys, get all the goats, sheep, donkeys, your cooking pots, axes and gear together immediately, we are moving south."

"Why Father?" asked Reuben.

"No time for questions now, we are going to your grandfather Isaac, and hurry up. Let's go!" Reuben heard his father's determined voice and obeyed.

So Reuben stuck two fingers into his mouth and made a loud sharp whistling sound. Then he waved and motioned with his arms to his other brothers that were far away to come down. They understood the sign language of Reuben's waiving arms. Immediately they herded together the grazing flocks and drove them over to Father Jacob and south. This was a rather slow process, because sheep do not walk so fast. Jacob told his wives and maids to fill all their containers with water and start walking. It was hasty. The boys and some servants walked up front as leaders of the herds, the others stayed on the flanks of the herds and some drove them on from behind. It was a great, but slow cattle drive. Jacob on his camel moved throughout the processional, urging everyone on and made sure nothing was left behind.

In time the children were getting hungry, so were the women and Jacob. The herds also needed time to graze. Jacob lifted up his arm high and called for a general stop. Everyone was relieved for it was already late afternoon. Now the cattle started grazing with intensity, they were hungry also. There was a river and the boys and servants drove them to the water.

The women, in the meantime, were very busy grinding grain for flour. Leah and Rachel had their heavy grinding stones hanging on donkeys. The maids were quickly grinding grain, a hard job. Jacob was making two fires, drove stout forked sticks into the ground and hung large copper kettles with water over the fires. He had the firepoles previously prepared. His wives in Haran were living in houses on one spot. Now they had become travelers. Jacob made sure the women learned how to handle the traveling lifestyle. He butchered some goats; some for Rachel's family, the others for Leah's. He told the women not to think about bread, just mix the wholegrain flour with water and make dumplings. Jacob had managed to take some breeding chickens along in a cage for eggs. He could not catch them all, it would have been too obvious to the neighbors. Leah and Rachel milked the goats and gave the children milk to drink. After about 2 hours the meat was done and the dumplings dumped into the boiling soup. The dumplings did not take long to cook. Jacob looked up to the sky and said a prayer of thanks to the

Lord, and half the people were eating. The other half were watching the cattle. Then the others took their turn eating.

Jacob let the cattle graze until it got dark. But now there was hectic activity. The boys and workers had to gather stones to pile them high in great circles and drive the goats and sheep and other livestock into it, to protect them from marauding animals. Every adult shepherd had a herd to guard with one of Jacob's sons, so that all would be safe. The sky was clear, no rain clouds to be seen. Jacob told his people they may as well sleep under the stars this night. They were told to keep little fires burning to scare animals away with a firebrand or torch, if need be. Jacob slept right away, he was very tired. Finally the others also lay down to sleep.

After a few hours Jacob woke up and took his night shift. He did not trust his boys to watch in the night nor his other shepherds. He walked around the fenced-in herds. He checked everything for safety, for robbers, for wolves. He did not see anything out of order. *Thank you, Lord.*

Very early in the morning Jacob awoke the shepherds and the older boys first. They had to drive their cattle to the water to drink. The women woke up to grind more grain. The maids' fingers wore sore because it was hard work. So, Leah and Rachel took over: "Crunch, crunch, crunch." There was a lot of grinding needed for such a large group of people. Jacob had the fires going already. The water was ready to be boiled, for dumplings again.

"Make enough dumplings to last for lunch, we eat them cold," ordered Jacob. So there was more grinding: "crunch, crunch, crunch," and more boiling. The children were ordered to find more firewood. Whoever did not try got a quick slap with Jacob's leather strap. There was hectic activity. Jacob made sure things went like clockwork. The cattle were grazing. The children had to have their milk, breakfast for the cattle herders, packing the extra dumplings in skins, hanging them on the donkeys, picking up the heavy grinding stones, hanging them in pouches on the donkeys. Jacob walked restlessly around, watching over everything, giving advice, making sure nothing was left behind. Finally, he saw everything seemed to be in order. The women mounted the camels with the younger children and Jacob climbed on his camel also. He raised his arm high, blew his whistle and called "proceed."

The herders called their flocks of sheep and goats with loud calls. The goats seemed to know where they were not supposed to go because that is where they wanted to go. So the men were very busy to keep the whole caravan moving. Leah counted her children and the maids theirs as well. With young children running every which way, the mothers could never be sure that all were in sight. All seemed to be in order. And on they went, south, always south.

When the sun was high overhead, Jacob called a stop again. The cattle needed water and the people needed food. Everyone had some dumplings. The women found plenty of sorrel near the river. They picked it, checked it for worms and gave the leaves to everyone and Leah ordered every person to eat them, like it or not. But they did like the sorrel; it was the only raw green thing they could get to brake up the monotony of the dumplings. The leaves tasted sour and rather good.

Then Jacob ordered everyone up again and on, south again. This time Jacob rode in front of them because he wanted to take the caravan higher into the mountains. There were too many people living in the fertile valley; he wanted to meet as few people as possible. Nor did he dare to go near other people's grazing grounds. And south they went, on and on, uphill and down.

At night they had dumplings again. Young Issachar complained, "I want steak."

"Me too," asked Gad, and Asher chimed in also, "Steak and cake."

"Quiet!" ordered Leah, "You eat your dumplings or you eat nothing. Understand?"

Grouchily they kept nibbling on the dumplings, and just then Father Jacob came over, and their complaints ended.

The second night started out much like the first night. However, they encountered a leopard who seemed to be hungry. One of the servants saw it first and waved to Jacob. Jacob grabbed his bow and arrows and ran over to where the man had seen the leopard. Word got out about it. Every man got his weapon ready. This would be a restless night. The women ordered their young children to stay close by, near the fire. They also had some torches along with tar at the tip. This could be held into the fire and in case of emergency, a wild animal could be burnt with it if it came too close. Jacob kept close watch. And as the blackness of the night sank down on them, outside of the perimeter of the campfires where the large cattle stood, two green dots were visible and coming closer. The children were scared but tried to be brave.

"Sh, sh," said Leah, "Father is watching." Then suddenly a howl was heard and a noise came from the ground where they had seen the two green eyes. Father Jacob had shot and killed the leopard. A sigh of relief went through all people. Even the sheep and goats, that had pushed themselves close together, relaxed. Jacob walked over to the leopard. It lay still. He poked it with his spear, it did not move, it was dead. Then he pulled out his long knife, and cut off the beautiful hide. He left the meat for the eagles. When Jacob carried the leopard hide to the campground, the animals became shy. So he wrapped it inside out, rinsed it in the river to loose some of the scent. Then he rubbed some salt on it to preserve and to dry it out and keep it from insects.

The rest of the night was uneventful. Women and children could go to sleep again. The boys beamed with pride for their father had shot a leopard in the dark.

~~~

On the third day Jacob found a shallow place in the river. He ordered everyone to cross it. No crocodile or other dangerous animal hindered them. So far, they were making progress. But Jacob was not relaxed. They had to move on and on. Even though the cattle drive went slowly but well, Jacob knew the hard part is still to come.

The boys saw bees emerging from a crack in a rock on the mountain. "Hey, bees!" Asher yelled. "Let's get the honey!" He was always trying to "organize" some food. Naphtali and Issachar lit two torches. Naphtali who was tall and thin took a heavy stone ax, Issachar carried the clay pot. Asher held the other torch. Naphtali and Asher climbed up the steep face of the mountain, holding on to small trees. Naphtali held the burning torch and the ax. Asher labored to haul the clay pot up the mountain. They held the torch with the firebrand to the bees' hole. The bees did not like the smoke and with angry humming left–but not for long. Issachar saw the bees surrounding him and yelled at his brothers to come down and hurry up. "Burn the bees," they yelled down to him. Issachar on the ground swung the burning and smoking torch around the buzzing bees and they stayed away from him. Then Naphtali, the oldest and strongest, slammed his ax against the slot in the rock to make it bigger. The other one grabbed the honey combs and deposited them in the pot. Asher then quickly slid down the rockface, put the jar down and climbed up again. There was more honey and honeycombs in the hole than they had expected. Then they put it into their leather pouches, slid down the rock face and all three ran as fast as they could away from the angry bees.

They could not run fast and had to keep swinging the torches at the bees until they stopped following them. Then the three walked over to Mother Leah.

"Mother, look, we have lots and lots of honey from the rock," exclaimed Issachar. Leah looked and was so happy.

Leah now could sweeten their dumpling soup with milk and honey. Everyone loved it. Suddenly Asher screamed, "I got stung from a bee! Help!"

Leah looked. Yes, one bee had been caught inside some of the honeycombs and had just emerged unto Asher's arm, the stinger still in him. She took a knife and carefully scraped the stinger out of Asher's arm. "Don't worry, boy, it will heal, be brave. Go, show it to your Mom. That bee will now die."

~~~

At Padan Aram, the neighbors of Jacob did not mind the folks being away to help drive Jacob's herds to a different grazing ground. It was natural. They would be back. They expected them to be back at night on the second day, perhaps. Maybe they were tired and something held them up. On the third day the people expected them to come back, they looked in the direction the camels had gone, but there was no dustcloud coming their way. By now they were all talking about it and discussing it. None of Jacob's wives or children or servants came back. Strange! Someone decided to better tell Laban.

Laban's sheep shearing was just about done. The fleeces were loaded on wagons driven by mules and oxen, ready for the fur processors and for sale. Laban could not believe his daughters were gone. He walked over to the huts his daughters and children had occupied. True, they were gone. Everything was gone. He asked the neighbors as to when they had left, what reason they had given them. The neighbors told them they had to help find new grazing ground for Jacob's cattle and they said they needed all hands to help.

New grazing ground, all right. That bastard, he escaped, he is afraid of me.

So Laban told his wife and children that Jacob escaped. Then he told his brothers, and he and they decided to get their camels ready and forcefully bring them back. Then Laban looked into his house if they stole anything from him. Nothing.

Wait a moment, where are my gods? My Egyptian, beautiful idols, for which I paid so much money? Where are they? He looked everywhere - gone. *Ah—, he is scared! Now suddenly Jacob does not trust his God anymore, he wants a little extra assurance, some extra good luck. I must get them back, they are my servants. I must force them to return, if necessary with weapons.*

Laban told his wife about the missing idols, and she agreed they should be returned. Laban and his brothers and some servants packed provisions and early the next morning they started after Jacob.

Laban, however, had an odd dream that night. He did not say anything to anyone about it. It seemed to be a heavenly dream, something he should mind. However, he still started the journey after the escaped son-in-law, together with his men and their weapons. It was not hard to follow Jacob's caravan because it had not rained and they could easily see the footprints of Jacob's cattle on the ground.

~~~

Jacob had a lot of cattle, sheep, goats, camels, and people that managed them. His older sons helped along responsibly, as was the custom that children had to work as young as possible. Jacob was on edge, for it was not easy to drive such a large group of cattle and people over new territory. He had to proceed carefully for there were other people living there through whose territory he had to trespass. Jacob rode a camel, that way he could be everywhere faster and he could oversee his sons, servants and cattle better. He needed supplies like tents, for in his father-in-law's area in Padan Aram people lived in small houses or shacks and adobes. So Jacob had to sell a number of cattle to trade for tents and other supplies. But so far things had gone fairly well for him and his huge caravan. However, Jacob had the feeling that it is too early to call it a sucessful venture. His servants would stay with him, he presumed. But he had to make sure they received good food and good care. Servants could not just run away from their jobs; there could be many consequences. However, when his workers see new territory, maybe a greener pasture somewhere else, one or the other just might take off and find himself a new master in the passing neighborhood and abandon the herd. Cattle left on their own and getting scared may cause a stampede. He did not need a stampede or any kind of upheaval. But, so far nothing bad had happened. Wild animals in the mountains were seen now and then, but with so many people surrounding the herds they were a bit intimidated. Jacob made sure all herds were safely fenced in at night either in a stone enclosure or thorn fence. If he saw an empty large cave in late afternoon, he would drive the ewes with their lambs in there for the night.

Leah and Rachel with their maids were very busy grinding grain, picking green herbs and cooking large meals for all the workers. They had to rush because when the sun sank down on the horizon it was totally dark until the moon came out or the stars. Cooking and care of children had to be finished by then. Then came a long night of rest. Leah did not always sleep all those long dark hours. She was thinking and planning what needed to be done the next day: what to cook, which maid should do which job, which sons were needed to carry food to the servants. Master Jacob would probably eat his meals with her sister Rachel and maid Bilhah, so she had one large mouth less to feed, although it still bugged her that she, as the Number One wife, did not have Jacob first for herself. But she did not spend time worrying, because their travels were far too dangerous to waste time on such minor details of the soul. Their escape route and their daily survival routine was on her and everyone's mind right now.

On the sixth day after his secret departure, Jacob and others saw a dust cloud in the distance coming toward them from the north. He knew that this was it! The long-feared encounter with Laban. Jacob told his servants to keep their mouths shut and talk only what he tells them to say. He told his wives and maids to be silent, look humble and demure and keep their children under control. "I want no sound out of them." He especially cautioned Bilhah to keep loudmouthed Naphtali quiet. Jacob rode to the front of the caravan awaiting Laban. Jacob's caravan was camped on a mountain.

Laban's riders, all on camels and armed to the teeth, camped in a hilly country called Gilead. Laban dismounted, and so did Jacob. Both men came together, Laban angry and upset, Jacob determind to stand his ground.

Laban exploded: "Why did you deceive me and take off with my daughters? You know they are my daughters!"

Not any more, you old fox, I married them they are mine, thought Jacob. However, his face remained calm and controlled.

Laban continued, "We could have made a beautiful farewell party, with singing, music and dancing. I did not even have the opportunity to kiss my daughters good-bye."

There he goes again how much he loves them when he connived their inheritance away, that cheater.

"You know, Jacob, that I am a strong man? Do you see my soldiers and armed men? I have the power to force you back into my employ and make you a slave for good. However, since I am a generous man and good, I won't do that."

"The God of your fathers told me," continued Laban, "in a dream last night, not to hinder you in any way and let you do your own thing. And I, good, generous and orderly as I am, am heeding that command of your God." A genuine breather of relief escaped Jacob's mind, but he, of course, would not let on. It bothered Jacob that his father-in-law mentioned "your God," as if He is not Laban's God also, when there is no other one. Laban should know that.

But then Laban continued, "Even if you took off like that you did not have to steal from my household!"

Now Jacob was surprised and he had to say something.

"Well, Laban, I thought you might take your daughters, my wives, away from me. I wanted to be safe. However, I did not steal anything from you, and that is a fact." And Jacob stood straight and tall and threw back his shoulders, "I did not steal from you anything. In fact, if you find anything in my possession that belongs to you, may that person die! Jacob made a wide sweep with his hand showing off all the dark and speckled sheep and goats and servants that he had bought, all his, legally and deservedly.

"Not true," replied Laban, "you did steal from me: My gods! I paid a lot of money for them, they enhanced my house and brought me good luck."

"The gods," exclaimed Jacob, "no, I did not take your precious gods. You may look around."

And Laban really started looking around. He looked in every tent, in every bag, in every box.

Someone in Jacob's caravan was getting more and more anxious. It was Rachel. She had secretly stolen those gods from her father's home. She believed they would bring her good luck. Going into strange territory, living in tents, not knowing how tribes and other inhabitants of the country would treat them made her scared, and she thought some extra good-luck items could not hurt. Leah, her sister, did not get that idea. She had learned to trust her husband's God.

Then Laban checked the camel Leah was riding on and the children's donkeys and camels and their baggage, while Jacob watched. When Laban came to Rachel, she exclaimed:

"Let it not displease my lord that I cannot rise up before thee; for the custom of women is upon me." She knew that men at that time kept away from women in that state, it was the custom. Laban believed her or his honor dictated that he believed her, and turned away. *Whew, that was close,* Rachel thought.

Now Jacob lost his temper and started yelling at his father-in-law in righteous indignation. "You searched all my possessions, as if they were yours, did you find anything? No. This is against my honor. I worked for you for twenty years, seven for Leah, seven for Rachel, and six for the herds, and you are still not satisfied. What is my trespass? What is my sin, that thou hast so hotly persued after me? When I came to you, your flocks were small. Your daughter could take care of them. Now, look how rich you have become through my diligent labor, all the flocks you have and even soldiers and all kinds of servants. Also, you changed my wages ten times, whenever it pleased you, and whenever you thought I got ahead too much you changed my wages around." Deep down in his heart Jacob knew that if you allow white rams and billy goats to mate with dark ewes and dark goats the kids will be speckled. And Jacob knew that he had fixed it that way. But he did not let on to his father-in-law that he had "helped along" with this blessing in his own favor.

Jacob further told Laban that whenever an animal was ripped by a wolf or got hurt, he would make good for it to Laban. He reminded Laban that no matter how hot it was, how cold, how windy, how rainy he was outside watching Laban's herds, and how thirsty he often got. Work and responsibility came first to him. Laban could not deny that.

However, Laban would not give in easily either. He reminded Jacob that his wives are really his daughters and their children are his, Laban's, because if a servant is owned by a master everything the servant has, does or owns belongs to his master. Laban really tried to rub it in to Jacob. But then he calmed himself again and, thinking what God had told him, he wanted to abide by His orders. He was a little afraid of Jacob's God and chose to better go along with His orders.

Then Laban suggested to collect a large pile of rocks, as a business contract. Then Jacob found a large stone and righted it up in the center of the pile as a memorial or contract. Then the men sat down to a hearty meal that Leah had already anticipated and prepared. *What an efficient woman,* thought Jacob.

In those days most people could neither read nor write. Papyrus was the only paper in existence and very expensive. People also wrote on stone or clay tablets or on white birch rind. Laban named the place Galeed, and said "May the Lord keep an eye on us while we are separated from each other." Jacob named the place Mizpah. Laban went on to say that "this pile of rocks means I will not fight you with weapons, and you must also not fight me with weapons, not now, not ever! Understand, Jacob?"

"Yes, Father Laban, I understand."

"However, Jacob, I must give you an order: don't you dare mistreat my daughters, now that I am not around to watch them. Treat them well. Remember, God is watching, even if I cannot keep an eye on you anymore.

In the name of the God of Nahor and Abraham, your grandfather, swear to me that you will be good to my daughers and stick to this agreement, and don't you take any more wives for yourself. Two wives, two special maids, and twelve children is enough for any man to handle. Agreed?"

"Yes, Father Laban, I vow to you." Leah and Rachel, when they heard this, were glad. Then Jacob killed a sheep and ceremoniously burned it up on a stone altar to verify his oath.

After all was done it had gotten dark. Laban decided that he and his warriors should not venture home in the night. They stayed on the mountain. Then early the next morning after another good breakfast, Laban kissed his daughers and all the grandchildren, said good-bye to them and left.

Jacob was relieved. He praised Leah for supplying all the meals. He praised Zilpah and Bilhah and the other younger maids for keeping the children quiet and under control. Rachel did not help with serving when her father was around because she had to act as if she had her monthly event.

One problem solved, now there might be another problem as yet, a bigger problem to come, but I will see, Jacob thought.

Jacob stayed a number of days near this place as long as grass lasted for his cattle. Also, the women had to bake bread, which always meant making a new clay oven. The women needed time to make sour dough and let it rise and bake. Also, Jacob did not want to race his pregnant cattle. So he took his time traveling on. He also needed time to check on all the cattle whether they were healthy or not, check their hoofs and see to it that all is well. His final goal was to get back to his father Isaac and his mother Rebekah. He longed to see them.

~~~

Jacob felt that the biggest battle is still ahead of him: The meeting with his brother, Esau. He found out that Esau now lived in the country of Edom, not close by his father anymore. However, a large caravan like his will not be overlooked. He knew Esau was, and has always been, a good fighter, and angry on top of it, and Esau would not forget anything, not the sale of his birthright with the lentil soup, nor the cheat about the inheritance. Jacob was thinking about that. He was mulling over the situation of how best to proceed. He thought about his very wealth; that part of it was God's blessing, but part of it was his manipulation. Would God, his God, the God of his grandfather Abraham and his father Isaac, protect him from his brother's anger? Jacob realized that he was not totally 'white' like the snows on Mt. Arrarat. His handling and managing were at best 'gray.' Would God stick to him anyhow? God sticks to the good people; will he be good enough for God? So that God will help him? Jacob thought about all those things.

After some time in the general area Jacob decided to proceed further south into the country that God had promised his ancestors as their inheritance. He also had told his wives and children about that land, that someday it will be theirs because the Lord had said so. Then his sons asked him:

"What about the people living there now? Will they let us?"

Jacob told them that when the time is just right the Lord will find a way. In fact, the Lord had told Abraham that those people living there right now are not bad enough to be displaced. That meant "leave things as they are."

Then suddenly, while the caravan had moved on further south, with the forested Lebanon mountains towards the sunset and the Hermon mountains toward the sunrise, and Jacob was alone, angels met Jacob in the fields. His eyes sprang open in wonder. He stared at them, they looked like young men in white clothes. He was elated: *My father Isaac's God does like me.* He could tell they were not mere men. They wore extremely white gowns and had a brightness about them unlike normal people. Then these angels looked at him, turned and walked further on and left him. Jacob was so happy that God is on his side, that he will get his needs met, that all will be well. "This is the place where God was."

He told Leah, Rachel and his sons about the angels. They were also very happy. Now Jacob called the place Mahanaim.

Leah was also happy and confident. She knew as long as the Lord is on her husband's side, even if he loves Rachel more than her, things with the caravan and their livelihood will work out properly.

His sons also were quite confident. They talked amongst each other about that. They presumed that they were like the cream on the top of the milk, the privileged people, the folks that can do no wrong, and everyone must move when they come. They did not say those things to their mothers, of course, and not to their father either. "Those old parents are somewhat old-fashioned, and still in their spirit under the invisible control of their grandfather Laban, out of habit. But we, the new generation, we are free men, and if anyone is not good enough, we will take care of them." Thus they talked amongst themselves by their camp fires at night. The sons of the maids were also just as intelligent and boisterous as the sons of Leah, and they also put their ideas into the fireside talks. All except Joseph, he was the smartest one, and often he acted as if he was a 'wise man of old' which they did not like. He also carried with him that clay pot with papyrus and Egyptian writing, and he could supposedly read it. His brothers commented on that sometimes.

"What is reading good for anyhow? Strength and work is the thing that gets you a livelihood. Reading and writing, 'baah' that's for Pharaoh's crouching scribes." They made sure Joseph got his fair share of work cut out for him, too.

After quite awhile, and when the grass was grazed off there, Jacob finally had his plan with his brother completed. They had to move on, though. Now Jacob chose three trusted servants, including the one who was mauled by the lion some years ago, and sent them to Edom to tell his brother Esau that he was coming back. He did not want to surprise him and be attacked unawares.

The servants found the tribe of Esau. They had multiplied and spread out, Esau being their ruler and father. Everyone knew Esau. The servants had no hard time finding him. After they had given Esau Jacob's message, they returned back to Jacob. Leah with daughter Dinah, Rachel, and everyone else stood up waiting for them to hear what Esau had said.

"We went to your brother Esau, and he is already on his way to meet you. He has 400 men with him."

"Oops! This does not look so good," said Leah.

"Did the men have weapons on them?" asked Jacob.

"Yes, bows, arrows, spears, a long saber in their sheaths, and looking as strong as bulls."

"And they were already on their way?"

"They were getting ready and saddling their horses and camels. However, we walked away, and after we were out of their view we ran to you, as fast as we could, to tell you about it."

His boisterous sons suddenly were rather quiet. They grabbed their weapons. Jacob seeing that, told them to hide them. "This is not the time to take up arms, pull your "tails" in like scared dogs and act humble. Just look at your size and your still underdeveloped muscles, you cannot fight those warriors of my brother. Forget it. Now, do your duty and keep down."

Jacob now rearranged all his cattle into two groups. The men swung sticks and staffs and with yelling and screaming divided the cattle. His two most trusted servants were put in charge of each group. Jacob told the first group to go ahead so far that the second caravan is not visible. In case Esau takes or attacks the first group, maybe the other group can run away, hide or escape.

"And you, boys, each go with his birth mother, and hide your weapons and act small, I want no words out of you during the confrontation. Obey your mother, Reuben, Simon, Levi and Judah. You look like grown men, but I want each of you to take a younger child on his hand, as if you are caring for them. Maybe my brother will think you are just young teenagers. And you, Reuben and Simeon, quickly cut off your long beards."

"Father..." Reuben exclaimed, "no, it's our honor as men."

"Shush! Not right now, if your skin is important to you. In a short time I want to see you as beardless teenagers. And make it quick! No more talk out of you two." He shouted at them:

"Do it right now. Understand? Your life and ours depends on it."

Now the other boys, especially Levi, who had some blond fuzz growing already, were grinning at their two brothers. Reuben and Simeon threw them a vicious and threatening look as if to say 'you just wait...' Joseph whispered to his mother, "Father is really nervous and upset. Do you think Uncle Esau will be that bad?"

Jacob and his servants hurried to get the cattle divided before Master Esau comes. They did not see any dust clouds as yet. Maybe they will finish before he comes. They were near the Jabbok River. Jacob told them to cross that river. It was not so difficult, for the river was wide and shallow on that spot and sheep, goats, camels, donkeys could wade through with some prodding and hitting. Leah, Rachel, and the other servant women also crossed the River Jabbok. The three youngest, of mother Leah, Issachar, Zebulon and Dinah found the shallow water so enticing, they splashed each other and tried to get all wet. But Leah scolded them and made them behave, at this most critical time. Then all sat there and waited for new orders from Jacob. But in the meantime the women started cooking for the ever hungry family members. Jacob stayed behind on the other side of the river.

"Where is Father?" asked Joseph. Rachel told him he stayed behind. "Is he afraid?" asked Leah's son Judah.

"You just keep quiet, boy. Father is responsible, and you know what to do, so do it."

"We are hungry," whined Issachar and Zebulon to their mother.

"Yes, yes, you are always hungry. We have no oven here to bake bread, so get busy and grind us some grain for dumpling soup again."

"I want steak," said Judah.

"Be quiet," answered his young brother Issachar.

"I like dumplings."

"Yes, yes, you like everything, except working," answered Simeon. "Boys, boys, be peaceful," admonished Leah, "and help with the fire."

Renate M. Schulz

The Angel Man

Jacob, in the meantime, was alone on the other side of the river. *Where is my God, now that I need him? The angels talked to me. But they did not say anything of great importance, just that they know me. I thought I was such a great guy.—Aha! Then the angels left. They left! That's it! I did not realize it, they left me. They left me, for sure. That is it! I am not good enough for them to stay with me. The Lord has not forgotten what bad things I had done in the past. Leah came to his mind. How often did she have teary eyes because I would not show her a smile or hold her hand or embrace her or say an extra nice word to her, all because I did not want my father-in-law to have the satisfaction of being right, that love will come. God's memory is awfully good. Better yet than Esau's. What am I going to do? I have no soldiers to fight my brother, and God is not on my side. Man, what a mess I am in? I have to talk to the Lord and see if I can make His face shine on me again. I must get His blessing, somehow!*

Then Jacob knelt down and spoke to the Lord:

"God of my grandfather Abraham, and God of my father Isaac, hear me. You told me, Lord, to go back to my land and to my relatives, and you would let everything go well for me. I am not worth all the kindness and faithfulness that you have shown me, your servant. I crossed the Jordan with nothing but a walking stick, now I have come back with these two groups. Save me, I pray, from my brother Esau. I am afraid—afraid that he is coming to attack us and destroy us all, even the women and children. Remember that you promised that you will make everything go well for me, and to give me more descendants than anyone could count, as many as the grains of sand along the seashore."

After that prayer Jacob stayed on this side of the river to do some more thinking and planning. He figured he should select his top cattle and have the servants drive them ahead of the group as a present for his brother Esau. Jacob figured correctly, that the Lord will do His part, but he also has to do his own part. Maybe this will please the Lord.

Suddenly there appeared a tall, muscular man who attacked him, not with weapons, just with his hands. He had a dignified face and blond hair. This man tried to pin him down on the ground–maybe kill him, choke him?

What is going on? Why does this guy want to kill me? I did not do anything to him? Well, if he thinks he is strong, I will show him a thing or two, I am strong too, I know all the tricks in fighting by hand.

Jacob kept on fighting the man, he had to because the man would not let go of him.

"Hey, what did I do to you?" Jacob managed to say to the stranger. "Am I on your land? I will move right away, you see my famliy and goods are already on the other side, I will leave too." The man kept on fighting him, saying nothing.

What does he want from me? We did not steal anything by trespassing through his land. It is common practice around here. And so Jacob kept on fighting the man; on and on, he was beginning to get tired.

Jacob wrestled the man to get rid of him, he tried all his tricks, he punched, kicked, even did kicks in the underbelly of the man, but that man did not seem to get hurt at all. Then Jacob tried his "grand finale", a hard punch to the chin of the man. *That ought to do it.* But it did nothing to the strong stranger. No matter how much Jacob fought him, this man had unending strength. However, the man also could not overpower Jacob.

After Jacob's last great punch to the man's chin, when nothing happened to the man, Jacob suddenly realized: This is not a mere man, this is an angel-man. Immediately Jacob dropped his arms in shock and awe, he did not want to fight God. But then Jacob realized *If this is God, I must not let him go.* Jacob right away grabbed the angel-man and held on to him tightly. *I need him for blessing and success.* Then the man slapped Jacob hard on his hip. Right away his hipbone jumped out of his joint and Jacob screamed in sudden pain. Then Jacob's hunch was confirmed: This is really not a mere man, this is an angel in human form. Now Jacob did not fight anymore. He held on to him, and begged him to bless him. In the meantime, it was getting light in the east and the angel-man tried to leave. But Jacob held on to him with all his strength. The angel-man said: "Let me go; daylight is coming."

"I won't unless you bless me," begged Jacob. Then the angel-man asked Jacob.

"What is your name?"

"Jacob," he answered, (Jacob, meaning the deceiver).

"From now on your name shall not be 'deceiver' anymore, it shall be 'Israel'."

"Now, you angel-man, please tell me your name."

"Why do you want to know my name? But I will bless you. You fought with God and man and you won. I'll let you have the victory." Then the angel-man blessed Jacob by putting his hands on his head and repeating the blessing of the Lord.

Suddenly the angel-man was gone and nowhere to be seen. Jacob was all alone in the grass. Jacob exclaimed:

"I have seen God face-to-face, and I am still alive. Amazing!" Jacob was happy. He gave this place a name called Peniel, to remember it for all times. Then the sun arose in the east.

Jacob had to cross the river Jabbok, get back to his family and herds, but walking was hard and painful. He was limping. He touched his hip, and felt through his muscles, *Yes, there was something different.* He pounded the bone with his fist to punch it back into the hip socket, it hurt him a lot, but it was not as it was before, it felt loose somehow. He turned around in all directions, looking for the angel-man, but he was nowhere to be seen. Jacob compared his normal hip with this hurting one and felt it was not the same. He pinched himself, *is this for real, will this stay like this forever? Maybe this is the punishment from the Lord for me, and after the punishment is over, things will be all right? How will I run after the cattle with this hip? I hope it will get better. If my hip stays this way, I know God is dead serious and I cannot play around with shady dealings.* Then Jacob remembered the angel man's direction, his new name.

Jacob practiced saying his new name: I s r a e l. It sounded good to him. I s r a e l. Then he waded through the river and walked back to his first wife Leah. He wanted to be proper and correct now. She is his first wife, so he felt he had to talk to her first.

He put his arm on Leah's shoulder and told her what he had experienced on the other side of the river. Leah was happy that God had visited her husband, and that their livelihood would now be safe because God had met Jacob. But in her heart Leah smiled, knowing that God did see all that Jacob had not done to her and that his limping is what is coming to him for not loving her. But Leah did not let on, of course. She knew now that God does not overlook things. Then Jacob told the episode of the angel-man to Rachel and they told it to all the others.

Esau

Soon Esau with his older sons and soldiers proceeded toward Jacob. This would be a great battle and his long awaited revenge toward his brother. His soldiers were ready to attack Jacob. They were tense but confident. Then a large herd of cattle approached them instead.

"Whose cattle is this?" inquired Esau from the man at the front.

"It is Jacob's cattle and a gift for you, Sir." And the servant made a deep bow before Esau. *Well, we cannot fight cattle, can we? A gift for me? What does my brother mean?* He saw they were very good, fat cows, goats, camels, in top shape. *I don't get it. But we will see...* It was getting late in the day. The herd of cattle had to be rested down for the night. Esau and his warriors also rested for the day. The confrontation would be the next day.

This was a restless night for Jacob and his family. The sun finally arose in the east. The women cooked breakfast but Jacob did not eat.

It was not long before Jacob saw Esau coming in the distance in a cloud of dust. He had his first group of cattle sectioned off and driven ahead of him as a gift for his brother, to gain his favor. Jacob did not know as to what happened to that first group that he had sent ahead, if his brother took it or not. Or if he even saw it.

Then he told his two maid-wives Bilhah and Zilpah to go ahead with their children, each having two. After another group of cattle walked Leah with her seven children. Then at the very end, in the safest place, had to be Rachel with Joseph. Then Jacob limped ahead of all the groups to meet his brother and his soldiers face to face.

In the meantime Esau saw another group of cattle coming toward him. *Still no soldiers, brother dear? What's on your mind? And what about all those women and children coming toward us? Where are Jacob's soldiers? My men don't fight women and children.*

Then Esau saw an old man, seemingly in his nineties, like his own age, limping toward him. He was dumbfounded. *Could that be my twin brother?* Esau gave that man a sharp look, he tried to see his face from the side, *Yes, it's him, my brother Jacob. My old, handicapped brother Jacob. What happened to him in those 21 years?*

Esau just sat there on his horse with his warriors, all speechless. Then he saw Jacob bending down to him seven times, as was the custom for an extremely respected person. When Esau saw his brother Jacob doing these actions, while limping, his anger and revenge dissolved and a compassioned love overcame him. He jumped from his horse, ran toward Jacob, embraced his brother and kissed him. He was so glad to see him after all those years; the cheating of the birthright and the inheritance seemed to be all forgotten and forgiven. The twins looked at each other and Esau was very happy. Esau realized only now how he had missed his brother and their companionship. There was a good seed inside Esau that one could not deny.

Then Esau asked him about that herd of cattle that they had passed. Jacob told him:

"It is a gift for you, so you would be good to me."

So there is reason for Jacob to apologize to me, his conscience is bothering him, even after 20 and 1/2 years.

Then Esau told him, "O sure my brother, I love you, things are good and even between the two of us, we are brothers. But I don't need the gift, all that cattle and servants, no my brother, I have enough."

"Please take it anyhow, I sorted it out for you. Please take it. It would make me so happy."

"All right, my brother, I take it." Then Esau ordered the cattle to be driven to Edom where he, his wives and children lived.

Jacob knew in his heart that if Esau accepts the gift then it is a contract between them, Esau would not make war with him. Esau accepted. Only now, after the accepted gift, would Jacob be sure that he could believe Esau.

Then Esau asked about the two women with their four sons, up front. Jacob told him how God had given him those two women with their children. Then afterwards, behind the first group is his first wife Leah with her seven children, also given to him by God's grace. Way in the back is his second wife Rachel with her son Joseph.

He did not mention to Esau that Rachel was his lover wife. Leah however saw in the set-up of the groups that Jacob still seemed to love Rachel more than her. But she had no time to think about it. She had to be strong and tough like leather. Strong people don't suffer from unecessary heartaches. She had learned to hide her soft heart inside a tough exterior and act as though nothing hurt her as not to appear vulnerable.

Then while the brothers talked and exchanged news, especially that their mother Rebekah had died, Jacob was sad. His good mother, gone. However, he had no time to think about it now. Esau offered to travel with him, his herds and family. Or at least leave some of his soldiers with him for protection. However, Jacob did not trust Esau's soldiers. All kinds of things could go wrong with them around and the children's loud mouths, and for his wives to feed all the hungry stomachs of Esau and his men. Jacob felt it is better to trust the protection of his God and travel alone and not be dependent on relatives. So Jacob told Esau about his young "weak" children and all the pregnant and milking cows, sheep and goats that cannot travel as fast as the soldiers, not even one day. They might miscarry. His young, weak children also, could not walk so fast.

"Please let me travel alone and slowly, I will follow, for we need time." Esau let him have it his way. They parted in friendship and disappeared. A great worry had left Jacob when they were all gone, he started laughing and relaxing.

Even if a number of good choice cattle are gone, he will bring the herd up again. Also the women relaxed and started getting dinner ready for a happy feast, as good as it goes while on the road.

Reuben and Simeon had heard that their father had called them "weak" when their great uncle Esau was there and found that statement utterly ridiculous. However, they were sharp and smart enough to have "looked" small and weak in the presence of their powerful uncle. Gad, son of Zilpah, had also heard that statement "weak" and he wanted to cut in, because he was a good runner and strong, but his mother's hand had landed on his mouth, shutting him up. She gestured with looks to be quiet until that young boy finally got the point and was silent.

"You could have gotten us into trouble before, Gad, trying to cut into the speech of our father while he talked to Esau," Naphtali needled Gad. Then Gad made fists to attack Naphtali. But Zilpah yelled at the boys to keep peace and not always fight each other.

"You are getting older, and I demand some common sense from you boys," said Zilpah. The boys obeyed the command of their mother, there was peace again.

Now that Laban was not around anymore, Jacob did not feel he had to pretend to be tough and not love Leah. He also had met God in the form of the angel-man and it had changed his heart. So, when Esau and his troup was gone Jacob had a sudden urge to give Leah a praise. He put his arm around her shoulder and thanked her for being a good partner, keeping the children in line and feeding everyone. He stroked over her blond but graying hair and gave her a quick, hard kiss. Leah was embarrassed and overwhelmed. Tears shot out of her eyes. Then Jacob left for his duties. Simeon had seen that love scene. His heart was not softened, he had not had his hour of conscience as yet. *Finally, that father of ours is doing his duty toward my mother, about time.* Reuben also did not have his hour of conscience with God as yet. Of course, they did not dare say that aloud. They were going to wait and see and watch their father how his life style would change, if at all, after meeting the angel-man of God.

Jacob then went to his servants and older boys and told them what to do and where to work, and to put the divided group of cattle back in order again.

Jacob wanted to go to Edom first to follow his brother. But after he thought everything over he decided that should not be. *Why should I be so close to my brother and all his children? That could cause problems. I will go to where my father is or the area that God told my grandfather that should be owned by his heirs, some day. Also, going from place to place is hard on the women.*

This was near the city of Shechem, in the land of Canaan. He pitched his tents by the town of Shalem. Of course, if he wanted to stay, he had to pay for the land. There lived a man by the name of Hamor, the founder of Shechem. From his decendants Jacob bought the land for a hundred pieces of silver. Leah was glad her husband had the money and they could now settle down again, after the long journey. Now they could build ovens for bread baking and make more delicious meals. Rachel, and especially Bilhah were happy, for now she could take better care of herself again. She enjoyed the good life. She also spent time to massage her hands, face and feet with cream from goat's milk. She wanted to look smooth. Leah had all those children and did not have that much time to spend on herself. But even if she tried she felt she looked just the same. Jacob and the servants and older sons were very busy building houses for themselves. They had to learn how to buy lumber, learn the prices for everything, and how to put wooden beams together. Quite often the women would hear a cry or a swear word when someone hit his finger with a hammer, until the young men got the hang of it. Then the cattle had to be kept together, fed, and watered. For this they chose the Jordan pastures. Jacob had to teach them how to make manure for fertilizer, because when a farmer stays on the same place he needs to fertilize in order to harvest. There was so much to do and to learn. It was truly a busy time. Jacob called his place Succoth. It was east of the Jordan River.

Jacob wanted to see his very old father. However, he could not get away alone to visit him. With the new place, the children, servants, the local population and the cattle, his presence was needed here. Also, his hip prevented him from moving around too much. However, his brother Esau told him that their father has a very responsible middle-aged woman taking care of him, and not to worry. So Jacob remained on the homestead for now.

Teaching About Adam and Eve

Jacob erected an altar to the Lord. He took rough stones and piled them on top of each other so they formed a table. He named the altar El-el-o-he Israel. Every seventh day, if possible, Jacob would order all of his family to do no extra work, just keep all the cattle in line, cook and eat. Then all would have to come to the altar El-el-o-he Israel and watch Jacob sacrifice a sheep to God. Then Jacob also told his children the basics of what he knew about God. He taught them that being good and orderly was enough and was demanded.

Jacob told his family at these occasions about Cain.

"Cain's feelings about the Lord were not as deep as Abel's. Remember, Adam and Eve were naked. It was warm in the Garden of Eden, they needed no clothes. Then, after they had picked the forbidden fruit and ate it, suddenly they felt they ought to be clothed. Somehow showing their whole bare body to each other and the animals and in the evening to God, while hiking around and talking, did not seem right anymore. Then they broke off large fig leaves and created some sort of covering for themselves. In the evening when they knew God would come walking and talking to them, they hid. However, God knew exactly what had happened, because His eyes see everything, even though Adam and Eve thought God sees them only when He is around."

"And then," cut in Joseph, because he had heard that story before, being with his father so often, "the Lord said to Adam…"

"Cut it out, Joseph, your father is talking," said his mother Rachel.

"Yeah," chirped in some other brothers, mumbling quietly.

"Joseph acts like he knows it all."

Then Jacob continued, "Then the Lord said in a loud and powerful voice: 'Adam, where are you?' Adam waited a few moments, but then crawled out from under his bush in his figleaf garment.

"What did you do? Did you not pick the forbidden fruit?" asked God.

"Adam said, 'Eve, the woman you gave me, picked it and led me astray.'

'Eve, why did you pick the forbidden fruit?'

'The snake told me if I eat it I will be smart.'

"Then the Lord cursed the snake and said that it will never evolve growing legs. He gave Adam a punishment, that from now on he will have to work hard and sweat, and still he would barely make a living."

"I like that part," whispered Bilhah quietly to Zilpah who was sitting next to her.

"Let the men work hard and sweat, what about the women?" whispered Bilhah.

Then Jacob continued and told how God punished Eve.

'Your husband shall be your boss.'

Zilpah, thought, *I would have wanted Joppa as a boss over me. Too bad, forget the past, live with the present,* she sighed.

"And," Jacob continued, "the Lord said you will bear children with pain."

"Don't we know that!" said Leah quietly to her daugther Dinah.

"Is it really that bad?" Dinah whispered to her mother.

"Well, it is, but also it is not. If it does not hurt that means the baby is not coming and both mother and baby can die. And sometimes mothers die. But men die in warfare, so it evens out."

Then Jacob told his family that very first great promise:

'I WILL PUT ENMITY BETWEEN YOU AND THE WOMAN, AND BETWEEN YOUR SEED AND HER SEED; IT SHALL BRUISE YOUR HEAD, AND YOU SHALL BRUISE ITS HEEL.'

"And I want you to repeat this sentence until you all know it. Now go ahead, repeat." They all repeated it several times until they all knew it.

"And you better remember it, or else," and Jacob pointed to his leather strap.

"Father," said Asher, "I hit a snake on the head with a big stick because it wanted to bite a sheep. Should I have stepped on it with my heel, as the Lord had said?"

"No, Asher, you did right, the snake would have bitten you. The Lord meant that an evil force, the evil force that enticed Eve, had gone into the snake, and that is why the snake could talk. You know snakes don't talk. The evil force was talking out of the snake. And the evil force will some day be crushed for good. Then everything will be well. We are waiting for that time. Some day some powerful God-man will come and crush the evil force. But in the process He will also get hurt. That is all we know right now. I have a hunch that that will not be the end of the God-man, there is more to come. My ancestor Enoch also "saw" there is more to come."

Jacob continued, "From that time on people must not go totally naked anymore. Those fig leaves were not reliable enough, not good enough in the eyes of the Lord. So the Lord took a sheep, killed it, let his blood flow out until it did not move anymore. Then the Lord pulled off the fleece from the sheep. He burned up the sheep on top of a pile of stones as a sin offering for Adam and Eve to repeat in the future. Then the Lord took the fleece and made two garments out of it for Adam and Eve to wear. And we are to do that also, to cover ourselves because we sinned, and God was angry. And since that time the Lord does not casually walk around with us anymore. That was sad. Adam and Eve were lonely. Now they could not ask God questions anymore. They could not ask how He made the world. We don't know how big or tall Adam was when he was created, was he a baby then or a grown man? What kind of teeth did lions have in the Garden of Eden so they could eat grass? and other amazing things. They wept and were sorry. Then Adam yelled at Eve that it is all her fault. Eve was angry at Adam and said, 'If you knew it was wrong to eat that apple, why did you take it from me?'

"'I am the boss,' said Adam, 'from now on I tell you what to do.' Then Eve turned away and ran into a thicket and cried."

"Too bad," exclaimed Joseph, "that it came to that. I would have asked the Lord what comes after the end of the earth, is it like a flat table, and would we fall off at the end? Or is the earth like a round pumpkin, and if yes, then how come we don't fall off?"

"My son," answered his father, "you ask too many questions."

"What did the Lord look like?" asked young Zebulon. "Did he have brown hair or black? And how tall was He?"

"Just like you, Zebulon, are looking somewhat like me, so did Adam somewhat look like the Lord, only a bit different. Adam looked like the image of the Lord. He did not mention God's hair or skin color or whether he was pale or sunburned."

Then Joseph asked another complicated question about Adam and Eve's first clothes from the first sheep fleece.

"Which half of the sheep fur went to Adam and which half went to Eve?"

"It is almost a thousand years ago since it happened. You ask too many questions." Everyone laughed at Joseph and his useless ideas.

"Did they treat the fur? It must have smelled in time," asked Joseph.

"They learned how to treat fur with salt. Adam and Eve were not really simple-minded, they had some brains, too. However, you children are distracting me, listen up!"

"Cain liked vegetables a lot, so he planted them. Cain had some sheep but not as many. And when sacrificing time came, the time to burn more sheep on a pile of stones for the Lord, Cain did not want to part with a sheep. He was too stingy. So he thought, 'I worked so hard for the vegetables and picked some nice ones, and I will burn these on a pile of stones for the Lord. "But, as you know, vegetables don't burn so well, and the smoke of them went not straight up to the Lord. It hung around the pile of stones like a cloud. That showed Cain that the Lord did not like his sacrifice. The Lord wanted a sheep or a cow or a goat burned up. The furs from them would also give them more clothes to wear to cover themselves, as the Lord had demanded.

"In time women learned to make long threads out of wool and linen, so now we don't always have to wear fur anymore, only for winter."

"Then, when Cain saw that the Lord loved Abel's sacrifice and not his, he got jealous and angry. The Lord saw it coming, a murder. So He told Cain: 'Why are you looking so angry, your whole face is contorted. If you do the good deeds then you are also accepted by me. But if you do evil, then the evil force [that had gone into The Snake in the Garden of Eden] will sit in front of your tent flap, your door, and wants to come into you and make you do something evil. I call it sin. However, you, Cain, have the power over the evil, you don't have to do it.'

"You, my sons, know the rest, how Cain killed his brother Abel. But now boys, this is enough for today."

"Leah," Jacob cried, "bring me something to drink, I am thirsty from all that talking. You boys and men now go off, do your herding, and don't you dare let a wolf get our cattle!"

Shechem

They lived a number of years in the area of Shechem and all went reasonably well. Of course, Jacob's number of cattle increased and so his sons and servants had to be on guard that their cattle did not run on their neighbor's fields and their neighbor's not to theirs.

People like Jacob considered cattle their wealth. The more cattle one had, the richer he was. They did not seem bothered by the possibility of new deserts caused by an increased number of cattle. They did not look ahead that far into the future.

As it is when a newcomer, especially a newcomer with wealth and a lot of children arrives, everyone looks at them suspiciously. So it was also with Jacob and his family. His sons could not make fast friends with the locals. They also remembered that God had told Abraham that He would give his descendents all this land someday.

When the boys were alone they discussed the situation. They imagined how nice it would be if all those inhabitants of Canaan were gone, they would not have to watch the cattle that much and would have free run of the land. They hesitated to ask their father. But they told brother Joseph, to ask father about that, as to when they would get all that land?

Their father had told them at another time, when watering their sheep, about the various wells in the country. Some were built by their grandfather Isaac. Enemies had chased Isaac away from some of them. Isaac retreated. The brothers would not have given in as did their grandfather Isaac. Jacob explained again how it was: Isaac dug several wells, first the Gerar well with very good water that the Philistines had closed on him. Then the Esek well, then the Sitnah well, and finally the other good well that the locals let Isaac keep, the Rehoboth well. "And Isaac did not fight the locals for the wells? He just moved on as if he was afraid to stand up to them? If we took the pain of digging a deep well, and remember how hard that is, digging and removing rocks and knowing how easily the earth can cave in on you and kill you," said Gad, "we would want to keep it. These locals, we better be on our guard!" Gad was tall and broadchested, like his mother Zilpah, and was sure of his strength. He raised his fist.

"Yes, brother Gad, I agree," said Simeon.

"But after that, the Lord met Isaac and blessed him," added Joseph. "You cannot always wait for the Lord, little brother," said Simeon. Joseph, who always hung around his father and was close to him, asked Jacob about that. Jacob told him that God had told Abraham that the inhabitants of the area were not bad enough to be eliminated, so that means not yet.

Levi, who always tried to mind rules and regulations, especially when they were in his favor, thought about all that. *Not bad enough yet. Hm! So, if they are bad then we, I...will see what the future brings. I have to watch those locals closely.*

He told that to his older brother Simeon. They sat there one evening, looking in the direction of the local town and thinking. Then Levi said to Simeon: "Do you think what I think?"

"No, my brother, I don't. What do you think?"

" 'Not bad enough,' had said the Lord. So, that means, if they are ever bad enough, I, we can...I don't want to say it. I am sure, now you know what I am thinking?"

Simeon produced a wicked little smile and said to Levi, "Don't say it, brother dear, now I know what you are thinking."

Jacob did not have to hire so many servants anymore, because his sons were now capable of doing a man's job. One day a strange sheep had meandered into Jacob's herds while Jacob's boys were guarding their sheep.

"Look, a lost sheep!" exclaimed one son. "This is not ours."

"Let's get it," said another one. And one quickly grabbed the strange sheep and took it aside behind the tent. Another son pulled his butcher knife, another quickly grabbed a large stone and knocked the sheep unconscious, another one cut his throat, they let the blood flow out, the sheep was dead without making a sound. Another one cut into the fleece and pulled off the skin. One cut open the sheep. Another one quickly dug a hole in the ground and buried the intestines. They worked fast and silently. There was a fire burning already. They put the pieces of meat on the fire and prepared for their outdoor lamb roast. It would taste good. They could hardly wait.

After awhile two local shepherds came over and asked if they had seen a wayward sheep.

"A wayward sheep? No, we have not seen a wayward sheep. Is one missing? Maybe you guys should watch it better. You know there are wolves around. But if we find one, we will let you know."

Mother Leah was told by her youngest son Zebulon about the sheep incident. She scolded her sons for their dishonesty. She told them it would have been the right thing to do to either save the sheep until it's owner shows up or bring it back. Now it was too late, it would only make the locals more suspicious of her sons.

Then the boys asked their mother as to when they can take over the land. Leah explained that their father had the angel appearance, and he is the one who can act.

"Did any one of you boys see an angel? Maybe a light with a voice?"

"No, nothing."

"Well, then," said Leah, "you cannot act. We need God's blessing for things or else we won't have good luck. So, you stay put and behave yourselves."

Outside, Zebulon, the youngest, declared, "I will tell Father about the sheep." Then Naphtali jumped him, held him by the throat and threatened to choke him if he did. Zebulon understood the threat and kept quiet.

Another time, the sons were guarding the goats. Goats always like to graze and nibble wherever people don't want them to go. So the boys were busy keeping the goats out of mischief. It was getting dark and all cattle was driven into the fences. Then the boys had time to play the game of senet, an Egyptian dice game. They had no fancy game board, so they just bound sticks together for the outline of the game board, and instead of a dice they threw small bones. Whoever lost had to be the first one up in the morning and start the work. The sons played that game often, but always when their father was not around. Jacob knew that with cattle and all kinds of wild animals around one cannot be too careful, not even at night. One goat bleated incessantly. Finally, someone heard it and went to check. This goat used to have a kid and today the kid was gone. The sons were so intent on the game they had not noticed it before. "Where is her kid?" they asked.

"You, Joseph, go around and look for her kid." Joseph walked around the compound and behind the tents. Then he saw in the distance a dark shadow and green eyes moving around. He held on to his spear tightly and walked over toward the animal. It was one of those wild dogs, baring his teeth, but then pulling in his tail and running away. What Joseph saw was the killed kid, the baby of the mother goat. Joseph walked back to his brothers and told them that a wild dog has gotten the kid.

"Too bad, too late. Did you at least kill the dog?"

"No, it ran away."

The next day when Joseph was at the house he told his father about the killed kid while his brothers were playing senet, again. Father, of course, rode over to the sons and criticized them and told them they should mind their business. The brothers cast evil looks at their brother Joseph for telling. But they did not beat him up, for he was too tall.

Renate M. Schulz

Rachel's Surprise

One day, while they lived in Succoth, Rachel noticed that although she was not so young anymore and thought she was becoming an old woman, that things were different with her. She was pregnant! *Oh how wonderful! Pregnant a second time. Just as I have asked the Lord, to give me another child.* Rachel was so happy. She told Jacob, Bilhah, Leah, Zilpah. A child in old age. How exciting!

"A brother for me," trumpeted Joseph, and made a cartwheel in joy and anticipation, "or a sister, my princess!"

"Oh, be quiet, you show-off. We have a sister for a long time already," said Zebulon, "and she is our princess, first of all." Then Joseph jumped and grabbed a branch from a tree and swung on it back and forth, yelling "a brother or a sister for me, for me, for me."

"Good, then Father will be too busy catering to you," retorted Zebulon. "May the babe slobber on your face."

I don't know, somehow my brothers don't like me. I can tell there is a feeling of anger towards me, thought Joseph.

Dinah

Young Dinah had grown to be a beautiful girl. Her mother taught her all the things a woman had to know such as grinding grain, cooking, weaving, planting, watering, preserving meat with smoke and salt, and explaining about herbs. She also told her all the rules of behavior a woman had to know and do.

"Be humble to a man. Do what your husband says. Remember, the man is always right, even if he is wrong. And don't ever let a man entice you to sleep with him, except with your own husband. Have many children. Know that if a woman is not a virgin anymore she is considered a whore and very low in honor. A virgin can be married off for a large dowry, and thus make her father rich. A 'used' woman does not cost much. The more your husband's family will pay for you, the more the woman is worth at marriage. Beauty, of course, also plays a part in the purchase price for a woman."

Dinah looked at herself in a metal mirror that her father had traded for her. Dinah thought she was beautiful. Her hair was lighter, after her mother. Her skin was white, like her father's. When she asked her brothers how pretty she is, they all agreed that she is beautiful, the only sister amongst all those boys. Dinah saw on market days how the local girls dressed and she wanted to be like the locals.

"Mother, please let me go to the local girls. Can I just go over to them?"
"Absolutely not. Some bad man might grab you, rape you, and your value is gone, gone, forever."
"Oh mother, you are too scared, nothing would happen to me. They may have done those things when you were younger, but now they don't do that."
"You may not go, and that is it. They also don't worship the true God. And sometimes they sacrifice a baby boy to those gods and kill him. Can you imagine? They burn him up like a piece of wood. They are horrible. And to a god that does not even exist."
"Oh Mother, I am so lonely here."
"You have maids to entertain you, all those brothers. You children can dance to drums and flutes. You can have a great time."
Then Dinah, barefoot at the moment, stepped outside in the dark. She looked into the distance where she saw the little lights of the town of Shechem beckening her.

"Squash," she had stepped into some cow dirt in her bare feet, and it popped through between her toes. Dinah started crying and cursing her homestead.

"Always animal poo, wherever I go. I am the princess of the cows."

Next time Dinah saw her father she mentioned that she wanted so very much to meet the local girls. She put up her prettiest smile to her father, asked him if she could help get him something. She knew her father had a hard time walking since he had met the angel-man. Her father looked pleased at his only daughter and how eager she is and how helpful and how pretty. Finally he said.

"Very well then, some day you can go." She embraced him and gave his bearded cheek a hearty kiss and ran back to Mother.

"Mother, Father said I can go see the local girls sometime!"

"He did?"

"Yes, he really did. Now we have to prepare for it."

She ran to her brothers and asked them to tell her when the locals have a party and make connections for her to be invited. Now Dinah was preparing. She asked two other servant girls of her father's to be her companions. A rich girl does not go alone, she has maids along. They were also excited about this opportunity. Now they sat together and developed plans and clothes. Dinah had seen the princess from Shechem once, a distant cousin of the local prince. She was about her age. She wore her black hair open with only a band of red beads on them, then sandals with red beads also.

"Real rubies, mind you," she told her servant girls. They listened with admiration.

"Should I not also wear that?"

"Yes, Dinah, you should. But I think a green smaragd would be better for you since your hair is light brown with a tint of red. You could even put some as a chain around your neck, and an arm and foot bracelet. You would not want to imitate the princess and wear red. A green silk dress to match the smaragds, the material imported from the far east. It would look great on you."

"How about a light brown dress, matching the color of your hair? suggested the other maid. "Or a pale pink?"

Then Dinah went to her mother and told Leah what she needed. She wanted a light green gown out of silk. She wanted a head band with green smaragds and sandals with the same green jewels on it to match.

"Hold it, my daughter, not so fast. Smaragds, also called emeralds, are the most expensive and rare jewels one can get, you are just a shepherd's daughter."

Dinah started crying and lamenting, "Yes, that is all I get, sheep, goats and cows, I am tired of them. I need elegant clothes to go with my elegant look. The young women in Shechem are dressed beautifully. What do I get? Cotton! Linen! Look, Mother," and she stretched her skirt, "how coarse. I am dressed like a slave." Then she took the edge of her sleeve to dry a tear. "Don't you have any feelings for me?"

"Daughter," replied Leah with a strict tone of voice, "you have good clothes, well-made and practical. You exhibit a sudden streak of haughtiness. Come off it and I will talk with Father about the price of a garment for you."

Next time the Egyptian merchants came around Dinah called her mother and made sure her father was there and had his silver and gold pieces with him. She was right there. Leah and Dinah finally found something suitable for her to wear. It was blue gauze, matching the color of Dinah's eyes. Leah also bought sandals in brown and copper bracelets with blue topaz stones worked into it. She found a blue headband also, to match the dress. Then Leah bought something less elaborate for the two servant girls. The material for one maid's dress was green thin cotton, decorated with dark blue and green threads woven into it. The other maid's dress was also thin pink cotton, decorated with dark red and purple. Then father Jacob paid for the merchandise. Dinah embraced him again and told him that he is the best father in the whole world. *A lovely daughter I have, so beautiful and so friendly.* He did not realize the sneakiness of Dinah.

Now mother Leah had to sew the dresses with the help of some servant woman. Dinah tried hers on again and again, asked for changes here, some tucks there, and enjoyed when the whole female household was centering around her precious person. *I want no one say to me at the party that I am the princess of the cows.*

Then Dinah and her two maids that would accompany her to the party put their heads together and quietly discussed something. Then they laid down their spinning and weaving and started dancing. Leah happened to walk by, she saw the girls dancing.

"What is going on here? Three women dancing in the middle of a working day? Have you lost your bearing? What is this all about?"

"Oh, Mother," explained Dinah, "when we go to that party there might be dancing. We cannot be so clumsy, others will make fun of our dancing. They will say we jump around like goats and have no breeding. We have to practice, just in case."

"All right, girls. You will yet give me gray hair." And Leah shook her head.

"You may dance at night. There is a full moon tonight. However, sometimes when these heathen dance they bow down to a man-made figure, an idol. Don't you dare do that! Understand?"

"But, Mother, what if everybody else bows down?"

"Then you just don't. That is why I did not want you to go in the first place. So, you promise me you won't bow down to an idol."

"All right, Mother, we won't. I know what we can do: We bow in the direction of the king giving the party."

Then Leah left the room, and Dinah went back to her loom to weave.

The three girls worked diligently, anticipating a lot of fun.

Then one of the maids told Dinah, she had seen brother Judah making a harp.

"A harp? That is wonderful!" exclaimed Dinah.

"I will talk to him tonight, and he has to play for us when we practice."

At night, after supper, Dinah could hardly wait to get a hold of Judah.

"Judah, I know you have a harp. We three girls have to practice dancing for the party. Please play for us."

"Aw, come on, Dinah, I am busy. I have cattle duty tonight."

"Oh, please, please, Judah. I am your only sister. If we don't practice we will be called clumsy country goats. Please, Judah."

"All right, girlie, but not long. And go behind those bushes where we are not seen. Understand?"

"Yes, Judah. You are my best brother." She tried to give him a quick kiss, and jokingly added, "even if you could use a bath."

"Hey, Sis, you want me to play for you, don't you?"

"Yes, yes, my lovely brother. You are the apple of my eyes."

"Now you sound better," replied Judah, and left.

Dinah also approached the male servants that would accompany them on the camels, to make sure they are clean and brushed and the saddles dustfree. The three girls were in high spirits.

The party day finally arrived. Leah gave the three girls a few last instructions: "Behave yourselves, bow down to your superiors, do not eat like a glutton, do not forget to say 'thank you' and 'please,' do not bow down to an idol that might be posted there, do not go into a room alone with a man, so as to watch your virginity." Dinah thought her mother would never stop giving instructions, she could hardly wait to leave. Outside stood three servants with their decorated camels for the girls to ride on. And off they went. The weather was sunny and not so hot. It promised to become a beautiful day. Leah stood and looked after them until they turned a corner by the tall rocks and were out of sight.

When they finally arrived, servants from the local king Hamor were already waiting for the troupe and welcomed them. The servants helped the girls off their camels and took them inside. The three servants then led the camels to a water trough under a shady roof. Jacob's three servants stayed by the camels and fed them and hung around and talked with the local men under the sheds.

King Hamor's son, whose name was Shechem, who the city was named after, then came and also welcomed the girls. The girls minded their manners, and bowed down to the queen mother and to all that were above them, as was the custom. They were led into the large hall. There was a long table prepared with all kinds of wonderful foods on it. There were a lot of fancy, well-dressed young women, all staring at them and smiling. Dinah and her maids were embarrassed and shy. They hoped that their clothes and their persons would be acceptable. They felt so inferior amidst all the others. Then everyone sat down to eat. Dinah and her maids ate, but not much, for they were too timid to be in such fancy company.

Shechem, the prince, looked at Dinah. He was impressed by her beauty and fancy wardrobe and courtly behaviour. His eyes met hers. She became shy and looked down, but answered his questions politely. Shechem smiled and talked with her; he made her feel at ease until she also talked to him. Then Dinah saw that the prince was rather young and handsome. After the meal a court jester came and entertained the guests. Everybody clapped and did have a good time.

Then there was a little dancing to drums and flutes. Dinah and the girls tried to be their best as not to act like country girls. They seemed to blend in with the other dancers. No one bowed down to an idol. Everyone seemed to be so happy.

And my mother thought they would bow down to an idol. I am pleasantly surprised, thought Dinah.

Then Shechem showed Dinah a closet where his father had weapons stored away; beautiful, decorated swords and arrows. She admired them. Shechem told her at what occasions those swords were used and which spear ever touched blood. Then Shechem told her there is more to see. "Come in this next room." He laid his arm over her shoulder and urged her into the other room, the wide door stayed open.

"Look here, there are my mother's jewels, do you like them?"

"Yes, sir, indeed I do." She saw a famous green emerald and remarked how beautiful it is.

"Not as beautiful as your blue eyes and dress. You look like a figure come down from the heavens on a sunny day," the prince remarked. She asked him questions about the jewels, their names, and what special occasion it was when they received them.

"There is more, little Dinah, come and see." He opened another door, and there was a bath level with the floor lined with white tile and a row of blue tile along the rim. The floor was also with a few blue tiles in diamond shapes inserted. Steps led down into the sunken bathtub. It was filled with crystal-clear water. White and blue towels were folded on a nearby shelf. There were several resting lounges surrounding the bath. On the walls were candleholders attached with candles in them, but not lighted. Dinah had never seen such a bath and was overwhelmed from all that glamour.

"You don't know what that is used for?" Shechem asked.

"Yes, I know, for bathing, of course. I just never saw one as beautiful as this." Then he led her to a resting lounge.

"And see these decorated blankets? They are made from the finest white lamb's wool. They are embroidered, too. It took a seamstress months to make them. Are they not gorgeous?"

Shechem reached out his hand and with one finger moved a little lever by the door. The door closed silently. Then Shechem gently made her sit down, and before the surprised Dinah knew what was going on he was raping her. She tried to get away but he was so nice and friendly to her she dared not get fresh, he even kissed her. His lips sealed her cry. She thought of her mother who probably never was loved that way. She felt a strong pressure also. Yet, when it was over, she felt used, misused. *Is this what they call a rape? Am I still a virgin, or am I not?* A foreboding feeling came over her. But Shechem did not leave her any time for meditating. He continued right on to resting next to her and saying endearments to her as well as embracing her. Finally, Shechem decided to leave the bathing room. Then Dinah saw a three-feet tall figure standing in the corner over the bath.

It was an idol with an ugly face. The face of the idol seemed to look at her as if to say:

"We got you, didn't we?" Dinah knew it was just a handcrafted thing and no god, but she had this beaten feeling, nevertheless. Later, Shechem showed her around his house.

Then it was getting late and time to go home. The local girls looked at Dinah in a peculiar way when she came back into the large hall. Their looks did not seem friendly. So Dinah called her two servant girls and told them it's time to go home. Others also started leaving the party. Shechem, however, asked Dinah to stay, and let just the servant girls go home. He kept his hand on her shoulder.

"I love you so much, Dinah," he told her quietly. "Stay longer," and gently, but firmly, held her by the hand. Dinah whispered something into the servant girl's ear and the servants with the camels left for home.

When they arrived home and Leah saw only the servants, she exclaimed:

"Where is my daughter?"

"She stayed behind," said the older girl in a quiet voice.

"The lord Shechem got a 'shine' to her, he seemed to love her and kept her there," explained the other girl. Then Jacob arrived and became concerned. He questioned the three male servants. They told them they had to stay in the shed by the camels and did not know what was going on inside the palace.

Now Jacob questioned the two servant girls. They told them everything they had seen and that the last they saw Dinah and Shechem go into the other room and they saw him showing her his parent's jewels in a closet. They told them that after the party Dinah came and told them to go on home, Shechem wants to keep her there and marry her and she is not a virgin anymore. The last phrase she whispered to them.

"What? What happened?"

That is all Leah and Jacob needed to hear. Their world seemed to cave in. Our only daughter, raped, like a common whore! Jacob controlled his anger. It was too great to just explode in words. He had to come to terms with himself. Such a thing is just too terrible to comprehend, in a country where virginity was so revered. Leah started yelling at the two servant girls. A sudden great anger came over her. She took her leather strap and beat on the girls, screaming:

"Why were you not watching your young mistress? Don't you know that it is your duty? You accompanied her. You two are careless and terrible and useless!" The girls just stood there, covering their faces in their hands and weeping quietly, while each received several hard lashes on their backs.

"Now off with you two," screamed Leah.

"Oh, Mistress Leah, please don't send us away, we will be more watchful from now on."

"Go, you two! Change and do your duty or else you will get more!" Quickly and quietly they disappeared, took off their new party dresses, looked at the red welts the leather strap put on their backs and behinds, put on their humble servant clothes and went to work. Even they knew something bad and serious had happened. Whispered words got around quickly. Everyone in Jacob's household now knew about this. They knew something will have to happen now, and wondered if it would be good or bad for them.

When the girls were working in the kitchen and Leah had calmed down a bit, she looked at them seriously.

"Tell me, you two, were you also raped? Did someone sleep with you? Did any uncircumcised man touch you?"

"No, Mistress Leah, we are fine."

In the meantime, Dinah's brothers were guarding the cattle. Some goats from the locals had run into Jacob's fields. The local shepherds came after them to drive them out again. Jacob's sons were angry and told them to watch better.

"You crooks," said Levi, "you allowed them into our clover."

" 'Crooks' you call us? See who is the crook. After your sleazy sister threw herself at our young lord, and then blamed him for raping her."

"Our sister? What are you talking about?" And Levi and Simeon tried to attack them with their fists.

"Peace, peace, brothers," implored Reuben, the oldest. Then turning to the locals, who were more in number, Reuben said:

"Don't mind my brothers. They are stupid hot heads and simpletons. We are friends." He stretched out his hands to them and managed to calm them down.

"Don't mind about the goats, it's all right; some day our cattle might run into your fields, we get along. Goodbye, may you have a pleasant day." Then the local shepherds trotted off, their goats before them, one waved with his hand.

As soon as the locals were out of sight and earshot Reuben exploded, "Don't you hot heads know what a precarious position we are in? Can't you count their number and our number? Is Joseph the only one around who can do numbers? Don't you know they can kill us? We are just a few. They are many. Be a little careful. Keep your anger inside you for good reasons or we will all be killed. Mind your words."

"We will, we surely will," answered Simeon and Levi, while casting meaningful glances at each other.

In the evening, Hamor, Shechem's father, was visiting Jacob to talk to him about the girl, Dinah. Even Hamor knew, this ought not to have been done, just stealing and using a woman without permission or bridal price, was not common between people of means. However, he was willing to pay the price, whatever it might be. He assured Jacob that his son Shechem was untouched as yet, loves Dinah and wants to marry her, and he would not do her any harm. She would have a good life with them. Then Hamor asked Jacob for the hand of Dinah for his son in marriage, now in a proper fashion.

Jacob listened to it all but did not come to a conclusion. He held off with a price and settlement to wait for his sons, as to what they would say. It was a world in which a man with more wives did not have total control over his daughters. The daughter's brothers had rights too over the sister and often more so than the father.

Jacob knew he ought to consult his sons before making any rash decisions. Jacob waited for Reuben, Simeon, Levi and Judah to come home from the fields. Issachar and Zebulon were still too young to be included in this decision-making.

Simeon and Levi, who had already an inkling of what was going on, came home. They had a plan already made for how to deal with the people from Shechem, but did not know as yet how to carry it out. As they listened to the conversation and the attempted deal-making of their father with Hamor, they saw their opportunity.

The sons of Abraham had to all be circumcised, God wanted it that way. In a country where water and sanitary conditions were not always ideal, circumcision was a good idea. Hamor wanted to become one with the tribe of Jacob Israel. He saw a trade opportunity there and a profit for his people. They could supply consumer goods and Jacob could supply the food.

Now the sons of Jacob, the older ones, started talking: "The men from Shechem should all be circumcised, just like we, only then we could become one nation. However, if you and the men of Shechem do not want to be circumcised, then we will just take our sister home again with us."

"A deal?" asked the sons of Jacob.

"A deal!" answered Hamor.

Then later on, when Hamor went home again, he told all his men about the "deal" with the Israelites. He explained to them all the good that would come out of a union with them. How beneficial the marriage of Dinah to his son Shechem would be to all. Hamor managed to convince them of all the good. Just one little obstacle is in the way: circumcision. He explained the procedure and the benefits of the act itself. Hamor also convinced the men even in this.

So all men who came out of the gates of the city were circumcised. The sons of Jacob knew it would take awhile to heal from the circumcision. They knew that the third day afterwards was the most critical and painful. Simeon and Levi saw their opportunity.

Then on the third day Simeon and Levi took their sharpened swords and went into the city during daytime hours when the women were working outside their city in their fields and vegetable gardens. The city streets were somewhat empty. These two brothers went into house after house killing every male with the sword. Of course, the men tried to fight back but where not prepared for such an attack and probably had a case of blood poisoning and fever besides and just could not resist Simeon and Levi's fury. Those two thugs managed to kill all circumcised males in the city, even Hamor and young Shechem.

And what did the women do who were left and watched all this? Nothing. They were too afraid to interfere and not trained for combat. Dinah stood back and watched her two brothers pull Shechem away from her and kill him cold-bloodily. What was she to do? They were her brothers, and she had to obey them. Streams of blood were pouring out all over the ground in thick burgundy color, sticky and wet. Wild stray dogs ambled over to lick it up and high overhead in the blue sky condors were sailing over the city.

Then the women came running home with their young daughters from the fields when they heard the cries and commotion. However, Simeon and Levi and some of their brothers commanded them all to give themselves up and become their prisoners. These women also obeyed and were held captive. They were told not to move or else they would forfet their life. Full of horror and fear, they stood there and watched as the other sons of Jacob and their servant men went into the city and sorted through their goods such as blankets, useful cooking pots out of copper, clothes, money and whatever struck their fancy. The women were full of fear and heartache for they knew their fathers, brothers and uncles had died, butchered and bleeding. Some girls' secret lover was now dead; they shed silent tears. Mothers cried for their sons, and pregnant women cried for the father of their future child, but quietly. They could not make a big show of tears for they feared they would then be killed also.

Joseph was not in on this massacre. Simeon and Levi had ordered him to have cattle duty that day.

Then, when the sons of Jacob had taken their fill, they marched all the girls and women back home to their father's homestead, with their sister Dinah in tow. Dinah was embarrassed. Just a few days ago she partied with these girls, now these girls had become her enemies. She felt as if she had also betrayed them. And indeed, a dark beauty of a girl, shot hateful glances at her. She had wanted to marry Shechem. Then Dinah showed up and Shechem lost all interest in her. Now even Shechem is dead and she, a princess, would become a humble slave maid. How hard is life!

Jacob and some others on the homestead saw the large group of people coming toward them and were wondering what was going on. Jacob called Rachel out of the house and told her to go look. Jacob had a hard time walking since he had met the angel, he walked with a cane since that time. Rachel looked and she saw they were only women: old, middle-aged, young and little girls.

Slowly the somber group approached the homestead. The women carried a lot of goods, drove oxen, cows, donkeys, sheep with them. Very strange looking indeed.

"What is going on here, boys?" asked Jacob.

Now Simeon and Levi answered:

"We killed all their circumcised men because our sister Dinah was raped. You know that rape should not be."

Jacob was angry. "Boys, what have you done? Shechem was otherwise an honorable man, so was his father Hamor."

"Should they treat our sister like a common prostitute? We won't allow that."

All other servants of Jacob that were free came together also and looked at the scene. Even Leah had left her vegetable garden and came to look.

"What will you do with all the women?" asked Jacob. "I don't need them, you don't need them."

Then they discussed all this quietly. Leah and Rachel noticed that the younger girls looked healthy and some even pretty. None of Leah's sons had married as yet. She figured, with a little training, these women could overcome their anger and become wives for her sons. Rachel was not so sure they would respond in love, but in time they could have normal love relationships. Finally, it was suggested that Leah's plan should be followed: the boys were each to pick a women for themselves as a wife. It seemed like a good solution. Who cared about love, about interests, about suitability? The wife was a cheap labor source and created for men's pleasure. And if she did not obey, a beating would always bring her around, so men thought. Then Jacob told his sons to send the rest of the women home with whatever plunder they did not need. The local leftover women were sent home again. Their gods had not helped them. They were sad, disappointed and angry. Even their priests who taught them about the various gods did not help them. Israel's God must be the stronger god, figured the Shechem women.

"Boys, boys, what have you done? You deceived them. Shechem was otherwise a fairly decent man. What will we do now? What will we do? Tell me. The other kings will all come together and fight us and kill us all. You too, my boys. This bloodbath will be a curse to you, Simeon and Levi! Remember! Now we cannot inform them about the real God, they hate us. What shall we do now?"

Jacob was worried.

The chosen girls from Shechem were all housed in a large tent and given food. The next morning Leah started training them their Israeli ways of cooking, sewing, weaving and general behaviour. She had to prepare them for their sons to become good wives. Their training would take awhile, and she, Leah, would be responsible, because she is the Number One woman on the compound and her sister Rachel is pregnant and pre-occupied with that. Leah was getting old and tired and just thinking about all her responsibilities made her head spin.

This was not a very peaceful night for the family of Jacob. Jacob was still thinking as to what to do. How to protect himself from an attack of the neighboring kings. And the sons of Jacob, now that their vengeance was cooled, were also starting to feel somewhat uneasy. They still felt it was their right to have done this. They discussed it all during the night at their campfires.

"Did not the Lord say to Abraham, that the people of the area are not 'bad enough' to be evicted? Now they were bad enough, and we killed them. It served them right." However, they kept their swords by their side and their spears sharp in-between guarding the cattle.

"So, how do we divide up the women?" asked Simeon. "Since we caught them, Levi and I should have first choice."

"I take the princess, the dark beauty," said Levi.

"You are not," said Reuben. "You two acted cruel and irrational, you have to have your punishment first. Right Father? I am the oldest one, I determine my choice first."

A loud protest from several brothers was heard. Father Jacob saw a problem developing.

"Peace, sons, shalom! If you want a good marriage you have to be good to your wives, you know that. Love does not grow on an acre of hate. Go slow."

"Sure, Father," said Judah, "if she adores my intelligence…"

"Haw, haw, haw," laughed the brothers and clapped their hands.

"Keep me out," said Joseph. "I am glad I am too young to pick one, you can have them all." And he left the gathering.

"Since you were home playing with your papyrus while we did the hunting, you don't deserve a women anyhow," said Dan. But Joseph did not hear this anymore to correct Dan's accusation; he was gone. "I take the princess," insisted Reuben.

"All right, Reuben. See if she will want you. I saw resentment in her eyes and behaviour," said Father Jacob.

Reuben left for the women's tent to get Shabola, the princess.

"You come with me, Shabola." He grabbed her by the arm and led her out. Shabola followed hesitantly and cast evil eyes on him and told him not to grab her with his dirty cow fingers.

"You stink, Reuben. I detest you. Your brothers just killed my future husband Shechem, and you want me to be happy? You probably want me to learn how to milk a cow. Poooh! I am a princess, and I don't love you." And she quickly stepped out of his embrace and stared at him.

"Slow, go easy, my fair maiden, know your place," responded Reuben. He then took her back into the women's tent to cool off.

"I will get you later."

In the meantime, it got dark and time to eat supper and then to bed.

Reuben wanted to make Shabola his wife this night, but some cattle they had taken from the Shechem people had to be sorted, and his presence was needed there.

Around midnight, when all was quiet and the other girls slept, Shabola was still awake and angry. She heard a whistle sound. She listened. There, it was again! Some man was sleeping near the door of the girl's tent to watch them so that no one would escape. He heard the sound, too, and raised up his head. However, all was quiet.

"Must have been some night bird." He waited. Nothing happened, all was silent. The only sounds were the hooting of an owl and some night creatures in the distance. He saw bats whirring through the night sky catching insects. The guard fell asleep again.

Shabola stayed awake. That whistle sound was familiar to her. Where had she heard it before? She thought hard about it for a long time. Suddenly it came to her: it was Shechem's brother. He could whistle like that. Shabola got all excited. She listened. But there was only silence. Then she heard the guard snoring. There, that whistle sound again! Shabola arose slowly and quietly and tiptoed carefully across the other sleeping girls toward the door of the tent. She waited. Silence. The guard kept snoring. She stood near his head. The guard kept on snoring. She stepped out, one step, two steps, still silence. She walked toward where she had heard the whistle. She stopped again. Slowly, carefully, as not to stumble over the tentropes and tentpegs, she advanced on. She was scared, but kept on going one careful step after another until she was out of the perimeter of the Israeli tent. Then she stood still and listened. In the distance she heard another such whistle sound. She advanced further toward the sound in the dark night. Then a cloud sailed toward the east, revealing the moon, brightening the night sky. In the distance, she saw a dark figure standing. It was a man. She walked over in his direction, hoping it was Shechem's brother. As she got nearer she saw it was Shechem's brother Belam. She was relieved it was not a robber she had followed.

"How did you get here, Belam?" Belam held his hand over her mouth to indicate silence. She understood.

Belam grabbed her and silently walked her away from there. They walked for awhile. Then, finally, under a tree, by some bushes stood a horse. Belam lifted Shabola onto the horse, then he swung himself on it behind her and they left the area. He let the horse walk, not run. He did not want it to stumble into a hole or over a rock outcropping or alert the shepherds in the distance. Finally, they arrived to a safe area near the town of Shechem. Only now did they talk. Shabola asked Belam how come he is alive?

"Your good friend Shechem was so busy with the enemy Dinah, so Father gave me the order to bring messages to Uncle Alam up north. And when I returned, I saw the carnage. The unwanted women also told me as to what had happened. They told me that you were captured.

"I am so grateful to you, Belam," said Shabola.

"Yes, and will you now marry your hero?"

"Yes. I will marry and obey you. May the gods that protected you give us good luck."

"Don't be so sure about our gods, they let us all down."

In the morning the people noticed that the princess Shabola was missing. The other captured girls did not know where she was. The guard had not noticed her leaving. Reuben blamed him and wanted to hurt him. But the other brothers laughed heartily at Reuben and his disappointment.

~~~

A few days after this, Dinah asked her mother if she is, perhaps, pregnant. Leah told her to wait awhile.

"Am I still worth at least six cows and some gold coins if I get married?"

"No, my poor daughter, now you are worth less." And Leah started crying again.

"My daughter, my only daughter!"

"Moma," said Dinah, "if I get a baby, I will love him or her very much anyhow."

"That is good, my daughter. Every child needs to be loved and cared for. A woman has the unique responsibility to house a newly formed human being, a responsibility that is truly a gift and which holds supreme value."

Some time later an older merchant came by to visit Jacob Israel. It was Moolah from near Shechem. He showed Jacob some merchandise to trade for cattle. Jacob knew Moolah had just lost his second wife in childbirth. He had four children with his first wife, and two with his second and the newborn baby. Jacob asked him how things go since his wife died.

"Speaking of that, Jacob, it reminds me. I need a new young strong wife again. Good women are hard to find. How is your daughter Dinah? Is she feeling fine?"

"Yes, very fine indeed," said Jacob. He had just heard the good news that his daughter was not pregnant from Shechem. However, he knew what Moolah was hinting, and worried wrinkles showed on Jacob's forehead.

"She is our only daughter, and a bridal price would be high."

"No problem," replied Moolah, "after her…experience, how can her price be too high?"

"I think," said Jacob, "we should wait a little while and let things cool down."

Moolah told his wife at home about a second woman, Jacob's daughter Dinah, who just got raped some weeks ago.

His wife knew Dinah was beautiful and well behaved. She did not want that kind of wife in her home. She was afraid Moolah might fall in love with Dinah. She told her husband Dinah might be as hot-headed as her brothers.

"Do not worry, woman, my leather strap can handle any wild 'heifer'."

"Yes, I believe that. Did you not hit your second wife on the third day after her last child? All because the baby cried too loud?"

"You women are inept creatures; you get what you deserve. Now be silent, I have spoken." And he left to go outside.

When Moolah was still talking to her father, Dinah had listened behind a curtain and realized that Moolah really wanted her. And she absolutely did not want to marry that old, fat, nasty man and be the maid for seven children and a Number One wife ordering her around.

Dinah discussed this with her mother. She asked about their two evil great aunts, great-uncle Lot's daughters. After Sodom had burned up and became a salt lake the two daughters said,

"There is no man in the world anymore who would want to marry us, so we want a child from our father."

"Shh, Dinah, don't talk so loud, what if the servant girls hear it?"

"Where they so ugly, Mother?"

"No, Dinah, they had just become poor. A rich man wants to marry a rich girl. Great Uncle Lot sat in the gates, he was some kind of judge also, with respect. The two daughters just did not want to marry a man of lower social status than what they were used to. I am sure they could have found decent men to marry. Vanity has its price."

"I won't be like that, Mama," said Dinah. "I marry whomever I can get, except that old, fat, mean Moolah. Do you know that Dishon, the cowhand, made me a wreath out of dandeloins? When I put it on my head I looked just fantastic."

"What else did he do for you, my daughter?"

"Oh, he found a beautiful rock in the river for me. I hid it under my mattress. And when Dishon looks at me, his eyes seem to penetrate my very soul."

"Take it easy, my Dinah. You know fathers determine who marries whom."

"Please say something to father, I rather be married to a servant man than to some old, fat nasty man with several children."

Leaving Again

As Jacob was still thinking and worrying about the slaughter in Shechem, God stepped in again and spoke to Jacob: "Arise, go up to Bethel and dwell there: and make an altar there to the Lord. Go to the same place where you fled from your brother Esau many years ago."

In the morning Jacob announced to his whole household to pack up and go.

"Go to where?" asked Rachel and Leah.

"To Bethel, where the Lord had met me personally for the first time."

"Leaving again?" said Rachel. "I am pregnant."

"It is all right, my love, it won't hurt you."

"Leaving our homestead, the houses, the barns, the land we purchased?" asked Leah.

"Yes, Leah, we will be traveling again. When the Lord speaks we must obey. Also, the Lord sees we are not safe here. He is right."

Bilhah was also upset about leaving. She liked the good life. They had a solid house here in Succoth and now they had to leave. This leaving was, sort of, like a second flight away from danger for Jacob, many years ago, and now again.

"It's all Simeon's and Levi's fault, your sons, Leah," said Rachel. "And we all have to suffer," chimed in Bilhah. Leah did not know what to answer to that accusation. She knew their stay in this solid community would not be appreciated by others. She knew that every leftover woman sent back, had suffered the loss of a husband, son, relative, brother or lover. Also, the princess Shabola had escaped. Leah had noticed her vicious looks and resentment.

However, it was time for leaving. Leah, Zilpah, Dinah and other maids immediately started packing. Leah also felt sorry, for they had a stable life in Succoth. *My garden, oh my beautiful garden! We will have to dig out anything that is just about ripe and take it along.* Leah did not like the violent nature of their sons. Often she urged them on to be more in control of their emotions. Then the boys assured her that they loved her.

They said, "Mother, you are home and don't know how the outside world is, we have to fight the enemies, the wolves, the weather, our cattle. Just don't mix in."

"But you know the Lord wants you to be good."

"Yes, Mother, but where are His rules? There are none."

"Your conscience, my boys, your conscience."

"Our conscience told us that Dinah should not have been raped. You know how important purity is before marriage."

And so their talk went on and on. Reuben even thought that Father was a ladies' man, *and what he did I can do, too. If I ever have an opportunity...*

Jacob and his family did not want the name Shechem to cloud their experience all the time, so they decided to call that city Jacob's Well. It was close by toward the east.

It took a long time to pack from Succoth, but finally they were done and moving.

As the caravan of people and animals traveled south, the temperature turned warmer. Traveling was hard that season, and the women especially, were moaning under the hot sun. They slung their cloaks and scarfs tightly around their faces as not to become sunburned.

The people saw different plants growing on the wayside and fields. Jacob knew those plants from before because he was born in this area. Leah, Rachel, the maids and children did not know some of the new southern plants.

On one day Zebulon, Leah's youngest, found some beautiful melons. They grew on long vines and hung over rock trellises. He liked those luscious-looking gourds that had green and yellow uneven stripes. He picked as many as he could carry and brought them to his mother. Leah thanked him and put them aside, for the food for this day's meal had already been cooked. Soon Father Jacob came home to Leah's tent to eat. When he saw the gourds he recognized them right away and told them they are called paqquoth (colocynthis) and are poisonous. They should get rid of them, dig them in the ground so no one will try and eat them. Leah was glad and thanked her husband and did as told.

"Thank you, husband. How can anything as good looking as those melons be so poisonous?"

"Just like the Paradise apple that Eve picked and gave to Adam, it tasted good but had consequences," answered Jacob.

On the route south, the boys found another strange fruit on a tree. It bloomed with small white pretty flowers and the fruit was green and olive-shaped but longer and narrower than an olive. This time they asked their father right away.

"Take them to Mother for pickling. They are called abiyyonah (capers) and are good to serve with meat. And always keep asking me before you eat anything new."

Everyone was excited about the new land they were entering.

After sometime they passed a swampy area. String-like plants grew there in the water. Jacob pointed them out to his family.

"This is papyrus or gome. From this plant they make parchment paper for writing."

"Yes, papyrus for me, Father. Please, I need more," cut in Joseph.

The caravan needed to ford a deep but narrow river. Jacob walked up and down to find a shallow spot for crossing, but could not find one. So he ordered his sons to get their axes, they will chop down some trees and make a float. He pointed out which trees were to be chopped.

"But wait for me, don't do any chopping." He climbed his camel and went along the river to maybe find a better spot to cross.

The young men waited and became impatient and started chopping a tree. Suddenly, the tree broke and fell in the wrong direction just where Asher was standing. They screamed for him to get away. He did, but still one branch hit him on the hip, ripping his flesh. Asher screamed. He immediately ran home to his mother.

Leah and Zilpah were very much upset. Leah washed his wound out with salt water and Zilpah had to hold him down. Asher screamed and wiggled. Finally they were done bandaging him up. Leah sent him into the tent to lie still and not go back. Asher gladly obeyed.

After sometime Jacob returned and yelled at his sons for being so hasty. "That tree could have killed you. You have to first study a tree where the heaviest branches are, so you can figure out how to cut."

"We are sorry, Father," said some of the boys. Now the work started for real. The sons were quiet and well-behaved. After awhile Jacob noticed that Asher was missing.

"Where is Asher?"

"Oh, he did not feel good and went home to Mother."

At suppertime Asher sat at the table, between his two mothers and tried to eat fast. He figured if Father is angry he just might send him to bed hungry, so he better stuff himself first. Then Jacob noticed that Asher did not look well.

"What is happening to you? Are you sick?"

Then the boys told their father that Asher got hit by the tree.

"See, I told you, you need to obey. But I won't beat you up this time, the Lord did it."

Now all boys relaxed, laughed and started their usual happy bantering.

After the meal, Jacob told the women about a certain plant people use in Gilead (for this was the area they were staying this night), and if Asher's wound does not heal right they ought to go find that plant. It looks like a leafy cactus and has a watery jell. It helps with wound healing and is called Balm of Gilead.

Asher's wound did not heal right away and he developed a fever. The wound was red and swollen. Jacob, Leah and Zilpah were worried. Leah made him drink. They put cold wet clothes on him to lower the fever. Asher had pain and felt sick. *Asher might die on me. What are we going to do?* Leah told it to her husband. Then Jacob interrupted his bridge building and went with his women to seek that plant. Jacob asked his Lord to make him find that Balm of Gilead. Finally, he found it. He was very happy and explained to the women how to use it. Now their son would be healed, and so he was. After this balm was applied, the large wound healed well, the women stopped crying and were grateful to Jacob's Lord. He had helped them out again.

Jacob knew that God wanted his people to be good and orderly and have no other carved idols or good luck charms. The women his son's had captured still had their little idols with them. Some wore earrings, bracelets, necklaces in the shape of idols. Jacob saw it but did not directly tell his daughters-in-law to take them off. So he told his sons to remove all those anti-God items. Jacob felt he needed God's favor. He wanted to make sure his God is on his side and no harm will come to his large family. When he saw all that idol-jewelry around the women, Jacob was sure God frowned on them. Then, when he planned to do the sacrifice on the altar in Bethel, they should also all take a bath and put on clean clothes. The God that they worshiped demanded a clean soul and clean clothes. Then his family gave Jacob all their good-luck charms and idols from wood, clay or metal. The maids took off their earrings also. Jacob took all that stuff and dug a hole under a large oak tree not too far from Shechem. Then the whole caravan kept walking toward Bethel.

It took many days to get near Bethel with all their livestock. But finally, they arrived there safely. The other people, whose places Jacob and his family passed, were all afraid of them. Nobody attacked them on the way. They were astonished how Jacob's sons could kill so many men single-handedly in the town of Shechem. People did not dare to arouse Israel's son's ire nor their swords or their trickery.

Then when they arrived in Bethel, they put up their tents again and set up housekeeping. Then Jacob located the rock from years ago and put more stones on and around it for an altar. Then he killed the sacrificial sheep, lit the fire and burned the sacrificial male lamb up to the Lord. The smoke of the sacrifice went up, and the Lord was pleased—for the time being.

All that traveling around was hard for old Deborah, Rachel's old nurse. Deborah had been the nurse for Rachel. When Jacob had left his father-in-law, Deborah had come along. Rachel was very pregnant, and Deborah wanted so much to see the new baby, but she felt so tired and exhausted and the traveling food did not do her old stomach any good either. She lay on her mattress pad and was so weak. Rachel and Bilhah tried to put a pillow under her head so as to make breathing easier for her. But it did not help much. Finally, Deborah breathed her last and her soul had departed. Rachel cried. She was so used to this old servant of hers. They dug a deep hole and buried Deborah properly as was customary for a faithful and respected servant woman. Her buriel place was south of Bethel and was called Allon Bacuth. Now another midwife had to be ordered for the upcoming birth for Rachel. The new woman had experience and was also trustworthy.

~~~

Then the Lord reminded Jacob, that although everybody still calls him Jacob, he has a new name now, the one He had given him beyond the river in Padan Aram: Israel. The Lord saw now that Jacob had earned his new name. That name 'deceiver—Jacob' was not fitting anymore. Now Jacob told everybody they must get used to calling him Israel.

God further told Jacob:
"I am God Almighty, be fruitful and multiply; a nation and a company of nations shall be of you, and kings shall come out of your loins; and the land which I gave Abraham and Isaac, to you I will give it, and to your seed after you will I give the land."
After this repeated promise, the Lord ascended again into the heavens. It surely was a successful sacrifice there on the mount of Bethel, because the invisible Lord spoke to him. Then Jacob Israel had his oldest son and another servant gather a large stone on that place, then some more stones on top of those so it would be a true monument. This was to remind them all that on this spot the Lord had talked to them. They did not want to forget. Then he poured a precious grape wine over the rocks and some oil to give it holy significance. The place was called Beth-el.

171

Rachel Gives Birth

After the grass was grazed off around Beth-el, Israel traveled on toward the south, toward Ephrath. Rachel found the constant traveling rather strenuous because she was very pregnant. The nights were warm and she could not sleep well. The baby was too lively in her womb. Of course, Bilhah helped packing and the male servants as well as her son Joseph and Dan and Naphtali helped folding up their tents. They made sure mother Rachel did not do any heavy lifting and packing. But it was very warm and she did not feel well despite their efforts. She was not young anymore, but otherwise the pregnancy gave her joy and peace. Now no one could say 'Rachel can produce only one, single, little baby. She is expecting a second one.' Jacob Israel, her husband, was also at her side whenever he could get away from other duties. He could not walk too well anymore after his hip was out of joint. The ligaments were looser than on his healthy leg. He preferred to ride a camel or a donkey rather then walking. He had gained some weight. He tried to sleep at Rachel's tent whenever he could, now that she was so very pregnant. His presence gave her consolation, if not physically, at least mentally.

~~~

His sons did not like their father's interference in the business too much. They did not want to be supervised.

When Jacob Israel had a family meeting where he talked to his family about the Lord, how it was in the beginning, in the beginning when Adam and Eve were the only humans on earth, his sons always felt as if their father wanted to lord it over them. They had somewhat hardened their hearts. They did not have to fear being beaten with a leather whip by him anymore; they were too adult for that. However, word would always leak out when they did not watch the cattle properly or played a rock game instead. Or if they just tried to have a good time at night and then wolves entered the sheep herds and tore a number of sheep apart. Or if they did not handle their neighbors properly and let their cattle graze into someone elses' field. If someone's sheep, goat, calf or chicken meandered into or too near their camp, the sons would always catch and butcher it, then lie about it.

Someone would always tell Leah what the sons had done, again. She would criticize her sons and tell them to be good and orderly. Mostly however, they just assured their mother that they loved her very much.

They said, "Don't worry about us, Mother. You are in this kitchen tent and don't get into the outside world, you are so protected. We are out there. We have to see how we get along."

She would sometimes shake her head at them, so did Zilpah. Then the sons told each other not to tell mother and father, and there would be no trouble.

Joseph was interested in the history of Adam and Eve. He also wrote down about the tower of Babel. He wrote down how the 'children of God' saw beautiful women from the 'daughters of man' and married whomever they pleased (Cain's descendents) even if they were not fearing God. Joseph had aquired more papyrus and wrote down whatever he had heard from his father. Then he rolled it up and stuck it into a clay urn. Joseph was intelligent and had a way of overseeing a situation and did not hide his talent. In fact, he was somewhat aloof toward his brothers. That made them hate him.

If there were disagreements in regards to grazing grounds or trades, their father usually ended up endorsing Joseph's suggestion. The brothers hated him for that also.

When Joseph was not around the ten brothers brought up the incident many years back when their father had said, "You are all equally important to me."

"Now we see, it is not so. Joseph from the 'love wife' is more important to him than we. He always hangs around Father. I never hear a strict word spoken to Joseph from Father," said Levi.

"Yes, that is true," answered Simeon.

Then Issachar mentioned that Simeon and Levi did the slaughtering in Shechem, that's why.

"Be quiet, Issachar," said Gad. "You did not help to prevent it either."

~~~

When they had almost arrived at Ephrath, it was time for Rachel to have her baby. The midwife was there. Clean water was standing in a pot, covered up to keep out flies. She knew that around a mother in childbed things had to be a bit cleaner than usual. She did not know why, but her mother had done it that way, and her mother's mother before her.

Rachel began to have contractions. They kept coming. Then the midwife told her to lie down because she wanted to feel her abdomen. She felt it once, she felt it twice, she felt it again some time later.

"Why are you feeling my womb so much, Mara?" asked Rachel.

"I don't like something here," said Mara.

"What is it, tell me," begged Rachel.

"It seems that your baby has turned and is in a sitting position and cross legged. But babies like that can be born, it just hurts more and sometimes they twist an arm or a leg or the neck while being born."

Leah heard about that also, as well as Bilhah and Zilpah, and of course, Jacob. They were tense. Jacob walked around, demanded more food, more drinks, he had to eat in order to get his emotions steadied.

Then, suddenly, Rachel got stronger contractions and a hemorrhage. With every contraction she bled a little more. Bilhah had to keep cleaning up. Now Jacob and the midwife were really worried. Rachel was worried.

Jacob confronted the midwife as to what was going on. Mara told him that the placenta sat toward the side and toward the front and she could not do much. Jacob looked in on his Rachel, their eyes met. Hers were pleading and Jacob's eyes developed tears. He left. Mara, the midwife, had also asked him to leave, because in those days men did not belong into a birthing room. It would also make the midwife nervous and the wife tense. Sometimes a nasty husband would call a crying woman a weakling. Childbearing women don't need that kind of talk from their husband. Mara saw to it that Rachel was as much at ease as possible under the circumstances.

Jacob walked back and forth behind Rachel's tent. He thought about God. Did he not just erect a monument to God? And did he not pour a drink sacrifice and oil and his best wine over the monument to honor God? Then why is his wife in such danger?

Just then someone came and told him that some cows had begun a stampede. Jacob yelled at them.

"I am busy, can't you see? Go do your duty, get them back, don't bother me." The boy silently disappeared and told the other brothers, including Joseph and servants that things with Mistress Rachel were not working out right.

Even Leah was worried. That had never happened to her nor to her maids. They always had more or less spontaneous births, all always went well at the end. She ordered Zilpah to cook more food and take over Rachel's cooking, since Bilhah has to help the midwife.

However, things with Rachel did not improve, she bled and bled with every contraction. Rachel became so pale in her face and the loss of blood made her weak. She almost gave up. The midwife gave her juice to drink, consoled and encouraged her to talk, everything imaginable as not to let her fall asleep. Mara knew if she fell asleep that would be the end, she won't wake up anymore. It did not do much good. Rachel felt so light as if she were floating towards the sky.

Finally, the baby started showing with more loss of blood.

"Here he comes," exclaimed Mara, "be happy, Rachel, it is a boy."

"I am too weak to enjoy this boy, I think I will die. Oh, how terrible! I waited for this child so many years and now he causes my death, and I am still rather young. Who will take care of that poor baby?" breathed Rachel with an even quieter voice.

"Don't worry, you will," encouraged the midwife, "and your sister will help."

"His name shall be Ben-o-ni," Rachel breathed.

"A boy, a boy," exclaimed Mara. Then Jacob came stumbling into the tent to look. He saw his wife's face, pale as fresh butter. He called her name, he reached for her hand. - Nothing - Rachel had departed.

Then Jacob stepped out of the birthing tent and cried a loud cry of sorrow. His favored love-wife was dead.

"The Lord did not help me, He really did not. And God knew it all along that it would be that way. God knows everything ahead of time. Dead, dead, my Rachel is dead."

Jacob cried and cried, tears streamed out of his eyes. It was getting dark, good that others could not see it. This time Leah was not jealous, her sister—gone, this was serious.

After sometime Leah hit the copper bell with a stick, time for dinner. Everybody came running, but Jacob had lost his appetite. Nobody smiled, no one talked. Such a horrible thing had never happened to them in the last twenty-some years. After dinner everyone quietly left the kitchen area and went back to work.

Then Jacob, when he had cried his fill, came in to see his tiny son. He needed to be breast fed. Leah took over.

She walked over to Rachel's tent to see about the baby.

"What is his name?" she inquired.

Jacob answered:

"Rachel called him Ben-o-ni, but it is a sad name. I will re-name him. His name shall be Benjamin."

"What are we doing about the burial?" asked Leah.

"Since it is summer and our family's burial grounds are too far away, we cannot transport the body over there and have no choice but to bury her here in the vicinity."

Then the servants were ordered to dig a deep grave. Mara wrapped Rachel in a large sheet of linen. Joseph and Bilhah's Dan had quickly taken lumber and nailed a casket together for burial. Jacob sat watching her body. When all was ready Jacob, Joseph, Dan and Naphtali slowly lowered the casket with ropes into the grave. Everyone threw a flower down on the casket and the grave was shovelled closed again. Then Jacob found another large rock and built a monument right on top of the spot. Then the somber group left, each to his or her duties.

Since Jacob Israel could not walk so well, he had hired a married servant by the name of Lotan for personal use around the campground. Lotan's wife had a toddler she was nursing. The little girl was already about three years old. As was the custom in those days, if a young mother died, another woman who was nursing would take over the nursing of the newborn infant. Leah held little Benjamin in her arms and he started crying loud and penetratingly. Then Leah handed the baby over to the woman. She sat down on a fallen tree trunk and nursed little Benjamin. Then she handed him back to Leah. The baby was satisfied, snuggled up to Leah and fell asleep. The baby wetted, it ran through the blanket, wetted Leah too. "The poor baby! How would Rachel have loved getting wet from him! I have to find Rachel's sheep fleeces and wrap the child into that. It must be somewhere in her tent. Leah entered her sister's tent. Mara and other women were sweeping it and doing some more cleaning up. Then, in the corner, Leah found the little sheep fleeces to wrap the baby's bottom into. She decided to take little Benjamin into her large tent for good. Her daughter Dinah would gladly help with the upbringing. She also ordered Bilhah to weave some more cloth from that Egyptian cotton.

It's expensive. However, little Benjamin should have another gown. I don't want people to say that I am a bad stepmother and make him wear old things. Everyone knows a mother loves the child of her womb. With a stepchild such as this one, people will be watching me. Maybe I will embroider it around the neck.

"Aaah, aaah," there he is again, crying. Leah stuck her head out of the tent and called.

"Dinah, come here, cuddle the baby, he woke up, and it's not time yet for the next feeding. I have to do other work right now."

Dinah ran over quickly, with a wreath of flowers on her head and looking guilty, while one of the servants disappeared behind a tent.

"Aaah, aaah."

Leah saw the wreath and knew what it meant. She gave her daughter a stern look and handed her the baby. *Has that girl already forgotten what happened to her in Shechem? She is not allowed to get involved with a servant.*

Dinah carefully accepted the baby and gently swung him back and forth. The little guy stopped crying. How fortunate that the new worker had a nursing wife. She was well-stacked and had plenty of breastmilk for little Benjamin.

Now Leah finally had her husband to herself, after all those years. However, she could not be happy about that. *Must it come to that? Now my sister is dead, dead, gone. Now I should be happy, but I am not. Lord, why did you let this happen? I did not ask you to take her out of my life. Sure, we did not like each other anymore since she took Jacob away from me, but then Rachel also did not like it that another woman should share her husband with her. Are you so strict, God? I did not really wish her death. Was I too jealous? Why, o why did this happen?*

How good, that in all this trouble, we still have Lotan's wife for breast feeding for the child. We will do a good job raising him.

Joseph now started asking questions. "Where is my Mom now?"

"She is in the deep hole in the ground."

"But that cannot be, where is her mind? She cannot be gone forever and ever?"

Jacob told him that his father Isaac told him, and Isaac's father told his father, that "when the 'Hero' comes, the 'snake-killer,' He will do something. Only we don't know when that will be and how it will be, but He will do something. Until that time she will be in the grave and you will not see her anymore. Get used to it." Joseph was somewhat comforted, thinking about the Hero to come. He looked at his tiny brother, stroked his little head and placed a gentle kiss on his pink cheek. Later Joseph asked Leah a question, "Where were my little brother and I before we were born?"

Now Leah really had to think hard. Finally, she came to a conclusion. She sat down, took long, lanky Joseph on her lap, stroked over his dark, curly hair and answered, "You both were in the mind of God, before you were born." Joseph stared into space to think this through. Then his eyes got all excited and he said, "Dinah and Zebulon are running to the swimming hole, I got to run too. - Bye, Aunt Leah."

~~~

The family of Jacob lived in the vicinity of Beth-el as long as their cattle had grass to graze. Jacob was very serious since his Rachel had died. He thought a lot about God and his missing wife and how God's blessing could possibly fit into his loss, and he did not see it. Often he also told Leah about God, whatever he knew.

Reuben's Deed

"What are we doing with Rachel's tent now since it is empty?" Leah asked her husband.

"Just let one of the boys use it. Whoever wants it the most, I don't care."

Then Leah transported Jacob's things from Rachel's tent into hers. From now on Jacob would be in her compound only. She liked that idea, but she did not like the reason for it.

Reuben thought he would take over Rachel's tent since his was getting old. Bilhah lived alone in her tent, but her tent was not too far away from the tent where Reuben slept. Reuben could not, or would not, stop peeking through cracks in the tent at fancy Bilhah now and then. Secretly, of course. Even though Bilhah was older than he, she was still good looking. She had not gained weight in her waist after the two children. She did a lot of weaving on a loom. She could do it well. Her merchandise looked presentable. Jacob Israel could sell it and get paid for it. Bilhah was profitable to him. Bilhah carried her head high and was self-confident. She paid no attention to any male.

Reuben's captured woman from Shechem had escaped, he had no replacement as yet, while his brother's captured women were still around and some had babies already. Reuben did not like that, nor did he go out to find a women, and he did not want a maid as a wife. One of the two maids threw pretty eyes at Reuben, and giggled loud at every joke whenever he was around. However, Reuben just glanced at her condescendingly, but would not show interest. Reuben wanted a woman of higher social status. Reuben had the desire to be noticed by such a splendid woman as Bilhah. However, she never paid any special attention to him. To Bilhah, Reuben was just a young upstart, nothing more.

Then one night Reuben gave in to temptation, stalked over to Bilhah's tent and greeted her.

"What do you want, Master Reuben? It is late."

"You know what I want, Bilhah."

"I am the concubine of your father, don't forget."

Reuben grabbed her and forced her to sleep with him. She could not do anything or fight him off, he was just too strong. Morals did not mean much to Reuben right now. Reuben wanted to be a conqueror and Bilhah to him was the prize. He felt he could do the daring thing - right now. Consequences were pushed so far into his background that he did not see them anymore. To Reuben this was the "here and now." When Bilhah tried

179

to say something, Reuben cut her off and determined that his father had not seen Bilhah for a long time, she is "free." So Reuben did what he wanted.

However, such things as sex with another man's woman never quite go by unnoticed. So it was here with Reuben and Bilhah also. Word got out to Jacob Israel. Jacob was furious; he felt cheated and stolen from, like a man that just been robbed.

He went over to Bilhah to inquire about it in a harsh tone.

"Could you not cry out, Bilhah? You know how wrong it is for you to let my son, my oldest son, the strength of my youth, touch you. You should not have allowed it. Where are your manners?"

"Master Israel, you know Reuben is strong and powerful, I could not do anything, talking did not do any good. This was a rape. Not mine, Reuben's morals are missing."

And Bilhah started to cry and lament.

"Why did you let me live here alone, so close to Reuben's tent? You did not see me for a very long time, not at all. Reuben thought I was free." Angry tears rolled down Bilhah's cheeks.

"You women are a lot of problems, and have to be watched like a shepherd guards his sheep. I have enough sheep to guard out there."

"Don't worry, Master Israel, I am old and will probably not get pregnant anymore."

Jacob Israel then became a little more quiet but still looked angry. Bilhah was a good politician. She told him to forget about the whole affair and be happy about the things that are still good.

"Look at my beautiful woven material," she said, to sidetrack him. "See these stripes. Aren't they gorgeous? And look at this color red. I dyed it with red beets. Then I had an accident, and the whole yarn fell into hot oil when I was cooking. I took it out with a wooden pole and washed it properly. However, after this the color red was really bright and would not wash out anymore. I discovered a new dyeing procedure. Now, if I take other colors in-between and then this red again, it will look very good. Have you ever seen such a beautiful piece of woven material? You should get quite a sum of money for it."

Jacob Israel looked, and liked what he saw. His mind became more relaxed.

"You know, Bilhah, I won't sell this piece. Keep on weaving it until it is large enough to make a gown out of it. A beautiful multi-colored gown for my poor son Joseph, who lost his mother. Joseph is a good boy, he has morals. He is a bit of a show-off, but he is good. I bought him more papyrus and he writes events down. Then he puts it back into his earthen containers that Zilpah knows how to make, closes it tightly, and thus preserves our family history. I am pleased with Joseph."

"There you go, Master Israel, you see it will all turn out to the best. I let you know when the garment is done."

"How is little Benjamin doing?"

"Fine, fine, Bilhah. My wife is taking good care of him. Good bye, Bilhah."

He bent down to her slim, and still youthful-like, figure and kissed her on the cheek and left.

Next time Jacob Israel saw Reuben in the fields he gave him an angry look, pointed his finger at him and said:

"That thing with Bilhah will not be forgotten; you will lose your first-born blessing! Aren't there enough single virgins in the land to find a wife for yourself? The princess of Shechem escaped from you, so what? Your first-born blessing you will lose. Another one will take your place."

~~~

Time went by fast. Herds of sheep and goats, cows and oxen had to be driven from one pasture to another one. Often they had to cross narrow ledges next to rocky mountain sides with bushes and shrubbery. In these hiding places wolves would gather. When the herds crossed those narrow passageways, Jacob's sons and their servants had to be extremely vigilant, have their bows and arrows ready to shoot everything away that might hurt the cattle. Others had shooting rocks ready in their pouches. Sometimes the animals could smell a carnivore and would not move. Then the men screamed and yelled violent curses at the animals and whipped the cattle by force until they moved. Their father Jacob Israel, although limping, was a watchful overseer. He himself, when working for his father-in-law, was a hard worker, so he expected from his sons and servants an equal amount of dedication. Sometimes a sheep limped. Then the men had to examine its foot. Often it had stepped on a thorn. They had to then pull or scrape it out and, if necessary, wash out the wound.

One time young Joseph stepped on a thorn when his leather sandals were getting old. He cried out in pain.

"Take care of yourself 'baby'," the older brothers said to him, but would not help. Joseph felt they liked their sheep more than him. However, he became tough and did learn to take care of himself. He was the youngest of the sons, except for the child Benjamin. The boys were a rough bunch. The younger ones could always go crying to their mother's shoulder later on when they were home. They did not dare to look vulnerable on the fields for fear of being ridiculed. However, when being endangered by outside enemies the sons would all stick together.

Every time an animal got lost or ripped by a wolf or lion Jacob Israel would inquire about it exactly, give advice or criticize. Often, young Joseph was the one who was sent out into the fields with food and orders. If Jacob wanted to buy something from a merchant, he would either ride out himself to where his sons and the herds were or send Joseph. Joseph would then give the orders to his brothers. He would say, "Father wants you to bring six sheep, four goats and one oxen home for selling." They would then sort out that number and drive them over to the road where merchants traveled and Jacob Israel would make the deal.

Isaac's Departure

Often Jacob's thoughts went to his very old father. He felt he should see him, as he being the one responsible for him, the one who received The Blessing. Leah also had mentioned it to him. Since he had not heard anything to the contrary, Jacob knew his father Isaac was still alive at this time, but getting really old and frail. He was now 180 years old. Jacob traveled over to the area where his father lived, in Mamre, near the city of Arbah, later called Hebron. Years ago, when Esau, Jacob's twin brother, was so angry at Jacob, after Jacob had cheated him, Esau thought his father is old, blind, and would die soon. He then wanted to kill his brother Jacob as soon as Father dies, after the funeral. However, neither thing happened. Time healed some wounds. The gifts of cattle that Jacob had given Esau healed some wounds, and the hip injury of Jacob also healed some wounds in brother Esau's heart. Esau figured God had punished Jacob and that is enough. And last, but not least, distant living quarters brought peace between the brothers.

Finally, Jacob managed to get away from his temporary homestead to see his father. *Will Father have forgiven me for cheating him with those furs around my arms and saying that I am Esau? I know I was not my father's favorite son; it was Esau. However, I am now with God, totally. I ought to have one last father-son talk with Dad before he departs. So he can depart in peace and leave his peace with me.*

Jacob Israel did not come too soon to visit him. Isaac was very weak and looked forward to departing this life and laying to rest his old body. Jacob arrived at his father's tent. He saw he was properly being cared for. He called out to Isaac and greeted him loudly (in case he was hard of hearing). Isaac then tried sitting up in bed. Jacob put a stiff pillow behind his father's back to help him sit erect. After blind Isaac touched his son Jacob and heard the stories of his life from him personally, Isaac was pleased and rested comfortably. He knew God's blessing, that he had given to him in error, did remain on his son, and that in the end everything turned out perfect, the way God had told his wife. Isaac knew now that his wife's "notion" was not a fantasy born in childbed woes, but was really God's will all along. This gave old Isaac peace of mind.

"I am so sorry, Father Isaac," said Jacob, "that you were blind for so many years. How did you bear it?"

"I tried to live right. And that is what you and your children should do at all times." Then Isaac lifted his finger and said, "The path of the just is as a shining light, that shineth more and more unto the perfect day." That speech seemed to have exhausted Isaac's strength.

He fell asleep after that. Jacob Israel sat by his fathers bedside for awhile. Then he arose and tiptoed outside and looked around at his father's livestock and property. He thought about what to do with it all, should his father depart…The next morning when the sun rose in the east, golden and bright, Isaac did not wake up anymore. He had gone home to his inheritance, to the eternal shining light.

Jacob Israel cried. Esau was given notice of his beloved father's departure. All the children and cousins converged on the site and around his deathbed.

A proper funeral was being prepared with spices for the deceased body of Isaac. The serving woman who had taken care of old Isaac produced a white linen sheet, and Leah also brought one from her home. Esau's oldest son's wife also brought a linen sheet. They wrapped Isaac's body in a sheet. Then they put a lot of dry myrrh and aloes around him and wrapped him again. At the end they wrapped the third sheet around him to hold everything tightly in place and tied it down so it would not open up. His sons Jacob and Esau built a proper platform and laid the body of their father on it. Then Jacob, Esau and the oldest of the grandsons carried Isaac's body to the family burial place in the cave of Heth in Machpelah, near Hebron, the cave that their grandfather had purchased from Heth. It was a very long, somber procession of people that walked past the burial casket. There was Esau with all his wives and children and children's children. There was Jacob Israel with his wives and children, some of whom were married already and had children of their own.

In that burial cave was Abraham and his wife Sarah, Rebekah, now Isaac, and there was room for more. Only Rachel, who died in childbirth while traveling, could not be buried there. Leah felt sorry about that, so did others. *Was it a bad omen that she stole her father's idols and then when he was looking for them, acted innocent? Is this the Lord's punishment for her? Is this Rachel's punishment for always trying to take possession of her (Leah's) husband, to be buried other than in the family burial place? That could not be. God is merciful and gracious.* So Leah's thoughts bounced back and forth, trying to come to a conclusion. They did not cry much for Isaac, because he had been very old, blind, weak and wanted to go to his eternal home. However, with Rachel missing in the cave, that only now came forcefully to their attention. They all felt sorry for it. But things in life don't always turn out as planned. Leah, now an older middle-aged woman, hoped that she would someday be buried in that cave.

Jacob thought he will someday see Him, the Lord, somehow, when his own departure will come. Leah was also hopeful and told it to her maid Zilpah. They were reminiscing and discussing Isaac's last words that 'the path of the just is like a shining light, that shines toward the perfect day...' Rachel's son Joseph asked for some more papyrus and carefully wrote down what his grandfather's last words were and then stuffed them in his clay pots.

After the funeral Esau took his wives with all their possessions, moved north to get around the Dead Sea and then crossed the Jordan River and lived east of there. Esau also had too many possessions to live in the same vicinity as Jacob Israel and all his possessions. Esau also remembered The Blessing that their father Isaac had given his brother, that he should live in Canaan, and he (Esau) near Mount Seir in the country of Edom. His old anger against his brother was long gone and buried. His sons sometimes tried to bring it up, but Esau had a good streak in himself, in that he "forgot," and let it be at that. Both brothers were now very middle-aged for their time and had experienced in their long life that the righteous road in life is always the best, even if at first it seems like sheer folly and loss. Leah likewise had experienced it: One has to do the right thing and be humble and patient, things will then work out.

Months went by with the usual cattle chores for Jacob's sons and servants and for Leah's own household chores. Her daugher Dinah had adjusted again to their farm-and cattle business. The episode in Shechem with the rape had cured her. She never called herself "the princess of the cows" anymore. She had seen that not all is as golden and shimmering in other cultures as it looks at first sight.

Tamar

Judah's wife was one of the women captured from Shechem. She was slim and beautiful. Then one day she had a bad cold that would not go away. Leah prepared special teas for her, with lemon or orange juice, with liquor or without. She just would not get better. Eventually she started coughing. Leah rubbed her chest with special greases like eucalyptus and put a warm woolen blanket around her. It did not help. She coughed more and even spit blood. At the same time she lost a lot of weight. Leah cooked her rich beef soups and other foods that she used to love. It just did not help. She got thinner and thinner. Then Leah and Judah realized that she had consumption. Soon she died, was buried and Judah was alone. There had not been a child as yet.

Judah did not like to be single. He remembered that he had a friend by the name of Hirah from the city of Adullam. He met a young women in that city, the daughter of Shua. Judah remembered seeing a young woman there that was single. Maybe his friend Hirah would know her name and inquire for him. So he packed his bags and traveled to Adullam and found Hirah at home. Yes, his neighbor's daughter Serah was still available. Shua and Judah agreed on a brideprice and Judah could take her home. Serah soon bore him a son named Er, after that another son named Onan. Then the Judah family moved to another town named Kezib. There Serah bore Judah a third son named Shelah. They were happy. Neither Judah nor Serah were very strict to their boys, because Judah thought his father had been too strict with them, so he wanted to do it better. It turned out that Er, the firstborn, became a bad boy and would not obey; he was also a bully. Judah looked for a wife very soon for his son Er. The parents often did that in the olden days, thinking that the young people themselves are too flighty to make a good choice. The Lord saw that this Er boy, just a young teenager at the time, would make serious trouble in Jacob's large family later on, so He killed him. Judah felt sorry that Er did not leave an heir, so he told Tamar, the widowed wife of Er, to marry his second son Onan. The first son born to Onan and Tamar would then be the heir for Er. However, Onan did not want to do that, raise a child for someone else, and instead practiced a certain form of birth control. The Lord did not like that either in this case. So, the Lord let Onan get sick and die also. Then Judah, still in charge of his young people, took Tamar back to her father's house. It was understood in the custom of those days, that Tamar would marry Shelah as soon as he was old enough. However, Judah was superstitious now and afraid that then, maybe,

Shelah would also die. So he let the young widow Tamar stay in her father's house and never called for her when his son was old enough.

Tamar did not like living alone as a spinster in her father's house and knew that she was not given in marriage to Shelah, nor was she free to marry anyone else, since she was "spoken for." She thought of a way to remedy the situation.

Judah's wife Serah had died, now he was a widower. He traveled toward Timnah for sheep shearing time. Tamar was told where the men would be. She quickly took off her widow's clothes. Then she put on other bright robes and a veil so her face would not be seen and sat on the road where her father-in-law would come past, pretending to be a prostitute waiting for a customer. Judah, being single again, fell for the trick and tried to use her. Tamar wanted to discuss the price first before she let him sleep with her. The price she wanted was a young goat and as a pledge Judah's seal, cord and his personal walking staff. He gave it to her and only then Tamar let herself be used by him.

Afterward the two parted ways, Judah to go home and get the goat, Tamar to go home and change her clothes again. Judah's friend Hirah took the goat back to his hometown to give to the prostitute. He could not find a prostitute, nor did any of the neighbors see one. Judah decided to forget about his pledge items or else everyone would laugh at him that he saw a shrine prostitute that did not exist. After some time Shua's wife saw that their daughter is pregnant. "Pregnant - by whom? What a shame! Someone, go tell Judah, she was to marry Shelah. Who did this terrible thing to her?"

When Judah was notified that his daughter-in-law is pregnant like a common whore he exploded in anger: "Bring her here and let her be burned to death. We don't allow such misbehavior." Old mother Leah heard about it also what may happen to Tamar. She thought that is going too far. In her long life she saw how easily men can fall into temptation for a woman. She urged mercy and caution, especially since Tamar is the daughter of Shua, Judah's friend's neighbor, and the reputation of her son wanting her killed.

She need not have worried, because Tamar had 'something up her sleeve:' the three pledged items. When Judah saw them, suddenly it dawned on him what he had done a few months ago, and who that prostitute was, sitting by the road. "Oooohh!" Judah was ashamed. Now he could not say much. The only honorable thing for him to do now was to take the pregnant Tamar into his home and be his wedded wife. Tamar gave birth to twins: Perez and Zerah. Judah made these two boys his heirs. Now Shua had become his father-in-law.

Berries

It was midsummer again and hot. Jacob and Leah were riding around the countryside, on camels, looking for suitable pasture. Leah loved to get out of her tent and home confinement and see the area from on top of a camel's back. They saw a small arbor with lots of berry bushes. Leah was excited about the discovery. She wanted to pick them. However, a camel has to kneel down when a person, especially a woman, wants to mount or dismount. This particular old she-camel was lazy and stubborn. She was afraid once the camel sits down it may not want to get up again right away and then her limping husband has to help out by fighting the stubborn beast. Leah thought better of it and rather sent the girls to pick the berries.

At home, Leah called the two kitchen maids (the same that went with their daughter to Shechem/Succoth), gave them baskets, and a young male servant with three donkeys to accompany them.

"Pick lots of berries," Leah instructed them. "We are a large family."

Leah would serve them raw as a desert. The other berries she would dry in the hot sun, put them in linen sacks and keep them for later. The girls were excited to go and Dinah also. However, Mother Leah saw that Dinah had not finished her spinning portion of flax.

"You cannot go berry picking, Dinah, you did not finish your job."

"Oh, Mother, I am devastated, I want to go along, please."

"First do your work, then you go berry picking. I saw you talking yesterday and loafing in the middle of the day. If you ever do get married, your husband will beat you if he finds you lazy."

"Oh, men, they are so evil. That is why I want no one, except..." and then Dinah kept silent. Pouting and sad, she went back to her fuzzy linen spindle.

The two kitchen maids put large shawls over their heads, because they did not want to look sunburned (a sign for a poor country girl). Then the servant brought the three donkeys. The three of them sat on them and got ready to leave.

"Now you watch those girls, keep bears, hyenas and wild dogs away from them," said Master Jacob.

"I will, I will, Master Jacob, trust me."

The young man had a small spear, a bow and arrow, a knife, and a sling shot along for protection.

"Now, first you cross that brook where the boys put the large rock in the middle for easier crossing, the donkeys can wade through the water. Then you cross that meadow behind the brook. Then you look to the sunset for a rock formation that looks like a face, go there and then turn east. There you will see a small forest with the berry patches. See you before sunset," added Jacob.

"Yes, Master Jacob, all will go in order."

And off they went, while Dinah was pining after them, throwing an angry look at her mother.

The group found the berry patch. They happily ate and picked and ate and picked. They gave some to their guard to eat also, who kept sitting on his donkey looking out.

Suddenly from the north, a noise was heard and bushes broke. The guard nervously got ready to shoot the animal that would show, but it was not a bear as he had thought, it was Amorite men with their swords. They were dressed in body furs and wore black beards. Their faces looked grim and aggressive, with their weapons stretched out toward him. He had no time to shoot.

The girls started screaming, dropping the berries and ran. When the servant saw there were more Amorite soldiers then fingers on his two hands, he got even more scared and gave the donkey a hard kick in the flanks and galloped homeward. He heard the girl's screaming no more.

When he arrived back at the family tents he yelled.

"Master Jacob, Master Jacob, help, help!"

Everyone in earshot came running.

"The Amorites kidnapped the girls. I could not do anything, they were too numerous, more than fingers on my two hands. I am sorry."

"Did you shoot at least one?" asked Master Jacob.

"No sir, I was afraid."

"No time to talk now." Jacob blew into his bullhorn, four short bursts, pause, and again four short bursts. This was the sign for war and attack. All sons and male servants that heard the sound ran for their weapons. Jacob climbed his camel and off they went, in the direction toward the berry patch.

Jacob's small army troop made the distance in a short time, in hot pursuit of the enemies, now that they knew the way. However, the grass there was trampled down, the berries spilled and some still in a basket but the girls gone.

So, they continued northward, following the trampled grass as fast as they could on camels and on foot, with their weapons ready.

In the distance Jacob saw indications of a nearby settlement. He lifted his arm high with his hand flat, the sign for stopping and listening.

Jacob's foot soldiers stopped, then advanced very slowly and stopped a good while in-between. Then they heard rough men laughing and talking and girl's voices crying.

"Let go of me, noooo, help, help, nooo, you are hurting me, help!"

Then more laughing male voices, and more crying from the girls. They could tell the crying girls were their servant girls. The Amorites had a different accent and language usage. This really turned on the fighting spirit in Jacob and his servant warriors. They could not wait any longer.

Silently and swiftly they ran from the trees, and before those Amorites knew what happened one after the other got his throat slashed or his belly punctured. The Amorites further away tried to run for their swords that they had put under a tree, but Jacob and his servant soldiers shot everyone of them with an arrow, a sling shot, or used their sword. The Israelites had advanced, so the other Amorites could not get to their pile of weapons anymore. More men came running to fight the Israeli men but Jacob's men were tough, fearless and overpowered them. The rest of the Amorite men with their wives and children fled. Jacob was pleased.

"Now pick what you want, men, you deserve it."

Jacob's men raided their huts and took what they wanted, giving the rest of the gold and silver they found to Jacob.

"Burn the huts," ordered Jacob. So the men burned down the Amorite huts. When all went up in smoke, Jacob and his men, together with the two frightened servant girls, left for home.

Jacob put the gold and silver into a wooden chest as an inheritance gift to his grandchildren. He did not know which ones as yet. He would wait and see who would be the most deserved; certainly not Reuben's, Simeon's and Levi's children. Those three were under his curse.

Jacob had delivered the girls into the care of his wife. The girls were red from crying and bloody from scratches suffered from the men, their clothes were torn, hair all messed-up.

Leah stared at the girl's appearance when they were alone in the kitchen tent. Their braides had opened up, bloody scratches covered their faces, hands and breasts. Their clothes ripped and disheveled.

"Is this what they did to you?" she asked. "Tell me everything, and now stop crying."

Dinah also came running and looking. Now she was happy that she had stayed home.

"Did they rape you?" Leah asked.

Shamefacedly, both girls nodded their heads and started to cry again.

"By how many men?" asked Leah.

"By two," said one girl.

"Me too," said the other girl. "A third man wanted to get a turn on us when your soldiers came."

"This is just awful!" exclaimed Mistress Leah. "These heathen 'wolves' have no morals. But our God gave us the victory."

"I am sorry," Leah continued, "but now I have to cut off all your hair."

"Must it be? My beautiful hair?" said one girl.

"Yes, it must. Those Amorites are unclean. They may have lice on their bodies. They may have diseases and other sicknesses on them. You would then carry it into our clean and healthy family."

"Get me the scissors," demanded Leah.

"Dinah, you get the water ready."

"Yes, Mother" said Dinah. She poured water into the large pot that hung on a hook over the fire to warm it up a little, while Leah cut the girls' hair and then threw it in the fire.

"When Dinah was raped you did not cut off her hair," lamented one of the girls.

"That was different. Shechem was young and untouched. Don't worry, your hair will grow back again. I am more worried about something else. If you get sick, we have no medicine for it, you will die. Did you notice if those men had clear skin?"

"No, Mistress Leah. Others held us down while we fought, we did not think of looking," both girls explained.

Now Leah's forehead got all wrinkled and she shook her head in worry. "Even more reason to use drastic measures, girls. I am sorry, but this will hurt. We have no choice and still no assurance of success."

Then Leah threw a lot of salt and vinegar into the bathing buckets and made the girls sit in it. "I hope this works." The girls cried because that sharply-spiced water hurt their wounds, but it had to be. They wiped their teary eyes.

"Girls, stick your hands also into the water, all the way," she ordered. "Your shorn heads also have to be washed in that solution." Leah stayed around to see that her orders were followed.

"Mistress Leah," asked one girl afterwards, "what if this procedure does not work and we get pregnant? Can we sacrifice the unwanted babies to the god Moloch?"

"Absolutely not, Sheba, who gave you that grizzly idea? Yes, what will we do?" Leah made a deep sigh and slowly and hesitantly she explained.

"We will have two little children growing up without a father. And it will be my and your duty to raise them right so they will become valuable human beings that believe and obey the true God."

When the procedure was over, Leah remembered the berries and told her husband about it. This time more warriors accompanied the girls and this time Dinah was allowed to go along. They got their berries.

Somehow the painful bathing procedure had worked this time, and the two maids did not get pregnant from those infidels. Leah was glad.

Leah's Memoirs

Time passed. Leah's household was smaller now. Her boys had their own families and Leah had more time to think.

Often when Leah thought of her children she was not satisfied. They did not always do the right thing. When they were little boys and they threw temper tantrums, she could just grab and hold them and give them a good spanking and the tantrum would "miracuously" disappear...However, now they were men and she was getting old. Her boys were not very interested in being good men. Her husband sometimes worried about their actions. Then that trouble with her only daughter...Leah thought she had trained her properly in the ways of their families and culture that a woman's highest goal is to keep herself untouched by men. She had taught it to Dinah. Had she not been firm enough? Was she not practical enough? Should she have more vigorously ordered the two servant girls to guard Dinah and not let her out of their eyesight? And so Leah thought and pondered as to what could have gone wrong that her children did not turn out as they should have. On the other hand, she wondered if her husband's decision of having more wives and Laban's cheating may have cast a bad shadow over their sons so that they figured "What Father can do, I can do too!"? Sometimes when the sons fought or were seemingly not honest, she felt a heartache. On the other hand, she knew none of her children had as yet met "The Lord" in a personal way as did her husband Jacob. She thought maybe, someday, they might yet turn and want to be good when The Lord will appear to them personally. She wished it so much.

Leah could not forget how Simeon and Levi had killed all the men from Shechem because one of them had raped Dinah. The punishment seemed too severe for her.

Then there was the incident with the slaying of the man. Her husband had hired another servant from another country. He knew all about cattle and how to breed a good stock. This servant was not a slave. He also had to help Jacob mount a camel and do other things that were getting too hard for him. Jacob had to pay him for his work. Anyway, this servant was watching the cattle in a certain meadow, while some of her sons were having a feast. The party lasted long and her boys were drunk and did not go back to the field to the hired servant. It was getting very late and the man was alone out there, being responsible for everything, with only two young teenagers helping him. Everything was peaceful, they kept close watch for

193

wild animals in the night. Then the man got hungry and ate something while sitting down. He fell asleep. Suddenly the two young boys cried out "wolf, wolf." The man woke up with a start, grabbed his bow and arrow and ran toward the area where the boys had seen the wolves. He could tell because the sheep were bleating and pushing against the stone wall. The man saw the dark figures of three wolves running away in the moonlight, each dragging one sheep with him. He shot one wolf and managed to rip the sheep out of its mouth. The sheep was wounded but still alive. The other two wolves got away with their sheep. This was a catastrophe! Two sheep lost because he fell asleep. What will Master Jacob Israel say? The rest of the night was calm.

Then around sunrise the sons returned, still feeling the effects of liquor. When they heard what had happened and that the hired servant had fallen asleep, they became so very angry. Levi and Simeon took oxen clubs and beat the man, again and again. The other sons did not interfere. The man fell down and finally lay still and did not move anymore. Now Jacob Israel was really angry. He knew from experience how easy it is to loose a sheep or goat to wild animals. It can happen. It had happened to him before when he still worked for Laban. But beating the man to death was terrible. Leah was upset about that much more so than about the lost two sheep. Her husband would not forget this slaying. He told his boys that this deed will go on their records. When their father said "This will go on your record," that was meant as a curse, and the curse would cause bad luck to the sons later on.

Then Leah remembered the time when they were selling grain on the market. It had rained heavily. The general road was soaked and muddy. The oxen pulled the cart slowly, because oxen walk slowly. Then the cart's wheels had gotten into a mudhole and were stuck. The oxen could not, or would not, pull the heavy cart out of the hole. What men then usually do is scream at the oxen and whip them with the bull whip and give a mighty shove to the wagon or the wagon wheels. This usually works. However, this time they could not get the wagon out of the mud. It was absolutely stuck too deeply in the mud. They should have unloaded the grain bags to the side of the road, even if the grass was wet, and then get the wagon out, and then throw some rocks into the deep hole to make it passable for the next time. But no, her sons…would not go through that trouble, they kept beating the oxen. And then screamed to the animals, "If you don't want to pull the wagon, then we will cut your rear legs so you cannot pull anything anymore." And they really did, they were so enraged. Another adult temper tantrum! Those good oxen! Her husband was very angry and told them again that this deed will also go on their record that Joseph is writing down. "Why, O why, can my boys not be moderate and controlled? From whom did they inherit that?"

Then Leah rememberd her son Reuben, how he slept with Bilhah. That will also go on his record. *Why does that boy not have any good sense in his head? What kind of an example is he to his younger brothers?* All those things worried Leah. Sometimes she wished that the Lord would appear to her boys to straighten them out. She could tell that her husband definitely got better or nicer to her after he had met the angel. Leah thought, *if only the Lord gave us some specific set of rules on what to do and what not to do, then the children would obey.* She mentioned that to her husband Jacob. Jacob said that man has a conscience; the conscience guides one. But Leah thought conscience is not enough, because some people have a very broad conscience; to them doing bad things doesn't mean much, while others are more careful naturally. Therefore, Leah wished God would give them commandments.

Teaching Grandchildren

Leah could only think of one thing that might help the situation: Teaching. Teaching them continually about the Lord. Reminding them about the Lord's dealing in the past and how God acted upon men's sins. Such as, for instance, the Tower of Babel, how the people wanted to ascend to God's throne. And when their tower's top reached to the rain clouds, heaven seemed as far away as ever. They did not reach God and had no way to control Him. But the Lord controlled them by confusing their speech, and so they had to stop building; a failure in communication.

To put thoughts into action, when any young grandchildren were around Leah or her husband would talk to them and made them memorize their family's history. Joseph had to write everything down. The boys had to learn to recite the names of everyone of their ancestors, starting from Adam, Seth, Enos, Cainan, Mahalaleel, Jared, Enoch, Methuselah, Lamech and Noah. They were memorizing the age of each man when he had his first son, and then how long he lived thereafter. Young Benjamin heard this all the time, as well as the maids or whichever child was around. They had plenty of time to do this on those long dark evenings under the tent. They had to memorize also the sons of Esau. Then the children were told by Jacob what particular good or bad thing anyone of those ancestors had done.

For instance, there was the good Lamech, father of Noah. Then there was the bad Lamech who came from Cain's family line, the cruel one, with the two wives.

Jacob mentioned Enoch, who after his first son was born, became god-fearing. Enoch announced, "The Lord will come with many thousands of his holy angels to bring judgment to evildoers." Enoch was righteous. The Lord honored him by taking him home to God without first getting sick and dying. And thus Enoch was spared the trauma of enduring the great flood during Noah's time. Leah thought about what an excellent departure from earth Enoch had. *I wish I could go like that, not getting sick and weak and finally dying. Just being taken up by the Lord, that lucky guy! Won't happen to me though.*

Then Leah did some thinking and came to the conclusion that their ancestor Methusalah must also have been righteous because he could die on his bed, shortly before the flood.

While Leah was thinking thus and reminiscing about her life, it was getting dark. Then, when the fire had burned down low and it was getting late and cool in the tent, Leah would shove some coals around and some wood chips, so as to save some spark on the fireplace for the next morning. That way she could more easily start the fire the next day.

Jacob Israel also talked to the children whenever he had an opportunity. Leah and whoever was around, loved those ancestral fireside talks.

"Time for bed now," old grandfather Jacob announced. Then the young wives took their little children and each went home to her own tent.

Joseph's Garment

After a long time Bilhah finished the beautifully colored garment that Jacob wanted for his favored son Joseph. She called Master Jacob over to her tent and showed the finished piece to him. Jacob looked at it, gave Bilhah a close hug in gratitude, took the garment and left. Joseph was not home because he was asigned cattle duty, together with Dan, Naphtali, Gad and Asher.

Joseph saw his half-brothers were doing evil again; like playing dice, drinking strong wine and not watching the cattle properly. There were lion tracks in the sand again further out and the boys were only trying to have fun while letting some hired servants watch the cattle.

"How terribly irresponsible of them," said Joseph.

When Joseph's cattle duty was over, he went home to tell his father about the four brothers whose behaviour was bad again because they were not minding their business properly and getting angry when he criticized them. Word got around about Joseph telling on them. They were angry at Joseph.

Then Jacob showed Joseph the beautiful party garment. Joseph tried it on. It fit. He kissed his father and thanked him. At that time the brothers were grazing their cattle near Shechem. Jacob Israel knew that every woman who had lost a husband, father or brother or beau in the massacre, would be their enemy in addition to the men who married them from other places. That is a lot of enemies. He feared for the safety of his sons.

Jacob then told Joseph to go out to Shechem and see if all is well with his brothers. Joseph took some food and water in a leather pouch, put on his colorful garment and went after his brothers. Joseph was seventeen years old, tall, very suntanned with olive skin, dark hair and handsome. Jacob Israel stood there and looked after Joseph with love and enjoyed the beautiful garment he wore, until he disappeared behind a rock outcropping. The sun shone brightly but it was not very hot. Jacob figured Joseph should make good time. Jacob's heart was glad: This son really did things right. He could not complain about him. Joseph also got along well with his stepmother, Leah. She sometimes admired him a little bit, but not too much because she did not want to love him more than her own sons. Besides, Joseph was still young and had not proven himself adequately in times of danger and wild animals. She was a very busy woman. The whole household rested on her shoulders. She was the wife who was responsible for everything: food aquisition, food preparation, clothing, and packing up everything when her husband moved to new grazing grounds. Leah was the last one to leave a campground, making sure the servants and maids had left nothing behind. Jacob Israel trusted her; she had proven herself over the years.

Leah's blondish hair had turned gray, but she still looked robust and healthy. It did not bother her too much that she was nearsighted and sometimes had to ask others what there was in the distance, if it was a person or an animal or just rocks with bushes. She could do everything close by very well. Then Leah also had to raise Benjamin, her nephew. She was now his mother since her sister had died. Benjamin was an energetic young boy, smart and sometimes reckless. He clung to his father and his older brother Joseph. Benjamin tried to imitate his brother and do what he did. If Joseph laughed heartily, then Benjamin laughed heartily. If Joseph wrote words, Benjamin would try words. Leah found that so amusing.

One time Benjamin was disobedient and refused to do what his father had told him to do. When father Jacob had gone away, Benjamin imitated his limp in a mocking-like fashion. A male servant saw it and told Leah. Leah got angry and said, "This is too much." She loosened her leather strap, grabbed the boy and under a constant stream of scolding beat him until he screamed and promised never to do it again. Now Leah knew Benjamin had understood. He would never do that again. Benjamin then left to play in the yard, while rubbing his behind.

It was up to Joseph now to teach his brother Benjamin how to shoot an arrow or a sling shot with a rock. His father would test him out now and then. They told him the story of the lion, many years ago, before he was born. They told him about the wolves and how important it is to shoot and hit the target. Often Benjamin sighed from all that pressure of learning to shoot, just like his brothers did in their young years. Eventually he became a good marksman also and could be counted on. Benjamin tested his skill with mice. He kept rocks handy in his fur pouch. If he saw a mouse running he stood very still and tried to hurl a rock at it. Sometimes he killed the mouse, sometimes not. Or he tried to outrun it and step on it before it could disappear into its hole.

~~~

During all this time Dinah was living at home with her parents and was unmarried, a spinster. She had not gotten pregnant from Shechem years ago and she was glad about that. It was not customary in those days to openly show affection. Sometimes men wanted to marry Dinah and talked to her father about her. They never missed mentioning that she was a "used" woman and therefore, less expensive to get. So far Dinah was able to convince her father, if necessary with hugs and kisses, that she should not be married off as yet. And Jacob, as an indulgent father, heeded her pleas. He also was not greedy enough to "sell" her off in marriage in exchange for merchandise, even if it was the custom in those days. Dinah helped mother and did housework. She could not quite avoid running into Dishon on occasion, who was just a servant, she an heiress of a rich man. Every time Dishon and she passed by each other, their eyes met. Right now she saw no way how she could marry this man. He had no wealth to buy her out with a good bridal price. He did not even own a donkey to carry their goods if they married.

One time Dishon was working in the fields with Jacob's sons. Of course, they were gambling again, against their father's orders. They told Dishon to play along. As luck wanted it, Dishon won some silver coins. The brothers handed it to him with a frown and threatened him that they would get it back later on. Dishon then took the coins and went back into the outer rims of the grazing grounds as not to be seen. He put the coins into his leather body pouch under his garment, out of sight. He also stuck leaves in his pouch to prevent the coins from jingling noisily and reminding the brothers of the money on him.

Then, what did he see? Two wolves were in a crouching position, just ready to jump at the sheep. Dishon screamed, pulled his sling shot and rocks out of his pouch and hurled them. It hit one wolf on the nose and blood was visible. The wolf turned and ran away, the other one followed. The brothers quickly left their game and gave chase. Zebulon, Leah's son, was a fast runner and managed to shoot an arrow after the second wolf. It missed. So he went and retrieved his arrow. Now the brothers realized they could not take the silver coins from Dishon, because their father would hear about it. So Dishon kept them and treasured them in his body pouch under his garment. At the next occasion Dishon met Dinah, he pulled them out and quickly showed them, and put them back again. Dinah knew what he meant. She began to hope that someday, maybe, there would be a way they could get married.

~~~

200

Joseph, in the meantime, was hiking toward his brothers to Shechem. He had no map. It was a long hike, about 70 miles or two full days of fast walking. After awhile the area looked rather strange to him, he did not remember ever seeing this part of the country. "Could I be lost?" He looked at the sun, considered the time of day, knew where he came from, but just could not find Shechem or Succoth nor his brothers and their cattle or anything familiar. Then he met a man who was working in his field. Joseph assumed correctly that he must be a local man who knows the area. He approached him and asked about the town of Shechem and his brothers, the Jacob Israel sons and their cattle. The man knew them. In fact he had overheard them talking. He told Joseph that they had gone toward Dothan. The man explained to Joseph the route toward Dothan. Joseph thanked the man and left.

It was still many miles toward Dothan. He had to cross the Jordan River again by swimming across. The water was cool and refreshing even if it was somewhat muddy. Dothan lay toward the northwest from where he was. Joseph had time to think. He remembered his two recent dreams:

He and his brothers were binding grain sheaves and putting them in piles so they would form a cone, to dry. In case it rained, the rain would then run down the grain cone. He then dreamed that his sheave stood up, but his brothers sheaves fell down and sort of bent towards his sheave as if to greet it.

His second dream was that the sun and the moon and eleven stars were bending down to him, as if to greet him.

Joseph liked those dreams. He could not interpret them, but he thought they were significant. *Could I ever become a great man? Could I ever become a ruler? What might the future hold for me? These two dreams are really special.* He had told his father the two dreams previously. His brothers were upset and would not believe that he actually had dreamed that. They thought he had invented them, and tried to be superior to them. Then, when his father heard the second dream about the sun and the moon also bowing down to him, he interpreted it correctly: He being the sun, Leah the moon, and the eleven stars his brothers. Father Jacob was upset, and scolded Joseph about those dreams. Now even he thought that young Joseph was a "smart aleck"-type of guy that wants to show off. But still, Jacob believed in his heart that both dreams were real dreams, and he was wondering about that. Dreams were held in significant regard, they meant something to him.

Nevertheless, his brothers had not forgotten this latest boast of their brother Joseph about the dreams, and assumed he wanted to be superior to them. They disliked him. He told on his brothers when they did something wrong. Their father liked him best. And so the brothers discussed their home situation again and again.

"Did Father not say to me, that we are all equally important to him?" said Naphtali. "Remember, way back when we were boys?"

"And now, Father loves Joseph more than any of us," mentioned Judah.

Then Gad (son of Zilpah) cut in, "Remember when I was guarding the sheep and was attacked by a band of raiders, and I chased and slew them? They could not withstand my fury. And Father did not give me any special reward? If I had been Joseph, yes..."

Then Issachar complained that "Father thinks I am lazy. Joseph just works hard to be Father's best son." However, Dan (son of Bilhah) who always tried to judge everyone and put things straight, laughed at Issachar and said, "Hey 'Issa' this one time Father was right. You do try to get away with things. If you get any fatter from eating and sitting around, you will..."

"Stop that, Dan, or you will get to feel my weight on you!" threatened Issachar.

"All right, all right, 'Issa' we are friends. We were talking about Joseph," said Dan, and retreated a few steps away from Issachar.

"Yes, he is from the love-wife, of course, what do you expect?" said Simeon. Their anger against Joseph was definite.

Joseph was honest, orderly and intelligent. Father Jacob could trust him.

Now, as they looked up, they saw a figure moving in the distance. They waited to see who or what it was. It was Joseph, of course. And he was wearing that colorful party gown! They did not get one, only Joseph had one, of course. Their envy and hatred mounted. "Now he is checking up on us again, that "..." and various curse words escaped from his brother's lips.

"Let us kill him," said Simeon. But he had said it too loud. Reuben, the oldest one, heard it. He told them:

"No, let us not kill him, and shed innocent blood, he is our brother. You don't do that to your brother, that would go too far. Just let us put him in that dry well." Rueben then thought to himself:

And afterwards, when they are sleeping, I will haul him out of the hole and send him home to Father, and give Joseph a severe warning.

With malicious eyes his brothers watched him come near to them in his fancy robe. Several ran to him, grabbed him; Joseph tried to get free, but they were stronger. They unceremoniously dumped him into the dirt cistern, that happened to be dry at the time. Joseph begged them.

"Please get me out of here, I won't do anything to you. Father sent me, he was afraid someone in Shechem might do something to you. He is concerned."

"Concerned? Father concerned about us? You liar."

It did do no good, they just left him down there. Reuben left because he had to go away to an errand. Reuben said to himself:

*Joseph should be safe in the dry well until I come back. After all, I am the oldest one and responsible. They wouldn't dare...*His brothers were really very angry. Reuben did not trust the safety of Joseph in their hands at all. But Reuben had to go for that errand and wanted to be back quickly. Joseph in the well was shocked. *How could they do that to me? I am their brother. What about my dreams? I rule over them? They are ruling over me instead. I know those dreams were true...*Joseph was upset, sitting in that dry well. He was getting thirsty and hungry. His brother Issachar threw a small chunk of bread down into the hole for him. Joseph caught it with his hands. He wanted some water, too. Issachar put a cup on a rope and lowered it down to Joseph.

"Babying along our perpetrator? Issachar?" asked Simeon.

"Well- don't forget we decided not to kill him," he answered.

In the meantime, a group of Midianite salespeople came past them with their camels and goods for sale and trade. The brothers went to them and showed them their prize: A young, strong, healthy man, caught down there in the dry well. The Midianites ordered them to pull him out. They did. They looked him over from all sides, and liked what they saw: Young, tall, slim, in perfect health, intelligent face, good teeth. They could earn a good piece of money for this slave.

"No, please, you cannot sell me. Father won't like that," Joseph lamented. But Simeon gave him a punch in the mouth that he bled.

It did not bother the salespeople. They were used to buying and selling slaves and the whining and complaining that went along with it.

"Yes, we will buy him, for twenty pieces of silver."

The brothers whispered to each other. They agreed it is better to sell Joseph as a slave than to kill him, because he is their brother, and they should not shed any blood. This was Judah's idea. "Agreed," answered Levi and Simeon, the spokesmen for the others. Joseph cried and begged them not to sell him, but it did no good. The money changed hands. The Midianites tied Joseph with ropes, tied him to a camel and walked off with him. The brothers felt good for the time being; their "smart" brother, who tried to be better than they, was gone.

They had not forgotten to take off his fancy robe before they sold him. Several of the brothers took that robe and put it on and imitated Joseph,

"Hey you, bow down to me, I am Joseph…haw, haw, haw." Then Dan and Naphtali insisted that since their mother had made that robe they should get it.

"No way," said Simeon, we divide it up equally, everyone gets a piece."

"Absolutely not," said Dan. "My mother worked on it so long, it is way too precious to rip it up. If you want it that much, keep it but leave it in one piece."

"Yeah, then we can all bow down to you, Dan," remarked Simeon. More laughter followed. Naphtali, tall and slim, quickly grabbed the robe and ran, Gad followed. They had their fun with it.

Even though Joseph was browned from the sun, his exposed skin would hurt from too much sun after sometime, but none of the merchants gave him a coat. That Joseph could freeze at night without his coat had it not bothered the brothers. They did not give him a replacement coat when they sent him off with the merchants. "Let the Midianites care for him," said the brothers to each other, while Joseph was being tied up with foot and hand chains and taken away.

At night, when Reuben came back to the campground, he walked over to the pit. Joseph was gone.

"Where is Joseph, the child, what happened to him?" he asked his brothers.

"We sold him for twenty pieces of silver to the Midianites; he won't bother us anymore. You want your share of the money?"

"You rascals, what have you done? How will we explain this to Father? Can't you ever be moderate? You always explode in extremism."

"No problem," said Judah. We will kill a goat, dip his fancy gown, which we kept, in its blood, send it to Father, and say a wild animal has killed him." They did just that.

Then they sent the youngest two, Naphtali (son of Bilhah) and Asher (son of Zilpah) home to their father. After about two days they arrived home. The two, with artificially maneuvered, innocent faces, showed Father Jacob the coat, and said, "Look Father, this we found, all bloody. Some animal must have killed the person wearing this gown. Could you find out whose it is?"

Jacob Israel recognized the gown; it was his son's. He let out an agonizing cry that vibrated across the campground. Bilhah came running. Dinah, Leah, and the servants watched from the distance.

Jacob cried out loud, "My son, my son, my son, Joseph is dead."

He then grabbed his outer gown at the neck and tore it apart and threw himself on the ground crying. Leah stood there, the woman in charge, what should she do? She walked over to her husband lying in the mud, for it had just started to rain. She gently put her hand on his shoulder and asked what this is all about. He pulled out from under him the bloody garment and pointed to his sons (the two standing there somewhat embarrassed), telling her that a wild animal has killed his son and his blood is all over the garment.

"May I see the garment, please?" asked Bilhah, and reached out her hand to take it. She had woven it and suggested she could wash it.

"No washing, no touching, all is out, all is over, all is for nothing," cried Jacob. "I will bury it with my joy and my hope gone."

Then Leah asked the two brothers a few more questions as to when it may have happened, and at what day Joseph had arrived at Shechem. They told them that they had left for Dothan, and Joseph never arrived there. Still Jacob lay on the ground crying with only his outer gown ripped open, not the undergarment. It was a custom in those days to show utter sorrow to rip open ones' outer garment and sit in ashes.

"Go away everybody," cried Jacob. "Leave me alone."

So everybody left the elderly man lying there in the mud. Then Leah told Asher and Naphtali to come inside, get some food and always go together for safety's sake, until they get back to their brothers. Naphtali and Asher took some food, but not too much. *We can buy some on the way.* They felt guilty and left as quickly as possible. They felt ashamed that their very own father is lying in the mud and crying like a baby. When Asher and Naphtali were out of sight and earshot of their parent's home, they laughed and slapped their hands together on how well they had performed, and nobody found out. When they returned to Dothan, the brothers asked them how it went.

They told them: "Father did not examine the gown of Joseph. Bilhah wanted to, and we were scared she would question us how an animal could remove a garment so well in one piece. We thought there for a moment, we would be found out and brainstormed for an excuse, but it was not necessary, all worked out well. Father and everyone believed us. Father would not let Bilhah examine the gown. We were off the hook."

"Serves him right," said Judah and Gad.

"Why does he have to love him more than us? He never gave us a party gown."

"And to think that my own mother wove it for him," added Dan. Then Issachar joined in and in his slow and careful way advised caution. He did not feel quite right about it. Reuben also was still upset. But the others urged them, now that they have concocted that lie, they all have to stick with it. It is done. And, no one must tell his respective wife either.

"And if you servants tell, we will kill you," threatened the brothers. The servants knew the brothers from past experience and were silent.

As time went on, the brothers started fighting about the Joseph case. Reuben criticized the others. Levi and Simeon, although hot-headed and impulsive, now had cooled down and found no other reason to be angry. Of course, they would not tell their wives at home either. This was their own private, dirty secret. They tried to make up being extremely organized and conscientious about their work now. Sometimes one or the other mentioned God and the extra connection that their father seemed to have to the Lord. Could the Lord up there in the heavens be angry at them?

"But he is not dead," they comforted each other. On the other hand, they were free individuals, and Joseph was now a slave, and no one knew what had happened to him, he could just be dead.

But sometimes when their young children asked about "dead" Uncle Joseph, the brothers felt guilty about having to lie again and again.

Jacob Israel kept a close watch on Benjamin now. He would not let him go far away anywhere alone. A brother or servant had to go with him for protection everywhere. Jacob heaped all his love on Benjamin, the last child from his wife Rachel. Benjamin did not like the overprotectiveness of his father, but he understood. He was also rather reckless and sly. The brothers did not mind anymore that Father heaped all his love on Benjamin now. They saw that the spirit of their father seemed broken after Joseph's disappearance. Their father, a robust man with energy and a keen eye for business, now often just sat around, doing nothing. Often Leah had to remind Jacob of sales and aquisitions that had to be made. She hated to be the driving force in the family, but they had to exist. Their sons were getting more careful in their work and tried to be good and more friendly while talking to their father. Their conscience bothered them.

The sons also saw that now, since Joseph's disappearance, they better be on guard about their own business and not rely on Father and Mother anymore. They became strict authoritarians to their servants and children.

More Teaching to Grandchildren

A number of years went by. Leah was getting tired more often, even if she had enough sleep. Sometimes she was tired of life itself, especially on very hot days and nights.

Her sons and the sons of the two secondary wives, Bilhah and Zilpah, also were married. She had many grandchildren to keep her busy, sometimes too busy. The grandchildren were a lot of fun to her because she was not wholly responsible for them. When the babies cried it was not her breasts anymore that had to silence them.

Jacob Israel tried to keep the grandchildren in the awareness of God. He told them the stories of their ancestors, how God had led their family, and what a unique family they were. Already the father of Abraham, Terah, did not want to live in Ur of Chaldaea anymore and moved. Jacob Israel told the children how God had called Abraham. He told them that Abraham did not know exactly where he was to go, but then God revealed to him by and by what he had to do. Jacob told them what his father Isaac had told him, how the people in Haran were astonished that he would pack up everything he had and just move because a God, whom they could not see, would say "move." He told them that going the way of God is always good and right even if in the beginning it appears senseless. Besides, Abraham had heard God's voice with his ears. He was clear on that. Jacob Israel further told and retold the happenings in the Garden of Eden about the first people on earth. He told them how a snake-like serpent told Eve she would get smart if she picked the forbidden fruit.

"And did she get smart?" interjected one of the grandchildren.

"No, not really. The only thing she and Adam learned was the difference between good and bad."

Then another grandson with a triumphant face pointed to his sister and said:

"Yes, and that is why I am the boss, and all men are bosses and all girls and women have to obey us."

But his sister would not succumb to his boasting and gave him a powerful punch.

Now grandfather Jacob had to interfere again.

"Children, children, no fighting. Have you forgotten what I just said before that God's ways are always good and right? Women have the ability to make babies, men don't. Women have to stay around the house and take

207

care of them, while we men go out and hunt animals and tame the camels and do all the physically harder work. Everyone has to do something. Men do some things and women do other things that men don't."

Peace came over the group of his young grandchildren again. The girls became proud that someday they can have babies, and the boys were proud that they will be the great famous hunters, entrusted with the honor of protecting their families.

Leah, even though now old and tired, taught her granddaughters all the womanly things that girls had to know. And when a mother had given her little daughter a spanking, they would then run to old grandmother Leah. She would take them in her arms and comfort them.

~~~

The loss of their boy Joseph never left the memory of Jacob and Leah's mind. Bilhah missed him also, since he was the son of her mistress. Jacob and Leah kept the parchments from Joseph safely hidden in his earthenware jars, away from flies, and other bugs and moisture. They were very sacred to Jacob.

Every time someone mentioned Joseph, Jacob started crying, took his walking cane and left the tent. Jacob could not understand how his God could let this happen to him, losing his son to wild animals. His sons were also rather somber and subdued, as if the spark of their life was missing since Joseph's sale. Leah thought her boys finally had grown up and realized life's seriousness. Neither Leah, nor Jacob Israel, could understand why their sons never laughed again with them. The sons, in turn, thought their father had become uninterested in life, buying, selling, dealing and planning since the loss of Joseph. He took it harder then they had thought.

Hezron and Shoshanah

It was late afternoon, the sun was lowering in the west and too dark for Leah's old eyes to do sewing, so she thought she may as well go look at the brook. She hiked over the short distance and sat down under a tree. She loved to watch the water spill over rocks and create eddies. Occasionally she would see a little fish glide by. As she sat under that tree surrounded by bushes she heard sounds. Lovely singing voices. Leah sat very still and listened to a young man's and a young girl's voices. Sometimes they sang together in harmony, sometimes in solo and then coming together again. Leah stood up and quietly, as not to startle them, walked closer to hear and see more. They were two of her grandchildren, but she did not know which ones, because she was rather near-sighted. They sang about raindrops, love and romance:

Raindrops, raindrops, lovely raindrops,
Oh, how my eyes are searching for you.
River floweth into the deep sea,
Raindrops, raindrops, make it full.

Raindrops, raindrops, lovely raindrops,
Wet my hair and that of my love.
River floweth into the deep sea,
Raindrops, raindrops, make it full.

As our God sends rain to the parched land,
So your love sheds raindrops on me.
River floweth into the deep sea,
Raindrops, raindrops, make it full.

As the raindrops joining the river,
So our lips will join in our love…

Then Leah saw them embracing each other and kissing, their lips touching a long time. Then she saw the two laying down in the grass together and more kissing.

"Hold it, stop!" she exclaimed. The two young people were surprised and shocked and jumped up. Now Leah walked closer. She saw they were

Hezron (whose father was Perez), Judah's grandson and the girl was Shoshanah, the granddaughter of Levi from his son Kohath.

"We weren't doing anything bad, grandmother, we just sang and got tired standing up."

"Yes, kids, but we don't do that. It is not a custom in our orderly family to lay together before marriage. Good thing I saw you. Besides, what will your future husband say when he hears about this, Shoshanah?"

"Future husband? Grandmother? I don't want a future husband, I want Hezron and no one else."

"And I want no other woman, I want Shoshanah and no one else," replied Hezron.

"You know the father determines who marries whom. Besides, you two are much too young. Don't you know that birds don't lay eggs until they have a nest? Don't you know that foxes first dig a den before they have puppies? What do you have? Nothing!"

"We have our love, we love each other until death. Love finds a way," said Hezron.

"And if I am not given to Hezron," replied Shoshanah, "I shall jump from a high cliff and kill myself."

"Me too," said Hezron.

A deep sigh escaped Leah. "You two children are talking foolishly, you would just end up in darkness with the Evil Snake. Very scary!

"But, all right, children, I will talk to your fathers about it. However, you in turn must do your duty and stay apart. Or else your parent's belts will make so many welts on your behinds you won't know how to sleep at night," warned Leah.

"Also, next time grandfather has a sacrificing, you two sing a Jehovah song for all to hear. Maybe grandfather will grant your wish. Music seems to touch him. He can never forget his Joseph."

"We will, we will, grandmother," promised the two.

Both young people embraced Leah and told her how good it is to have someone sticking to their side.

Then Leah whispered something into Shoshanah's ear and searched her face.

"No, grandmother, we have not."

"Good, good, I came just in time."

Leah walked home again and sat down on a large stone near her tent. The stone was warm from the afternoon sun.

So, I am still good for something, watching over the young ones.

Then Shoshanah came by and told her not to tell mother that "we were…deep kissing."

"Please, grandmother?"

"All right, children, but remember what I said to you. And practice your singing around the common court grounds, not behind the bushes. Don't forget to make a song for the Lord Jehovah how great He is."

"We will, Grandmother, we will," promised Hezron.

~~~

Later Leah thought again about her life. It had been hard and lovely, both. Hard was the work, hard the coolness of her husband, but lovely were the children and all the joy they brought into her life. It was also good that she was married off. She had not enjoyed being an unwanted girl, it felt so shameful. She had felt so dejected. And then her father married her off. Was she happier being married without love and romance or would she have been happier staying single? No, single was not her piece of 'raisin cake.' This was much better. She was grateful to the Lord, for in the end He had made everything well. A lot of fights could have been avoided had her husband stayed with one wife. That was the bad thing in her and the other women's lives.

Leah was grateful also, for when she was very sad, she could go to a quiet place and talk to the Lord, and afterwards felt protected like a dove sheltered in the cleft of a rock when a heavy thunderstorm strikes. Somehow the Lord's presence comforted her even if she did not hear his voice nor see his face.

What would her death look like? How would it be after death? She did not know. Her husband believed that death would not be the end of people. The Hero that will kill the Evil Snake, someday, as the Lord had said in the Garden of Eden, will be hurt himself. However, since that Hero is of God, somehow he could not die or he would be resurrected again and that, in turn, will have consequences for people. Also, ancestor Enoch spoke of a judgment or reckoning. So Leah figured that death is not the end, there is more...Leah was hoping to see the Lord someday. Jacob and others had heard his voice. That means He is living. But where? It must be high up in the sky, higher than the Tower of Babel, higher than the stars. Leah could not quite understand it all. But she knew there is an answer to it. Sometimes she watched the heavens and the stars looked like windows into heaven, but otherwise they were unrevealing. Jacob told her just to trust the Lord, that is all we can do, and do what He told us to do for now.

Now it became dark outside and cool. The sun sank golden in the direction of the great water where the ships were sailing. She had never seen that great water but others had told her about it. She hoped that one day her husband would drive the cattle close to the great western sea so she could taste and smell it. However, he told her there is no grass there, it's all built up with houses, stores, and boat landings.

Leah went inside and put a large wool scarf around her shoulders for warmth. It was almost time to prepare something to eat. She looked to see if Zilpah needed any help. Zilpah was reliable.

Leah smelled fish being fried. Zilpah had started supper already.

The fish came from the great lake to the rising of the sun, called Lake Kinnereth. They were camping near it. It was a beautiful area, with gently sloping hills to the water's edge. Fishermen were fishing there. Her husband had bought some fish. Also, her sons and grandsons tried their hand at fishing. They were cattle people and fishing was rather new to them. At first the young grandsons did not catch any. Then one friendly fisherman told the boys that they have to adjust the lure to the fish: A large fish wants a large lure, a smaller fish a smaller lure. Some fish like to swim in shady waters near the edge by trees, others prefer the open water. The boys were all excited when they caught a fish and yelled.

"Dad, Mom, I caught something." However, immediately no fish were around.

"Sh, sh," said the friendly fisherman, "you are scaring them away. Now sit very quietly for a long time. Can you do that?" Some boys could, others preferred to leave and play.

"Well, here comes our fisherman," said grandfather Jacob. "Let's see what you caught."

"Nothing."

"Nothing, Amos?"

"The fish all swam away."

"Go back, my boy, and learn to fish, now go…" encouraged grandfather Jacob. So Amos had to go back and try again, very quietly this time.

The Wadi and Sodom

When the grass was grazed off near Lake Kinnereth it was time to move on, south, way south. Jacob preferred to skip the area in the center of the country this time and drive the cattle near the Dead Sea. Jacob had the herds stop southwest of the large salt lake, called Dead Sea. The land was drier there, for it had not rained for awhile. However, in the lower laying places grass still grew. There were also wadis (dry riverbeds). Leah's tent was set up near the edge of a wadi. The grandchildren played down in the wadi with rocks and had fun.

Some of the grandchildren heard of the salty Dead Sea. Since their tents were west of it and not too far away, their parents allowed them to hike over to test the waters. They took skins with drinking water along. The land was rocky and getting hotter the closer they came to the Dead Sea. Finally, they saw the large lake down below. They carefully climbed down towards it. The ground was hot from the sunshine, but they wore sandals. Now they would see how an object could swim in that salty brine. They threw some broken clay shards into the water. They swam. It was very exciting to them. They tasted the water, but they spit it out immediately. It tasted terrible, absolutely salty. Whoever had tasted it drew a quick mouthful of drinking water from his water skin to rinse his mouth.

When they came back to the homestead, the children were all curious as to why the Lord had turned the good water to salt. They asked their parents. "Go, ask grandfather," they were told. They promptly walked over to grandfather Jacob and a young boy asked the question. Jacob Israel hesitated as he looked at the boy.

"How old are you, my boy?"

"I am ten and in the next rainy season I will be eleven; I am big and we want to know what the people in Sodom did that their town became a salty lake. Dad said you would know."

"Well," said grandfather Jacob, "that is difficult to explain to you."

"No, Grandfather, we want to know," chirped a few other grandchildren. "Tell us."

With a deep sigh old grandfather Jacob hesitantly and rather diminutively started:

"Your grand-uncle Lot had two visitors, men, who stayed overnight in his house. The men from Sodom had seen them go into Uncle Lot's house. They wanted to steal their clothes away and catch them without, and bother them and maybe even kill them. But the two visitors were no mere men, they were angels of God; they looked just like men. Angels cannot be hurt by humans, you know. So the angels made the door disappear from the house of Uncle Lot. The evil men could not find the door to get in. The angels also told Uncle Lot and his wife and two daughters to get out of that town; the Lord will punish all those evil people and will kill them. Uncle Lot and Aunt Gira, his wife, were slow in packing. Finally, toward morning the angels had convinced Uncle Lot to leave right now. They left with their bundles of clothes and money. They were not supposed to turn around and look as to what would happen to Sodom and Gomorrah. However, his wife felt so sorry to leave her nice home, good garments, furniture and linens. She had a beautiful ceramic pot, a real piece of art. She stuffed her jewelry and her new roll of silken cloth in it to take along. The four of them now hurried out of Sodom. Aunt Gira was muttering all the time how senseless it is to leave everything just so, and run, just because two men, that supposedly were angels, told them so. However, her husband and her girls left the city, so she ran along with them. Father Lot ran first, then his two daughters and the mother ran at the end. The clay pot was getting heavier for her all the time until she thought she could not continue on. 'Help' she called.

'Drop it,' said Lot, 'we have to get out of here fast. The angels said we should hurry and run.'

'Mom,' cried one of the girls, 'maybe I can help you carry some stuff?'

'Don't you dare,' yelled their father. 'Run, run, don't look back, hurry!'

"So they kept running. They did not hear their mother's footsteps anymore, but kept running. Suddenly they heard a loud scream from behind them, it was their mother's voice, 'Aieeeee!'

'Run, run,' called their father Lot, 'don't look around.'

"Finally, Uncle Lot saw a dark cave in the mountainside," so continued grandfather Jacob, while his grandchildren listened with rapt attention. "They climbed up and ran right into it. They did not even check if there was a bear or anything in it. They just plopped on the ground exhausted."

'But, Father, where is Mother?' asked the girls.

'I guess she did not make it.'

"Then Uncle Lot's eyes got all watery when he realized that he had lost his wife, never to see her again. He wiped his eyes with his sleeves. 'Can we look out of the cave now, Father?' "

'No, absolutely not. Just rest here for awhile. Be sure to mind God's rules, girls. You see, God can be very strict.'

"Lot's wife did not obey the angels and turned around and looked back. Immediately her body turned into a salty stone pillar. There is a slim tall rock further west, that's her."

"If Great-uncle Lot did not look, how do we know about it?"

"Good question, my boy. Your great-grandfather Abraham was on a hill in the distance and saw the fire come down from heaven and burn everything up. And all because the men of Sodom were so evil." Then the boys and girls all fell silent and thought about that disaster that killed Uncle Lot's wife and the people of Sodom and Gomorrah. Then one boy looked at his grandfather and assured him, "We won't do that, Grandfather. We won't try to steal men's clothes and bug them."

"Right, children, then the Lord will be pleased with you," answered Jacob Israel. He was glad that his young grandchildren accepted this short answer for now. He did not want to explain the evil of homosexuality to them at this age.

After several weeks Jacob looked northwest. It looked like rain. He liked that. And then the sky turned dark and darker, the clouds became really black. Leah also saw the blackening sky. It meant west/northwest of them was a thunderstorm going down. Now Jacob heard the thunder and lightning and getting closer.

Then they heard an ominous sound like a distant waterfall. Jacob knew what it was: A rush of water. Jacob shouted to the servants and to all:

"Get the sheep out of the wadi! Fast, fast!"

The servants had also seen the black sky. All frantically ran and yelled at the sheep and used their long shepherd staffs to push them out fast. The goats were smarter and had escaped to higher ground on their own. The cows were also moving up the wadi slopes. Animals sometimes can sense when danger threatens and try to escape. The sheep were not as smart, they needed pushing.

Leah also quickly ran and pulled in her laundry from the outside. She and the young mothers yelled at their children to come in. But sometimes, childern don't want to obey immediately. Suddenly a roaring wall of water rushed down the wadi toward them. Leah saw two little boys that were still down in the wadi riverbed, the water rolling toward them. She forgot that she was old, just ran and jumped toward them right into the water up to her waist, grabbed the boys and held on to them with an iron grip and managed to pull them up on high ground. Just in time. The little boys coughed and spitted and screamed, but they were safe now. A lesson learned.

Leah breathed a prayer of thanks to the Lord. The mothers of the two boys ran through the pouring rain toward the wadi, screaming the names of their children that they found missing. Then Leah showed them the crying boys at the door of her tent. How happy they were!

"Thank you, thank you, mother-in-law." They trotted off with them going home to their tents, slowly. No use running, they were all soaking wet by now from the first rain drops. Now Leah had to change to dry clothes. Her health was not as stable anymore. She hoped she would not get sick. Dinah put some more dry sticks on the clay hearth for a bigger fire to warm up her mother.

Upstream a heavy thunder-and rainstorm had come down, the water could not penetrate into the dry ground fast enough and rushed down the dry riverbeds, turning them into raging streams. The children watched in awe as the rain now started pelting down on their tents, like a band of drummers gone mad. It was so loud they could not understand their words. Father Jacob checked the ropes of the tent on all posts, making sure the wind won't wreck them. But Leah, after changing clothes, her heart beat so fast, she had to keep walking around to walk off her excessively spent energy or die of a heart attack. That sudden cold bath had been too much for her. After awhile she wrapped herself into a woolen blanket and went to bed. Dinah made her a cup of hot tea with special herbs.

The rescued sheep stood close together, the little lambs nudging close to their ewes. Brown water cascaded down into the wadi running downhill to the south. Some sons of Jacob threw their upper garments into a tent, ran out into the pouring rain and Simeon guided them to roll rocks into the stream further down to stop the water and create a quick pond for later use. Water was a precious commodity.

Only one sheep was seen being taken away by the water. Reuben jumped on a camel and in the pouring rain went after the rushing currents to see if the waves may have spilled the sheep on low rocks. Perhaps it could be located and saved. After awhile of seeking, Reuben spotted what was left of the sheep, and in the distance he saw a young lion running away with the other part of the sheep in its mouth. It was too late.

When the cloudburst was over, the children ran outside and started throwing mudballs at each other. A little guy was hit in the face and screamed. Then the mothers heard it and ran after their boys and ordered them to wash themselves clean. They said:

"Don't you ever throw mudballs again, one could get his eye knocked out."

"I didn't do it," said Moshe, "it was Sapha."

Then Sapha received a few slaps on his behind from his mother for hurting the toddler. But in general, the children had fun watching the water and the mud and playing in it.

The rain was wonderful for the grasses and plants. Everything grew so fast and the people were happy. The cattle grazed and got fat.

Eventually, Jacob saw it was necessary to move to new grazing grounds again. This time they moved southwest. There was a good river flowing westward to the great sea. Then there was also a shady forest for pitching their tents in. Jacob told his family that this forest was planted by his grandfather Abraham, called the Hain Mamre in Beer-she-ba. He also planted a special terebinth tree that was fully grown by now. Abraham would preach in this place and call upon the name of the everlasting God. The people who lived in that area were called Philistines. They heard about Abraham's preaching also. However, they were not very easily convinced about the real God. With their made-up gods they could do what they wanted; truth to them was of secondary importance.

Father Jacob warned his sons and grandchildren to be careful and not pick any fights with the locals. "Remember what happened in Shechem, how we had to leave for our own safety, and leave that comfortable house."

Leah liked the Hain Mamre and the beautiful shade. So she took some of her grandchildren along for tree hunting. They found several saplings, one for each child. They dug them up, put them in claypots with water and carried them to the Hain Mamre.

Then they carefully planted the saplings on the outskirts of the forest to expand it. Each child had to water his own tree and keep it growing. They also broke off small branches and made a cone fence around the young saplings so no rabbit or dear would bite off the young little trees. Tree planting was fun to them.

"And when we move again and come back here in so many years, your little trees should be tall. You will see. If we need lumber, we can just cut down a tree, thanks to great-grandfather Abraham," Leah explained. "Every time we cut a tree, we plant a new one."

The Drought

Nothing of particular interest followed, just the usual care of cattle and moving when the time came.

The children of the Jacob Israel clan had multiplied. Their life was not all labor and sweat. They also made youth fun and dancing festivals. Father Judah had become a good harp player. Old Leah had been able to convince the men that Shoshanah and Hezron should be married together. They just loved each other too much. It would become a bad marriage if she was ripped away from Hezron and given to the man her father had chosen when she was a little girl. Shoshanah and Hezron were also good singers. They sang together. Hezron also played a flute to youth dances and family gatherings. Some of the songs they had made told about God and his love and mercy. Another song talked about the Lord punishing evildoers. When that particular song was sung, they would beat the drums fast and hard. Hezron would put intensity into those lyrics and moved his arms up and down, with his fists imitating a smashing hammer. The listeners would get goose-pimples when they saw Hezron and cousin Libni perform this. They liked the feeling of being emotionally aroused and sometimes tried to jump and dance along, wild and hectically. However, great-grandfather Jacob remembered the idol dances that the local people did, jumping around some man-made god. When he saw some young folks were getting too wild, he would blow his whistle to tune things down. The evening with a festival would always pass too soon for the young people. Then old father Jacob would blow his whistle again - "Time to go home and get some rest," before a new day with new duties.

Then followed a rather dry year. There were two rainy seasons in that land: a spring rain and a late rain. The spring rain did come but less than in other years. Therefore, the meadows and plants were not as plentiful as before. The late rains did not come at all. Everyone looked at the sky. They were outdoors' people and could tell the weather by studying the clouds and the winds. Sometimes it looked as if it would rain, then the wind came up from the desert from the far east and chased all rainclouds away. All women and shepherds had to be extremely careful with their fires now. A forest or meadow fire would be devastating. The grass was drying up. How was Jacob Israel supposed to feed his cattle? So he told his sons to sell some cows, sheep and goats. The camels would hold out longer; they could take dry weather better than the other animals.

Leah's garden would not grow properly. She took a pail and walked to the nearest brook and watered. The children and daughers-in-law also helped. Vegetables could not be purchased. City people were also in need. People were often in bad moods and fighting was everywhere because of heat and drought. Jacob Israel had to interfere often to monitor his grandchildren as well as his sons and their neighbors. Still the sun shone from the sky bright and strong and hot. Life was hard and the nights brought little comfort.

Jacob mounted a camel and rode northward to check out if they should move their herds and tents. However, the people there also told them that further on it is just as dry as here. So Jacob Israel decided to stay near the brook, a little water is better than none. Also, Leah and the women did not want to move before the harvest of their vegetables, few of them are better than leaving everything behind. So they stayed.

Leah could not produce the fresh spinach and other vegetables properly, and there were so many grandchildren that needed it also. Leah sometimes sacrificed some greenery for her children or grandchildren or pregnant daughers-in-law. After sometime her stomach gave her trouble and her digestion was not good anymore. She often felt sick. She always wished for a green salad, a pomegranate, some oranges. Leah still had some pickled caperfruit sitting in olive oil and vinegar which helped to make foods tasty, but the greenery was missing. Oranges were especially hard to find. Other people were hunting for fresh fruit and vegetables also, near rivers and brooks. Whoever got there first picked them first. Then people would hide their almost ripe orange or two in their pocket so no one would try to take it from them, if they managed to get it before someone else got it first. Jacob's family took water from the brook that became shallower and shallower. Everyone was worried what was to become of them. Finally winter came and with it cooler temperatures. Now the drought was easier to endure. Jacob Israel and his sons still had some grain left for their food, but now it was rationed. No one was allowed to sneak into the food stash and help himself. It was a hard winter even though there was hardly any snow in that region. There was an elderly couple in a local village. They had only one unmarried son, who had gone on a trip. When he returned and entered the home, both parents were dead. Neighbors were shocked when they heard about it. There was no water in their drinking bucket and on the cold stove he found ashes only. That one cold night with light frost must have done them in. Extra blankets lay folded on a shelf. They must have died of the cold in their sleep.

Then finally, the next year a spring rain came again. Everyone was elated. The daughters-in-law quickly broke up the dry ground and inserted seeds into the earth and covered them up with loose sticks and branches. They wanted to keep birds away from their vegetable patches. Now the rivers and brooks carried more water again. It was so beautiful, this spring rain. Children opened their mouths and tried to catch some raindrops.—But then the rains stopped. The plants stopped growing. Everyone started checking out the sky again. Now they had to go to the rivers and brooks again to fetch water for their plants. There were also more insects on the plants now. The plants with their slow growth could not very well outgrow the bug infestation. The older children had to chase rabbits away day and night to save their vegetable patches. Bigger boys had to sleep outside to guard their vegetables. They picked thorns and thistles and made tight fences around them so that other animals would not eat their meager plants. Later on there was another rain, but again, not as much as was needed.

Dinah

Jacob Israel decided that he had too many servants to feed and still too many animals to take care of in this drought. So he sold more cattle. He also let go of a number of servants.

There was Dishon, the servant. He still secretly loved his master's daughter Dinah. Jacob Israel gave Dishon a long look and asked him where his family comes from and if he thinks his father is still alive. Dishon told Jacob that he comes from the Lebanon area, closer to the ocean. He told him that in his homeland are many forests and that sometimes where there are a lot of forests there is more rain. Dishon knew what Jacob was thinking, that he would be let go now. He figured, *What does it matter if my request is preposterous? I, a servant, making a request from the master? I will now be sent away anyhow, what does it matter if I appear out of order?* Then Dishon deeply bowed before Jacob and told him of his love for his daughter Dinah. He showed Jacob Israel his silver coins (the ones he had won in a game) and tried to use them as bride price, if Jacob would give her to him. Dishon knew those few coins were not enough but since the times were bad he had nothing to lose. Jacob was totally surprised. He looked up and down on Dishon, *What a nerve that fellow has! Is he serious?* He smiled and told him to wait. Then Jacob took his cane and walked over to Leah's tent and told her about this. Then Leah remembered her daugher mentioning her love for Dishon a long time ago. She was surprised too. She sat down on a little stool and thought for awhile.

"Yes," she told her husband, "the times are so hard, and the fields so dry, and no one of means asked for her daughter's hand as yet who was acceptable to Dinah."

Leah further said to her husband, "Dinah is much too choosy for her own good. Maybe she should marry that man, even if he is only a servant. Besides, Dinah is getting older, and marriage would be the best for her future."

"However, I would suggest not to take his silver coins as bride price if that is all he has. Let him keep those few coins and move away from here, to Lebanon where Dishon said his family is living. Instead, add something to their trip. I will bake her some bread. Why not give her a camel or a goat, so they have enough to start a household? Who knows, maybe in Lebanon is more rain. We don't want our only daughter to go there bare and poor."

Jacob thought that was good advice. He went over to Dishon and announced:

"Yes, you can have Dinah."

Dishon bent down before Jacob and thanked him and gave him his silver coins.

"No, keep them, Dishon. Go home to your family and use the coins for a new livelihood. I will also give you a camel and some provisions. And treat my daughter well, the Lord will see you." Then he called Dinah. She had been watering the garden.

"Dinah, I decided you can marry Dishon and move away from this dry land." Dinah was so surprised and happy, her whole face lit up like a candle in the darkness. She stepped inside where Dishon and her mother were standing.

Then Jacob Israel laid his right hand on Dinah's head and his left on Dishon's and said:

"Follow Dishon and be a good wife to him. And may you have many children that believe in the real God of Abraham, Isaac and my God Jahweh, and may our families in later years always be friends with my people."

Dishon bent down deeply before Jacob. Jacob blessed him and let him go. Dinah was so happy, tears came out of her eyes and she wiped them with her sleeve. She embraced her father and thanked him.

"I like a love-marriage. My good father!"

She kissed Leah and gave her a hug also. Leah quickly put a few necessary items together that a wife would need, such as a large leather needle, a spindle, an extra copper cooking pot with some clay dishes inside and a blanket. Leah felt Dinah worked long and faithfully at home, she deserves something as a dowry. She then packed it all up in skins. Zilpah was already working on some bread dough for their travel. It would take hours to finish the bread. She stirred the dough well, kneaded it carefully to make sure the sour dough would rise properly. With all the sudden excitement Zilpah wanted Leah and Dishon to have good bread on their trip. Jacob Israel handed Dishon a new watering skin from his stash and Dishon immediately walked to the little brook to fill it up for the next morning.

Then at night, the sons heard about their sister having been given to Dishon. They were upset that they had not been asked first. They considered it their right. They came to their father and wanted to have a word with him.

"What is it, my sons?"

"You are giving our sister to a servant? Father? Is that so?"

"Yes, my sons, they make a good pair, and they will move away from here. I gave them a dowry also and nothing that you say will change anything. This is my command. Now, leave me alone."

The sons shook their heads and left.

"Father is getting old, but so stubborn."

"Let them go, the fewer people we have, the more food is left for us," said Issachar. Eating well and resting was his specialty.

"Yes, brothers, since Joseph is gone, Father…"

"Don't you start that again," countered Simeon. It was mostly Judah's idea." Judah was ready to blame Simeon but Reuben interfered.

"We have to keep peace and have to keep a normal face about this. Now, go and do your jobs. Fighting will change nothing."

The sons had peace with father since Joseph was gone but it seemed the blessing and the joy were also gone.

Dishon and Dinah were given an old tent to spend their first night together in it.

The next morning before sunrise, Dishon and Dinah arose to leave the campground. Leah was sad, now her only daughter is leaving. *I am so used to her. Dinah was always friendly to me. She never gave me a bad word. But on the other hand, staying here in that drought is no way to live. So, may they go and find a better livelihood.* She wiped a few tears from her eyes. Leah held her daughter in a long embrace. She had the feeling that she would never see Dinah again. A lump seemed to form in the back of her throat, but she wanted to be brave, and tried hard to make a happy face. Dishon and Dinah then loaded the camel with their few possessions. Jacob and some servants that were up already watched them. The camel Father had given Dinah was old and walked wobbly, but that way no robbers would want to take it from them. Dishon saw the good in everything, even an old camel. They looked happy. Dinah already had said her farewells to Zilpah and the other maids, the sisters-in-law, nephews and nieces and her brothers the night before. All the people stood watching as the two left with an old camel loaded full of bundles and bags, and the very important brand-new water bag. With their spirits high and with confident minds, Dishon and Dinah left the homestead. Father Jacob called a "May the Lord protect you on the long trip" after them. Dinah was glad about that, they needed some good luck. Just then, the sun arose in the east. It was a pale sun, promising no rain. The brothers still shook their heads.

"This marriage did not enrich our family. He gives her away like a poor man would. Strange, very strange!"

Then the couple turned a corner and disappeared behind a hill, leaving a dust cloud behind. They were gone. The place looked so empty and forlorn to Leah and Jacob. Leah leaned on Jacob for a good cry, but Jacob said, "Come on, come on, don't be so sentimental."

Won't Jacob, ever change? He is as cold and hard as Mount Arrarat. And my mother—if I could go to her—, oh my mother, she is dead and gone too, the spot of her grave won't comfort me either. Leah felt as if all sorrows of the world would crash down on her just this moment. Leah went into her tent, laid down on her bed and cried alone, long and hard. She loved her daughter. Some grandchildren wanted to go in and comfort Leah, but their mothers told them to leave grandmother alone, she needs time to grieve. When Leah's eyes had no more tears left, she arose from her bed, wiped her face and went outside.

"Grandmother, grandmother, I love you," exclaimed a couple of little girls and embraced her.

"Yes, children, I love you, too."

Suddenly, there was a noise and a breaking sound of clay dishes. A small grandson had accidentally knocked them over. As fast as his little legs could carry him he raced away and hid in his mother's tent under the blankets.

"Oh, oh, what are we going to do? I gave Dinah some of my dishes. But we will somehow manage. Maybe Issachar's wife has some extra ones. We cannot make new ones right now."

Zilpah's father had been an earthenware worker, a potter. He would take clay and form beautiful clay pots, water pitchers and bowls. Zilpah had often watched him as a child. Now and then, when she had time, Zilpah also worked clay and formed containers. But now, with all that drought, she could not use water to mix clay. All water was needed for drinking, cooking, watering gardens and cattle. It was really sad how all the people looked at the bright sky that did not produce a single raincloud.

Jacob had to sell more cattle and let go of more servants. The servants all went away to Lebanon and other areas. Jacob lost track of them.

Jacob used to have a lot of servants before his sons were grown. Now he counted his people that were left, they were 74, including all his sons, their wives, the children and servants. *Still a lot of people to be responsible for in this drought. But my Lord had helped so far, he will help in the future.*

He talked things over with Leah. She suggested he should talk to people and listen if there is an area that still has rain and grain. Maybe in another country. "The boys should get busy and look around," Leah said to Jacob.

"Did not your father Isaac say one has to do right in every situation and then you have the shining light that shineth more and more unto the perfect day?"

"That means we just have to do what we can and leave the rest up to the Almighty. He holds rainclouds in His hands."

"Yes, Leah, that I will do." Then Jacob called for his sons and told them the plans that Leah and he had made for them: To go to Egypt and find out if there really is grain." Someone had mentioned it to him. The sons looked at him doubtfully.

"Yes, boys, go ahead, make the trip and get going. We need food."

They then sat together at night and made plans. Such a long trip needed preparation. They would take donkeys, not camels. That way they would look more humble. It might help. Father would give them money. They would all go together as a group except young Benjamin. They did not want to "baby" him along; Father would worry too much. They also discussed the route and drew lines in the dirt with sticks were they would travel. In a few days they will leave.

A small granddaughter by the name of Anna (whose father was Asher) was excited about her father and the uncles taking a big trip. She asked her grandmother one question after another: about Egypt and the trip, as well as the mighty king Pharaoh there. Then she switched to the great hero-to-come, the snake killer. "Will he bring food? What will his name be? Will he like me? When will he come? Is my dress pretty enough to receive him when he comes? What will you and grandfather say to him when he comes?"

"Oh, little Anna, I am an old woman now," explained Leah, "I am sure, I will have departed this life by then. But, if you are nice and God-fearing, maybe you will see him. Or maybe one of your daughters-to-be will see him."

Then her father Asher cut in and told her not to bother grandmother with so many questions and concentrate more on the 'here and now'. "How is your weaving coming along? I see your loom sits idle."

Oh, Asher," replied Leah, "let her talk. The hero will come, definitely, he will, and maybe Anna will see him. If she seeks him, she will find him. You too, Asher."

Then Leah rested on her pallet for a while and little Anna ran happily to her loom to weave some more.

Leah Goes Home

Their mother Leah still did not feel good. Often her head felt hot. She did not remember feeling that way when she was young. Also, the wish for green leaves and precious fruit was always there in her mind. Issachar even promised to bring her an orange or two from Egypt, if they have any.

Then one morning Leah did not get up. Jacob waited for breakfast. Zilpah tried to step in and fixed him food. Then Jacob told Zilpah to go and take a look at his wife what might be ailing her. She did not usually oversleep so long.

Zilpah went into Leah's part of the tent. Leah lay on her back and just stared ahead and did not move at all. She called Jacob. Jacob took his cane and walked to Leah's bed. There she lay, very still. He talked to her, "Leah, my wife, speak to me!"

Leah moved her one hand, but no sound came out of her mouth.

"Maybe she is thirsty," suggested Jacob, "give her something to drink."

Then Zilpah got a cup of water, she put a rolled-up blanket under Leah's head so as to be higher. She but the cup to Leah's mouth and poured some water into her. But Leah almost choked. Zilpah quickly slapped her on the back. She did not know what to do.

"Let it go, Zilpah," said Jacob, "maybe she needs more rest."

Then Zilpah called the granddaughter Shoshanah and told her, she has the honor of watching over her grandmother, so no mouse, rat, fly or bee would bother her. Shoshanah grabbed a feather fan, sat down next to her grandmother and fanned her. Zilpah then took over the household and told everybody what had happened to grandmother Leah.

All the grandchildren and daughers-in-law came over immediately and stood around her bed. Many took her hand. Leah pressed their hand to show them she is alive, but she could not talk. Time and again Zilpah tried to force water into her mouth, and Leah did not drink. Then Zilpah just wiped her lips with water, that was the least she could do for her. The sun was up and another dry day had started. The sons came home from the fields to see their still and silent mother. They kissed her but could not help her either. Then Zilpah took a piece of straw, cut it to size and tried to make Leah drink from the straw. It did not work. Everyone was silent or whispered only. They felt this was the beginning of the end for their mother and grandmother. The great-grandchildren played outside and were hushed up to be silent. It went like this all day and night. Then came another hot morning. Jacob urged Zilpah to try and try again to give Leah some water or food, but she just could not swallow. In fact, it looked as if she would choke on it every time. Then Zilpah wetted a cloth and wiped her dry lips and tongue, and Leah's face also, to make her more comfortable.

Then the next morning Leah did not stir. Jacob took her hand and expected her to press his hand as she had done the day before, but Leah did not respond. A tear worked itself out of his eye. He was not as devasteted as when his Rachel had died, because Leah was old and old people do die. Still, his life would be lonely.

Then, in the evening of that third day, when nobody else was in the tent except Zilpah, she saw Leah's body make a jerk-like movement and her lips moved, her eyes went to the tent ceiling and she suddenly spoke.

"Judah, Judah, your offspring, The Hero...I see him," and Leah's face looked as if a light shone on it, in that dark tent. Zilpah quickly turned her head up but there was no light or anything at the tent ceiling.

Then Leah's head fell to the side and Leah was no more. Zilpah quickly called Jacob. Jacob saw Leah had departed this life and had gone to her resting place, wherever the dead go that had hoped and believed in The Hero, the snake killer, the one God would send.

Zilpah told Master Jacob Israel the last words Leah had said. She had to repeat them to him twice, and Jacob pondered them in his heart.

All the maids and daughters-in-law started the death wail that was customary when someone had died.

Now the funeral had to be prepared. It was a great funeral, worthy of the first wife of a rich man. A caravan was prepared. Leah's body was wrapped in spices and linens. All the family members turned their cattle over to servants to be free for the pilgrimage towards the town of Mamre, in the land of Canaan, to the field and the cave of Machpelah, the family burying ground. Her sons cried after her, they had loved their mother.

Zilpah walked straight and tall, knowing that now the master will take her as his main woman and not Bilhah. *Because Reuben had slept with Bilhah, Jacob Israel will probably not want her anymore. It's my turn.* Zilpah threw a triumphant look toward Bilhah. Bilhah acted as if she did not care. Zilpah held on to young Benjamin to be his new mother. Zilpah knew that Jacob had promised his father-in-law, way back in Mizpah, that he would not take another wife anymore. So she felt rather safe in her new position. *Or could he? Now that his wives are both dead, would he perhaps be freed from his oath? I am determined to serve him on hand and foot, so he won't get any ideas, and I better watch that Bilhah, nevertheless, and those younger maids...* She was determined.

227

The march to the burying cave was started early the next morning. After the funeral, Jacob remembered how it was when Judah was born. Leah had asked him to name the child. He had chosen the name of Judah. The name sounded so hopeful to him, as if great things would come from this boy's offspring. Now Jacob knew, he just knew, The Hero would come from the lineage of his first wife Leah, from her son Judah, sometime in the future. His wife had seen it. That thought comforted him. Jacob now saw that even though his marriage to Leah was not planned by him, still the Lord honored it and He would even make The Hero come from her offspring. *God's ways are surely strange but wonderful,—my Leah.*

Jacob wiped some tears from his eyes.

The End...

About the Author

I have been married for thirty-nine years to the same gentleman. We raised six well-adjusted children who are, in my opinion, a blessing to today's business climate and the working world. One son went into the Christian ministry after working as a scientist for a time.

We always go to church and I love to listen to challenging sermons. I noticed that pastors often mention Abraham or his sons from the Old Testament of the Bible (the Jewish Torah). However, some other events in the lives of these patriarchs are mentioned seldom, some never. Some episodes are not suitable for young children.

I am stepping into this vacuum because I love to read about conflicts. However, since we are not to add or subtract from the Bible, and I am stepping into it and am supplying the missing links that surely were there, my story slips to the level of a novel.

I was born in a farming area before electricity was installed there and can still remember how it was "in the olden days." Romantic love was not always a necessary ingredient for marriage. How might Leah, the first wife of Jacob, have felt? And, can women of today learn from her? This is the message I liked to portray in this novel.